GW00507958

ECDL
Made Simple

ECDL
Made Simple

Business Communications Development Ltd

MADE SIMPLE
BOOKS

OXFORD AUCKLAND BOSTON JOHANNESBURG MELBOURNE NEW DELHI

Made Simple
An imprint of Butterworth-Heinemann
Linacre House, Jordan Hill, Oxford OX2 8DP
225 Wildwood Avenue, Woburn MA 01801-2041
A division of Reed Educational and Professional Publishing Ltd

℞   A member of the Reed Elsevier plc group

First published 2000
© BCD Ltd 2000

All rights reserved. No part of this publication
may be reproduced in any material form (including
photocopying or storing in any medium by electronic
means and whether or not transiently or incidentally
to some other use of this publication) without the
written permission of the copyright holder except in
accordance with the provisions of the Copyright,
Design and Patents Act 1988 or under the terms of a
licence issued by the Copyright Licensing Agency Ltd,
90 Tottenham Court Road, London, England W1P 9HE.
Applications for the copyright holder's written permission
to reproduce any part of this publication should be addressed
to the publishers.

TRADEMARKS/REGISTERED TRADEMARKS
Computer hardware and software brand names mentioned in this book
are protected by their respective trademarks and are acknowledged.

British Library Cataloguing in Publication Data
A catalogue record for this book is available from the British Library.

ISBN 0 7506 4835 X

⚜ Typeset by P.K.McBride, Southampton
Icons designed by Sarah Ward © 1994
Printed and bound in Great Britain

FOR EVERY TITLE THAT WE PUBLISH, BUTTERWORTH-HEINEMANN
WILL PAY FOR BTCV TO PLANT AND CARE FOR A TREE.

Contents

3 Word processing 79

Preface

This book was designed to cover two aspects of instruction and training: To enable the user to follow the instruction, either as part of a tutor-led course or as a self-study guide. It is specially aimed at those users who have little or no experience of computers and the applications described within it. The aim is introduce the computer and its application and then to bring added value and skill-building instruction to the user.

This book covers the ECDL syllabus version 1.5, and is based upon the Microsoft Office 97 suite of applications.

Further information on the course in general, and availability of courses can be obtained from:

Business Communications Development Ltd
14 Cavendish Road
Southsea, Hampshire, PO5 2DG
Telephone: 01705.750137
Fax: 01705.751304
e-mail: info@hitweb.co.uk
Website: bcdtraining.co.uk

Screenshot permissions

Microsoft: Screenshots reprinted with permission from Microsoft Corporation.

Microsoft Windows, Windows NT, Microsoft Word, Microsoft Excel, Microsoft PowerPoint and Microsoft Outlook are either registered trademarks or trademarks of Microsoft Corporation.

Apple, the Apple logo, Macintosh are registered trademarks of Apple Computers, Inc.

Business Communications Development Ltd, has attempted to include trademark information for products, services and companies referred to in this guide. Although Business Communications Development Ltd has made reasonable efforts in gathering this information, it cannot guarantee its accuracy. All brand names and product names used in this book are trade names, service marks, or registered trademarks of their respective owners. Business Communications Development Ltd are not associated with any product or vendor mentioned in the document, other than its associated company, Hitweb Ltd.

Limit of liability/disclaimer of warranty

Business Communications Development Ltd and the authors have used their best efforts in preparing this book. Business Communications Development Ltd and its authors make no representations or warranties with respect to the accuracy or completeness of the contents of this book and specifically disclaim any implied warranties of merchantability or fitness for a particular purpose. There are no warranties which extend beyond the descriptions contained in this paragraph. No warranty may be created or extended by sales representatives or written sales materials. The accuracy and completeness of the information provided herein and the opinions stated herein are not guaranteed or warranted to produce any particular results, and the advice and strategies contained herein may not be suitable for every individual. Neither Business Communications Development Ltd, nor its authors shall be liable for any loss of profit or any other commercial damages, including but not limited to special, incidental, consequential, or other damages.

EUROPEAN COMPUTER DRIVING LICENCE and ECDL & STARS Device are trade marks of the European Computer Driving Licence Foundation Limited in Ireland and other countries. Business Communications Development Limited is an independent entity from the European Computer Driving Licence Foundation Limited, and not affiliated with the European Computer Driving Licence Foundation Limited in any manner. This publication may be used in assisting students to prepare for a European Computer Driving Licence Examination. Neither the European Computer Driving Licence Foundation Limited nor the Business Communications Development Limited warrants that the use of this publication will ensure the passing the relevant Examination. Use of the ECDL – Approved Courseware logo on this product signifies that it has been independently reviewed and approved in complying with the following standards:

Acceptable coverage of all courseware content related to ECDL Syllabus Version 1.5. This courseware material has not been approved for technical accuracy and does not guarantee that the end user will pass the associated ECDL Examinations. Any and all assessment tests and/or performance based exercises contained in this publication relate solely to this publication and do not constitute, or imply, certification by the European Computer Driving Licence Foundation Limited in respect of any ECDL Examinations. For details on sitting ECDL Examinations in your country please contact the local ECDL Licensee or visit the European Computer Driving Licence Foundation Limited Web site at http://www.ecdl.com.

References to the European Computer Driving Licence (ECDL) include the International Computer Driving Licence (ICDL). ECDL Foundation Syllabus Version 1.5 is published as the official syllabus for use within the European Computer Driving Licence (ECDL) and International Computer Driving Licence (ICDL) certification programmes.

1 Basic concepts of IT

The components of a computer

Types of computer systems

Personal Computer (PC) IBM Compatible

A PC is a computer designed for a single user. The term 'PC' is generally used to identify an IBM compatible system – IBM set the standard and other companies followed. A single PC is often referred to as a stand-alone system, indicating that it is not connected to a network.

The popularity of PCs has grown at a phenomenal rate in recent years. They are to be found in homes, business, industry, schools and the Armed Forces. The majority of PCs run the Microsoft Windows operating system.

The Apple Macintosh computer

The Apple Mac is also to be found in many homes, and is the favoured system with organisations that specialise in the production of graphics, publishing and multimedia products.

The Apple Mac was the first computer system to use a Graphical User Interface (GUI), more on that later.

Mainframe systems

The mainframe was at one time the only system generally available. IBM made its name and money selling its mainframe systems. Mainframe systems, are large compared to a PC, and process and store large amounts of data and support many users simultaneously.

A mainframe computer terminal usually only consists of a monitor and a keyboard. There is no local processor or storage device, as the mainframe handles these functions.

A mainframe computer normally supports a network system and may be found in many locations such as: multinational companies, military defence systems, telephone companies and universities.

The component parts

We are only going to deal with the PC, IBM compatible system. Computer systems are generally referred to as either:

a desktop system

a tower system – this one has separate speakers

The case

Whether the system has a desktop or tower case, it is what is inside the case that is of interest now. Here you will find most of the major components on a computer system.

Externally only two or three components are readily identifiable – all storage devices:

- The CD-ROM, or DVD drives.
- The floppy drive.
- Possibly a tape backup device.
- A Zip/Jaz or LS-120 (high-capacity removable disks) drive.

We will return to these items in due course.

Plextor's 40X internal and external CD-ROMs

Jaz drive

HP CD Writer Plus 8100i

Front panel controls

The controls on the front panel of the case are fairly universal, irrespective of type or manufacturer, and you may expect to find:

- The main power On/Off switch.
- A Reset switch.
- Several LEDs (Light Emitting Diodes).

Computer interface

Most external devices are connected to the system at the rear of the case, at the 'interface'.

The monitor

The monitor is used to display the computer output. There are two main types of monitors.

The **CRT (Cathode Ray Tube) monitor** comes in a variety of screen sizes, starting at 14-inch and progressing up to 21-inch.

Screen size is measured diagonally from the top left to the lower right corner.

Mitsubishi CRT type monitor

Monitors are generally classified by their screen size, but other factors to be considered are:

- **Dot size**. The maximum dot size should not exceed 0.28. The lower the number the better but at a greater cost.
- **Refresh rate**. This is the number of times per second that the screen is updated. A rate of 72 Hz, or higher, is recommended.
- **Resolution** is the number of horizontal and vertical pixels (screen dots). Lower resolutions, 640 x 480, give larger images, so you can see details more clearly. Higher resolutions, 1024 x 768 or more, give smaller images, but show more information at once.

The second type of monitor, is the **Liquid Crystal Display (LCD)**. This employs newer technology, and offers distinct advantages. It:

- Takes up less space on the desk.
- Is lighter in weight
- Uses less power.

Mitsubishi LCD type monitor

3

Environmental Protection Agency (EPA)

The EPA developed an energy saving system, known as Energy Star, which is now incorporated in most monitors. Energy Star technology reduces waste, and hence pollution, by switching the monitor, after a set period of inactivity, into a 'sleep mode', which uses less power.

If yours is an EPA Monitor, the use of a screen saver actually defeats the EPA purpose.

Purchasing a monitor

When buying a monitor, look for these signs, which indicate environmental protection though technology, good health and safety principles in design and screen emissions.

The keyboard

The keyboards is an *input* device – typing on it sends instructions to the computer. Keyboards come in several different shapes and styles.

Digital Free Wire, cordless keyboard

Traditional QWERTY keyboard

The mouse

A mouse is a hand-held device used to select or move items on screen. They also come in several different shapes and styles.

 Microsoft Intellimouse Trackball

Microsoft Intellimouse PRO

The modem

The modem is a device that the computer uses to communicate to other computers, fax machines and suchlike, over the standard telephone lines.

Modems have increased greatly in speed and reliability in recent years. The current standard is known as V90 56K x2, and has a reasonable good data transfer rate.

If you wish to access the Internet, then a modem is a must. For more information on this subject, go to Chapter 7 page 203.

3COM (US Robotics) V90 56K Message Modem

ISDN modems

There are specialist modems used for ISDN (digital telephone) connections. For more on this subject, go to Chapter 7 page 203.

Zoom Telephonics ISDN Fax/Modem

Other peripherals

The scanner

A scanner is an input device that captures a picture or photograph from a paper copy and displays the images on the screen.

Suitable software, such as Optical Character Recognition (OCR) can be used to scan in text documents and then converts the text for use in a word procesing package.

Most scanners usually come with a cut-down version of specialist graphic editing software as part of the package.

Agfa 310 flat bed scanner

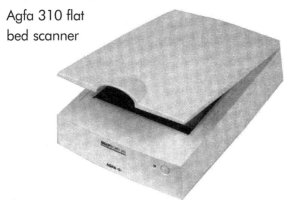

The printer

A printer is an output device, which converts copies of electronic documents to paper format, which are known as hard copies.

There are an abundance of printers on the market, ranging from:

Dot matrix printers

These use a set of pins which impact on an inked ribbon. The print is of fairly low quality as it is made-up from a series of dots.

Inkjet printers

- An extremely popular type of printer.
- Produces high quality print.
- The ink is usually a water-based product which degrades over a period of time.
- Do not allow print to come in contact with water, because it will run.

HP DeskJet 670C printer

HP DeskJet 1600C

Laser printers

- High quality print output.
- Does not use ink but a toner, hence no problem with dampness, etc.
- Laser printers are generally more expensive to purchase and to run.

HP LaserJet 6P/6MP printer

One of HP's advanced workgroup LaserJet 8000 series of printers

Inside the computer

The case contains a number of other important sub-units, that make up the computer system.

The motherboard

This is the main circuit board of the computer – all other items or units connect or plug into it. There are various types of boards available.

AT motherboards are old and have been largely replaced by the ATA motherboard.

ATX Slot 1 motherboards support both the Pentium II and III processors.

There are also other types of motherboards, designed for certain processors. They are referred to by the type of processor housing, e.g.:

AT Super Socket 7

ATX Super Socket 7

CPU Super Socket 7

TMC A15VG+ Super Socket 7 motherboard

Take note

Some motherboards will support more than one processor, usually the Pentium II series.

The TMC T16NBD Slot 1 ATX motherboard (66-100MHz)

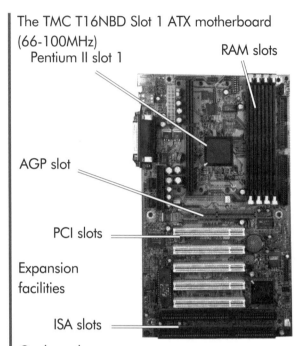

Pentium II slot 1

RAM slots

AGP slot

PCI slots

Expansion facilities

ISA slots

On-board systems

Motherboard technology has advanced leaps and bounds in recent years. It is not unusual to find some or all of the following built-in to the motherboard:

- Two channels for the floppy drives.
- Four channel EIDE support for hard disk, CD and LS-120 super floppy drives.
- VGA support for the monitor.
- Various types of SCSI support.
- Sound facilities.

The Central Processing Unit (CPU)

The CPU is the main chip in the computer. It processes instructions, carries out calculations and controls the flow of information through the computer. The CPU is the computer 'brain'.

CPU manufacturers

Intel is by far the greater producer of CPUs. Their processors are known by names.

- The current Intel processor is the Pentium III, with speeds from 533 to 750 MHz, and has generally replaced the Pentium II CPU.

- The Pentium II, with speeds from 233 to 500 MHz. With the introduction of the Pentium III processor it is unlikely that you will be able to purchase a Pentium II CPU.

Intel Pentium II CPU
Shown here without its fan
and heat sink assembly. CPUs run at
high temperatures so need these to keep cool.

- The Celeron, socket 370, is a fast inexpensive CPU. Based on the Pentium II, but with less built-in memory, this was designed to meet the needs of home and budget users.

Other manufacturers of CPUs

AMD offer a range of CPUs, such as the AMD-K6-2 and AMD-K6-3 series, and the recently introduced Athlon, Slot A CPU.

Cyrix with their range of 6x86 and Media GX CPUs.

Some AMD CPUs

AMD-K6-2 CPU

AMD-K6-3 CPU

AMD Athlon, Slot A CPU

Computer technology advances in leaps and bounds. With the operating system upgrades, applications upgrades, CPUs are not being left behind. New CPUs are in the pipeline, as are faster speeds for the current range of CPUs. Intel is currently working on a new CPU, aimed specifically at larger network systems.

Take note

Processor speed is measured in megahertz and the higher the number, e.g. 450 MHz, the faster the computer. However, if you have a fast processor but only a limited amount of RAM, you will not be able to get the best out of your system. CPUs and RAM, together, produce the speed.

Random Access Memory (RAM)

RAM, found on the motherboard, is a temporary storage device. RAM is only active when the computer is switched on and powered up. Any data still in RAM when the system is shut down, or subjected to a power failure, is lost never to be regained.

There are a number of different types of RAM with differing speeds and compatibility requirements.

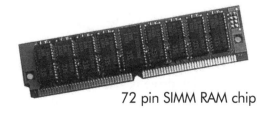

72 pin SIMM RAM chip

7

Expansion slots

There are usually a number of spare slots on the motherboard, for expansion or upgrading. Generally there are only two types of slots used on current systems. The slots are known as ISA, the older slot and PCI, the newer slot.

There are usually several of each type of slot on each motherboard, thus allowing the user a degree of flexibility. You preference, wherever possible, should be for the PCI slot cards.

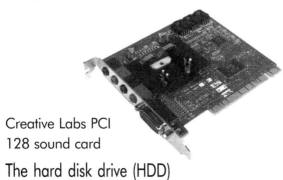

Creative Labs PCI
128 sound card

The hard disk drive (HDD)

The hard disk drive, also known as the fixed disk, is mounted within the computer case. Currently the minimum HDD storage capacity is 13Gb which is rather large.

The HDD is connected to the motherboard via a special ribbon cable to the EIDE (Enhanced Integrated Drive Electronics) socket.

The internal view of a 3.5 inch hard disk drive

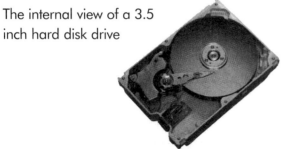

The floppy disk drive (FDD)

The floppy disk drive is also connected to the motherboard, by a similar type of cable as used by the HDD, though this has a different type of connector. The FDDs capacity is typically limited to 1.4Mb, thus limiting its usefulness.

The CD-ROM drive

The CD-ROM (Compact Disk-Read Only Memory) drive is connected to an EIDE socket on the motherboard, by the same type of cable as that used by the HDD.

CD-ROMS use a disk similar to audio CDs, with a capacity of 650Mb. You can only read files – you cannot store your own on a CD-ROM.

CD-ROMs are gauged by the speed that they run at and this is often referred to as 36X or 40X. The higher the number the faster the CD-ROM will function.

Digital Versatile Disk Drive

The DVD is gaining in popularity and is now quite often fitted in new computer systems as standard, instead of the CD-ROM. The DVD has a capacity of 5Gb.

Panasonic LF-D101U, a rewritable DVD RAM drive.

The Power Supply Unit (PSU)

The PSU connects to an external mains supply, converting it from 250 volts Alternating Current (AC) to Direct Current (DC), with voltages between 3.3 to 12 volts. Power consumption is between 200 to 250 watts. Compare that to the average household bulb of 60 watts.

A fan within the PSU draws air out from the case to assist in keeping the components cool.

Operating systems

An operating system (OS) is the link between the hardware and the software. It ensures that all the components, that make-up the computer system, function together and efficiently.

When you start your computer, the operating system is started first. Applications software, such as MS Word can only be started after the OS is loaded. Without the operating system the applications cannot and will not function.

MS-DOS

Microsoft Disk Operating System, MS-DOS, was the earlier and a command line OS. The user performed tasks by typing in short text-based commands, which the PC then executed.

Windows

Windows is the follow-on OS after MS-DOS and likewise is a Microsoft product.

Windows is a Graphical User Interface, GUI, operating system. Instead of typing in commands, the user performs tasks by selecting icons, small images, or selecting commands from menus. GUIs makes it easier to use the OS, speeds up operations, and are more user friendly.

First generation Windows OS still required the presence of MS-DOS, because the two systems functioned together. MS-DOS had to be installed first, followed by Windows, which basically sat on top of MS-DOS, with the GUI. Windows still used various MS-DOS facilities, as and when required.

Other Operating Systems

Unix

Unix is a powerful OS that has been around for sometime now and is enjoying a revival in some areas.

Unix is used on many computer systems that support the Internet.

The Apple Macintosh OS

The Apple company produced the first GUI for computers. Unfortunately, due to Apple Mac's marketing policy and strategy, they really lost out to Microsoft over time.

Unix and Apple Mac OS are mentioned simply to indicate that there are other operating systems available, other than Microsoft products.

A short history

MS-DOS was basically the first OS for PCs and over a period of time, numerous versions of the OS were released.

GUIs arrived with Windows and most users first encountered Windows at version 3. Windows was upgraded to version 3.11, which in many ways was the forerunner of the next OS – Windows 95.

Windows version 3, by the introduction of the GUI, was a major step forward in operating systems for PCs.

Windows 95 was the next major step forward, still using a GUI. This time however, the GUI had undertaken a major revamp. It was even easier to use, and allowed the user to carry out tasks and actions much quicker.

Various patches and upgrades appeared for Windows 95, until the arrival of Windows 98.

Windows 98 still uses the 95 GUI, with increased functionality and facilities.

New Technology (NT)

During the transition and development of the variously mentioned operating systems, Microsoft was developing another system, called New Technology, NT for short.

The earlier versions of Windows NT used the same style GUI as that used in Windows 3x operating systems, up to NT version 3.51. With the introduction of Windows NT version 4, the switch was made to the Windows 95/98 style GUI.

Windows NT was developed specifically as a more powerful and secure operating system for business and industry.

Windows NT OS appears in two forms, the Workstation user system and the Network version, known as NT Server.

Platform

The term 'platform' refers to the type of operating system used by a computer. MS-DOS, Windows 3xx, Windows 95/98, Windows NT and Unix are all platforms.

You cannot run any Windows applications on MS-DOS, though you can run most MS-DOS applications on a Windows platform. This is due to the fact that Windows has 'backward compatibility'. Within Windows, there is a section of the software that is specifically written to cater for MS-DOS applications.

Functions of the OS

Other than ensuring that all the components of the computer work together, the OS has many other areas of responsibility and functionality.

File management

It is the OS that is responsible for all file management aspects on the computer. To this end, Windows has a particular program for file management, called Windows Explorer.

File Naming

Under MS-DOS and Windows 3, file names consisted of a maximum of eight letters followed by a full stop, a period, and then a three-letter extension for example, '.doc'

With the introduction of Windows 95 there came a far more sensible file naming system using long file names. This permitted the user to use up to 255 characters, in place of the original eight. The name is still followed by the full stop and a three-letter extension. This system allows the use of more descriptive names, making file recognition and management that much easier.

For more information on file management, see Chapter 2.

Utilities

The OS also provides a number of utilities, smaller programs, as integral elements of the OS to assist in the efficient performance of the computer. For example:

Disk formatting

Before a disk can be used on a computer, it must be formatted, in a manner that the OS will recognise. It is the OS that provides the program to format the disk.

See Chapter 2 for further information.

Computer performance

If the computer finds a fault or error on any disk, there is a program within the OS to deal with this problem. This is called Scandisk. It conducts a series of checks on the disk and will attempt to fix any faults found. Scandisk will advise the user on the current status of the disk on completion of the scan.

Defragmentation

Because of the way data is stored on disks, there will come a time when you will notice a slowing down of the system when attempting to open files. This is due to the fact that often the file is broken down in to smaller sections. These sections are then stored in different locations on the disk, fragmentation.

The procedure used to overcome fragmentation is known as Defrag. This locates the various sections of the files and moves them, if possible, next to each other, in contiguous locations. This will assist in opening the files quicker and free up wasted space on the disk.

Networking

Windows 95/98 supports networking, with all the necessary software included as an integrated part of the OS.

The only additional requirement to establish your own network, assuming that you have two or more computers, is to install the Network Interface Cards (NIC), and the appropriate cabling and connectors.

Plug and Play

Windows 95/98 supports Plug and Play technology. What this means is that the OS will detect any new hardware that you install and load the necessary *drivers*. These are short programs that support the hardware items connected to the computer, and allow them to function.

File storage

FAT16

MS-DOS, Windows 3.x and Windows 95 use a file storage system known as FAT16. The FAT (File Allocation Table) remembers where the various parts of a file are stored on the disk.

FAT16 is quite wasteful in the way it stores data on the disk. To overcome the problem of wasted space, Windows 98 introduced a new system known as FAT32.

FAT32

FAT32 is more economical in the manner that stores data on the disk. Less space is lost and the system is more efficient.

There is a problem however, only Windows 98 recognises FAT32. Be careful if you elect to use FAT32, you do have a choice. If you pass files to colleagues and friends who are running MS-DOS, Windows 95 or Windows NT, then those disks must use FAT16.

NTFS

New Technology Filing System (NTFS) is used by Windows NT operating systems. Only NT OSs can read this filing system, and it is through the use of NTFS that Windows NT gains some of its increased security features.

With the introduction of Windows 2000, yet another filing system will emerge. This new system is based on NTFS but it is believed that there will be no backward compatibility with the original NTFS system, thus making it reliant upon Windows 2000 operating systems.

Customisation

All Windows programs permit the user to customise the computer set-up and the user interface. Windows 98 provides increased functionality in this area, for instance:

Twin monitors

Windows 98 allows for up to two monitors to be connected to the same computer. This is particularly useful if you give presentations (see Chapter 6). You may have your own monitor adjacent to the computer or you may set it up, along with the second monitor for audience use.

To run two monitors, you must install a second video card in the computer, and of course you will require longer cables.

Other features

There are more features within the OS, and they are not all listed here. Read the appropriate user handbook. Failure to even scan the handbook briefly will almost certainly result in you not being fully aware of the capabilities and functionality of the OS.

Internet browser

Microsoft includes its browser software, Internet Explorer, with the operating systems. The browser is necessary if you intend to access the Internet.

See Chapter 7 for more details.

Programs and applications

Application software

The term application software, such as that contained within the Microsoft Office suite, refers to a number of different programs specifically written to accomplish specialist tasks and functions.

These applications are used to write letters, manage finances, to create databases, to draw pictures and to play games.

Application software is platform-related. That is to say, you must have the appropriate operating system loaded to run the application.

When application software is released, it has a name and a version number. Inevitably, even after considerable testing, the software will have faults in it, known as bugs. The software manufacturer will periodically issue an update or 'patch', designed to correct the various problems. When applied to the applications, the patch will also update the version number of that product.

It is important to be aware of what version your software is, particularly if access and security are concerns to you.

MS Word – word processing

This application is used to produce letters and a variety of other types of documents, which would, until the introduction of computers, have been produced on a typewriter.

MS Excel – spreadsheets

This application was specifically written to manage and analyse finances and information as well as create charts and graphs.

Excel can also be used to create simple databases.

MS Access – databases

This application was specifically written to create databases, to enable information and data to be assembled and collated.

Access is a powerful application that lends itself to simple databases, such as a list of names and addresses of your friends, to more complex ones such as stock control and ordering in warehouses and supermarkets.

MS PowerPoint – presentations

PowerPoint produces a series of slides, including audio and video inserts, to be assembled for presentation to audiences.

MS Outlook

Outlook is much more than a Personal Information Management (PIM) system.

Outlook lists your contacts, assists you in organising your time and such like, but much more:

● Outlook produces and manages your electronic mail, e-mail.

E-mail is covered in Chapter 7.

13

- If your computer is connected to a network, Outlook provides a group working facility to enable, a team for instance, to collate their activities, meetings and so on.

Outlook is well worth investigating more deeply, in time. There are many features not readily apparent on the surface, such as tracking and logging the time you spend working on a particular document, spreadsheet or database. This feature is particularly useful if you are self-employed and charge for your time by the hour.

Application integration

All applications within the MS Office suite are written by Microsoft and therefore support cross-application functionality. What this means is that instead of each application carrying out similar functions independently, the same functions are centrally located and each application accesses these functions.

Through the use of integrated functions, the applications do not waste precious space on the hard disk. Further more, as a consequence of integration, many of the menus and toolbars, within the applications, are very much the same, in respect of look, content and feel.

Naturally there are specialist menus and toolbars specifically related to the particular application.

Because of the similarity and layout of the application GUI, user training and experience is much easier and quickly transferred.

Summary

Applications are platform-specific and will not function without the appropriate operating system.

Integrated applications are frequently cheaper to purchase rather than buying each application singularly.

Furthermore, by purchasing a suite of applications, cross-application and functionality is greatly enhanced.

Storage and memory

Storage devices

Permanent storage

All storage devices such as hard disk drives and floppy disk drives are known as permanent storage devices. What this means is that any data that is written to the drives can be retrieved and reused at a later date.

The action of shutting down the computer and turning off the power will not result in the loss of this data.

These types of drives use a magnetic medium on which the data is stored. That is why it is particularly important never to use any other magnetic material in the vicinity of computer disks. The magnetic influence will corrupt and destroy the data stored on the disk.

Identifying disk drives

The operating system employs letters to identify the various drives installed in a computer system.

If only one hard drive is fitted, it is allocated the letter C and this is known as the Root drive.

If other hard drives are fitted, then they will be allocated the next available letters.

Most computers now have a CD drive installed and it too is allocated a drive letter, usually the letter D.

So, we have the letters C and D but what happened to A and B? The letters A and B are reserved solely for the use of floppy drives.

It is uncommon to see more than one floppy disk drive installed these days and it is always allocated the letter A. Even though there is not a second floppy drive installed, the letter B is not available for use elsewhere.

If a second drive unit is installed at a later date, the user must set up the drive through the computer BIOS, and only then will the operating system see the drive.

Consult the documentation that came with your computer for more information, such as what type of BIOS installed on your computer.

Types of storage devices

There are numerous types of storage devices available. Some, such as the hard and floppy disk drives will permit the user to read and write to the disk any number of times. Other storage devices will only permit read actions.

CD drives

The average CD disk has a storage capacity of 650 MB. Compare that to the everyday floppy disk, which has a capacity of 1.44 MB.

There are three types of CD drive:

- **CD-ROMs** can only be used to read data, you cannot write, save files, to a CD-ROM.
- **CD-R** drives permit the user to read from the CD any number of times; however, the write capability can only take place once. You cannot go back at a later date and perform another write action to the same CD.

- **CD-RW** drives permit multiple read write operations to be carried out on the same CD, until such time that it is, of course, full.

CD-ROMs do not require any specialist software, other than the appropriate drivers. Whereas the CD-R and CD-RW drives do require specialist software to function and cost a great deal more.

DVD Drives

Digital Versatile Disks, come in two types:

- **DVD ROM** looks just like a CD-ROM, in shape and size but stores over 26 times the amount of data. A standard DVD disk can hold over two hours of high quality video with improved CD quality audio.

  The DVD-ROM will also read standard CD disks. Storage capacities vary from 4.7 GB to 17 GB, making them ideal for distribution of large multimedia applications.

  DVD players are now also available for use in the home for viewing full-length feature films.

- **DVD RAM** also looks very like a CD-ROM drive and has the same features as a DVD ROM drive. The difference is that the DVD-RAM allows the user to record data. The DVD-RAM is a read-write system

  The recently introduced Panasonic LF-D101U is a DVD-RAM system. This drive has a capacity of 5.2 GB, and will also read the Panasonic optical disk. About the only thing it cannot do is write to the standard CD disk.

Other permanent storage devices

The optical disk

This requires a special drive unit to write to the disk. The first series of optical disk had a storage capacity of 250 MB. The current series of disks now have a capacity of 650 MB.

The super floppy

This recently introduced drive, is rumoured to eventually replace the older floppy disks. The super floppy is known as the LS-120. The figure 120 indicates the capacity of the floppy disk. It is 120 MB, compare that to the older floppy disk with a capacity of 1.44 MB.

The external appearance of the LS-120 drive is almost identically to that of the old 3½ inch floppy drive unit.

The LS-120 will also read and write to a 1.44 MB floppy disk.

Memory

When the computer is running and you decide to use one of the applications, the essential elements of the program and data are loaded into the Random Access Memory, RAM.

There are a number of different types of memory and their locations vary, as follows:

CPUs have a limited amount of memory, built into them. This memory is known as **internal cache** or primary cache or L1.

Working in conjunction with the CPU cache is another memory cache, known as **external cache**. This resides on the motherboard and consists of Static RAM (SRAM) chips.

In the Pentium II and Pentium III CPUs the external RAM is built into the CPU, this makes accessing the cache much quicker.

Random Access Memory (RAM) is the main memory of the computer.

Memory is not a permanent storage medium – RAM is volatile. This means that any data stored in the RAM will be lost when the computer is switched off.

Accessing data

As already stated, a certain amount of data is loaded into the internal cache of the CPU. If the processor cannot find the data it needs in the internal cache, it looks in the external cache for the data. If it cannot find the data it needs in the internal or external cache, the processor then looks in the slower main memory, the RAM.

Data movement

Each time the computer requests data from RAM, the computer places a copy of the data in the memory cache. This process constantly updates the memory cache so that it always contains the most recently used data.

As a consequence of the movement of data to the internal and external cache, these memory areas will quickly become full. So not only is data going into the cache, it is also being moved out. The older data, that has not been used recently, is moved out down the chain.

Another memory area that the computer uses is sometime called a Swap file or dynamic memory. This is an area on the disk drive that the operating system reserves for its own use. If the computer system has limited amounts of RAM installed, this area on the hard disk is used more often. This process slows down the access time considerably.

Operating systems

Different operating systems use memory in different ways. In the older Windows 3xx, the OS generally set swap files. The user could change the size, providing the hard disk size was adequate and space was available.

Windows 95/98 uses a dynamic system. What this means is that the OS automatically adjusts the size of the file as and when necessary.

Take note

Do not confuse 'storage' and 'memory'. Both are memory mediums but handle data in two completely different ways. For instance, the HDD stores data, through the use of a magnetic medium. If the computer is switched off the data is retained.

RAM stores data but only while the computer is switched on. RAM requires a constant supply of electricity to function.

The basic units of stored data

The aim is to introduce the various terms used, their relationship and how it all comes together in the computing process.

Bit

A bit (*b*inary dig*it*)is the smallest unit of information that a computer can process, and is usually represented as either 0 or 1.

Byte

A combination of 8 bits is referred to as a byte. Each byte can represent a single character or letter. For example: the letter A = 01000001.

Kilobyte

One kilobyte, abbreviated as KB, is 1,024 bytes. In terms of space in a document, it is approximately equal to one page of double-spaced text.

Megabyte

One megabyte (MB) is 1,024 KB or 1,048,576 bytes, roughly equal to a 300 page paperback.

Gigabyte

Gigabyte (GB) is 1,024 MB or 1,073,743,824 bytes.

Terabyte

One terabyte (TB) is 1,024 GB or 1,099,551,627,776 bytes.

Records

A record is a small amount of data that is stored, processed, and retrieved as a single convenient unit. It is a group of related facts describing one item contained in a number of separate locations called fields.

Databases are made up of fields and records. Any number of fields can be used to create a record. For instance, if you are creating a database of your contacts, it may have a field for the details: first name, last name, address line1, address line2, address line3 and so on.

The rows of data within a table of a database, are its records. Each row of information is considered a separate entity that can be accessed or sequenced as required.

Files

A file is a set of data with an identifying label held in a computer storage device. Files are the end result of writing a letter, of creating a spreadsheet or the database.

Applications may well call their particular end product by a different name. For instance, a letter created in MS Word, would usually be called a document. Remember the three letter extension after the filename and the period, *doc*. This is an abbreviation for 'document'.

It is irrelevant which application, or how that application refers to files created by it. For instance, Excel produces a spreadsheet, but when stored on a storage device, it is a *file*. Likewise an Access database is a file.

For further details on files and file management, please refer to Chapter 2, *Using the Computer*.

Using a graphical user interface

Windows and Macintosh operating systems use a Graphical User Interface system, GUI (pronounced 'gooey').

A GUI is a visual means of interacting with the computer and provides an easy means of issuing instructions and commands without the user having an extensive knowledge of commands and programming by using windows, icons, mouse and pull-down menus.

The GUI system uses small pictures, known as *icons* to represent actions and commands. The interface is also made up of a series of *menus*.

The menus, once activated, open a drop down list containing further commands. Even more menus may be concealed within the initial drop list and this system of menus is known as cascading.

Icon method

Icons are a visual means of issuing instructions, for instance 'print the document', by the use of one mouse click on the appropriate icon.

To issue the same instruction to the computer, using the menus, would require three separate mouse actions, which is still quicker than the older method of command line instructions.

Menu method

Though the use of icons is normally a quicker method of issuing instructions, menus often offer greater flexibility. For instance:

Refer back to the icon method of printing a document; one click on the icon was all that was needed however, to print the document using the menus required three separate actions to do the same thing. Now suppose that you only wanted to print the one page. The icon method could not be used as it prints the entire document.

Using the menu method opens a print dialog box, which offers a number of options for printing the document. For instance:

- Print one page.
- Print a range of pages.
- Change the printer properties.
- Change choice of printer for the current print job.

The application window

Each application window consists of a number of different areas:

For instance, the MS Word application window, starting at the top:

- The strip along the top is the Title bar. When it is coloured blue it indicates that it is the active window.
- The Title bar will also list the document name, and subject to customisation, the file path as well.
- Below the title bar is the Menu bar usually with nine drop-down menu lists.
- Below the Menu bar is the first of the toolbars, usually the Standard toolbar.
- Below the Standard toolbar, usually, is the Formatting toolbar.

Each of the three items listed above can be customised by you, with additions and subtractions being made to the content of the menus and likewise to the toolbars.

The overall appearance, such as which colour scheme you prefer, whether the ruler is displayed, and any additional toolbars that you may wish displayed permanently, can all be customised.

Standardisation

With the majority of application suites, standardisation and integration has greatly improved. For instance, the majority of the icons that appear on the Word Formatting toolbar will also appear on the Excel Formatting toolbar.

This increases your productivity, in as much as that, having already used one application, you can immediately apply that knowledge to the second application.

The same applies to the drop-down menu contents, even to such a degree that different software companies are conforming to a common standard layout.

Customisation

As touched upon previously, customisation allows you to set up the screen display, and suchlike, to best suit your preferences.

Within the operating system, there exists a means of changing the screen resolution.

This is particularly useful for anyone who is visually impaired. By changing the resolution to a lower setting, the images will appear larger on the screen, thus improving the visibility for the user.

Productivity

Productivity is increased. This is due to the fact that you can often, on the click of a mouse button, issue instructions extremely quickly, and then proceed to another task without having to wait for the last instruction to by carried out and speeds up the work process tremendously.

To gain the maximum use of any application, it is necessary to experiment and try out the various options available.

Use the online Help system, via the Help menu on the Menu bar.

Further detail

For further detail on the layout and content of the various applications covered by the ECDL course, please refer to Chapters 4 to 7.

Multimedia

Multimedia, literally 'many media', for example, using sound, pictures and text to make a more effective, understandable presentation.

Multimedia CD-ROM disks

A CD-ROM disk can store multimedia presentations. The CD disk is currently the main medium used by the multimedia industry, though the introduction of the DVD disk will impact on its future greatly in time.

You will recall from previous sections on this module, that the CD disk has a capacity of 650 MB, which when compared to the floppy disk, is considerable. However, when compared to the DVD disk, which has a capacity in the region of 5.2 GB, the CD disk has its limitations.

DVD multimedia

DVD multimedia, in the computer and home entertainment environment offers far greater opportunities for advancement.

Already on sale, on the High Street, are DVD players and full length feature films. The systems connect up to the TV in a similar manner to that of the video recorder.

Current DVD home entertainment systems do not offer a record facility, as do the video recorders, though this will change shortly.

Computer DVD

The initial DVD systems for computers were read only, though available now, at some cost, are read-rewrite units. The system offers several features that make it a very attractive item. For instance the unit is not only able to read and write to DVD disks; it can read CD disks and optical disks as well.

Cost is of course a major consideration with any recently-introduced new technology.

Some examples

There are numerous multimedia products on the market, such as encyclopaedias and teaching aids – particularly on computer subjects.

If you are a classical music buff, the extended audio disk will be of interest. With all the necessary hardware installed, you can of course play the audio disk through the computer.

So what's new? Well before playing the music, it installs a small program that is also on the disk, and then whilst playing the music you can research, from the audio disk, the history of the music as it is played.

Multimedia and the Internet

More and more areas on the Internet and for that matter, company intranets, are using multimedia.

Intranets are much the same as the Internet except that they are run on private networks within organisations and are not normally accessible to the general public.

OnLine shopping

Imagine that you have decided to do some shopping on the Internet. You are going to place you weekly grocery order with your local online supermarket.

Imagine how boring it would be once you are logged on, to simply have a screen display listing products and a series of tick boxes. Not a very good sales pitch.

Now imagine, you log on, a voice greets you by your first name, which is picked-up from your log-on process. You are then advised of the store's special offers accompanied by the appropriate images of the products.

By clicking on a series of buttons, which identify the various sections of the store, you are taken to that section and you select the items you require. Quite often there is an image of a shopping basket and to select an item, you simply left-click on it and drag it to the shopping basket and drop it in.

While you are placing your order, the supermarket computer is checking the availability of products and suchlike and if there is a lack of stock, you will be advised of such immediately and possibly offered an alternative item if one is available. If you decline the alternative, you are will be advised of the anticipated delivery time.

Quite a difference to simply a screen with lines of text and tick boxes!

Drawbacks

There are of course certain drawbacks to such a system.

How often do you go to the fresh produce section? You almost always pickup an item and feel it for freshness and suchlike!

When the supermarket is assembling your order for you, are they so discerning? Of course they would have us all believe so, but this is an area that requires further investigation on the part of the user once again.

Tip

Multimedia lends itself ideally to the application covered in Chapter 6, *Presentations*.

Developing a computer-based system

Business use

When an organisation, or for that matter an individual, decides that they require a computer system, either from new or upgrading current systems, there are a series of steps and procedures that should be followed.

The following is essential to the process:

Systems analysis

Identify the requirements – the input processes, the output and control mechanisms operating in the current system.

Systems design

Specify the inputs, processes, outputs and control for a new system, designed so as to overcome the shortcomings of the old system.

Program design

Using a high level programming language to write the programs necessary to perform the processing operations required by the system specification.

Feasibility study

Is the proposal economically, technically and socially practicable?

Program testing

With real time and test data to iron out any bugs and test the system to extremes.

Implementation

Either parallel, direct, phased in, or a pilot system.

Training

Is re-training required, if so prioritise the training requirement. Key personnel head the list.

Conversion of files

Will the new system read old formats or will manual conversion be required.

Maintenance and monitoring

To deal with any problems that come to light after implementation and to maintain and upgrade the system as and when required, either in programming or through the introduction of new hardware.

Home use

An individual's assessment

As an individual, the procedure is much less complicated and the overall deciding factor will almost always be that of finance.

The following are a number of questions that you should take into consideration when thinking of buying a computer for personal use:

Finance

The first consideration is how much can I afford? If money is no object then the assessment is somewhat easier, though it should still be carefully thought out.

Requirement

What do you want or expect the system to do? For example, is the use solely for adults or will children have access to the system?

Security

Is security going to be of importance? If so, then the type of operating system required should be carefully considered. For general home use and low-level office requirements Windows 98 would be satisfactory.

If security is likely to be a problem then maybe Windows NT will meet your security requirements. The increase in security has a corresponding increase in price as well.

Applications

What applications will you require? Will the built-in Windows 98 word-processor meet your requirements, or will you require compatibility with applications in use at the office.

Multimedia

Almost all systems come pre-packaged with CD drives and sound cards and speakers. It is worth checking just to be sure.

Brand names

Do you go for a brand name, for example an IBM or Compaq computer, or buy a clone by mail order. There is a great deal to be said for purchasing clone systems. There are many good deals to be had at slightly lower prices.

Monitors

Careful consideration should be given to the monitor size. It is suggested that the minimum size that should be considered is 15-inch.

What does 15-inch mean, what is the actual viewable size? In many cases the actual viewing area on the screen is less than that stated, because some of the screen is behind the moulded plastic case. Be aware, always check.

Games

Do you intend to play games, if so then a good quality joystick is required. You are limited when using a mouse to control games.

Disc size

This is less than a problem today than it used to be, however, still check the size.

RAM (Memory)

A system with a fast CPU will be degraded by a lack of RAM. The more RAM the better and more efficient the system.

Always remember that the OS has a minimum RAM requirement as do the applications. Minimum requirements for a modern system is suggested as 128 MB.

Warranties

Ensure you understand the warranty offered, and do you purchase an extended warranty?

Pay particular attention to monitors in respect of warranties. Many mail order houses offer what is known as swoop-out warranties. If the monitor becomes faulty, a simple telephone call will generally have a fully re-conditioned monitor at your door the next working day.

No need to return the faulty item to the High Street store, it is taken back by the delivery service and most warranties are for three years.

Applications and use of computers

The importance and growing use of computers

Throughout history there have been numerous technological introductions and advances that have resulted in major impacts upon the way of life and approach to manufacturing.

The arrival of the computer, though initially slow to affect us, has in recent years made tremendous changes to almost all ways of life and work. The computer, whether it be a mainframe, mini-computer or the PC, has impacted to some degree or another on almost everyone's life. This may take the form of a person actually using a PC at home, in the office or in the way they work, for instance in a car plant where a considerable volume of work is now automated.

Computers are ideal systems to carry out unattended repetitive actions, with a very high degree of accuracy. This is seen particularly in manufacturing industry.

Computers have lessened the risk to people by their use in dangerous areas and processes, for instance in the nuclear industry and by the police and armed forces in bomb disposal.

The above fields were mentioned to highlight the use of multimedia. In both of these fields, visual, and often audio, requirements exist. The use of a computer coupled with video and audio equals one form of multimedia.

Development continues at a pace within the computer industry, in the form of new CPUs arriving on the market, new systems of data storage such as the DVD RAM, and the continual upgrading of operating systems and applications.

Surrounding the introduction of the new or upgraded applications there is also the introduction of new or expanded use of computer systems and applications.

Computer systems in business

There exist numerous systems and platforms in use in business today, for instance:

Banking

- Automatic Transaction Machines, better known as cash machines.
- Automatic cheque readers. These not only read the cash details, etc., by the use of magnetic or other medium, but also monitor the number of cheques issued by the individual or company, to determine if a new cheque book is required. Once it detects that the user is down to their last four or five cheques, the system initiates a process that will order and dispatch a new chequebook.
- Cash transfer, whether national or international.

Stock Exchange

- Trading on numerous Stock Exchanges is now conducted by the use of computers. There were some problems in the earlier days. The systems were designed, and programmed, to monitor the sale of stocks and

25

shares, and should there appear to be a run on them, the system automatically initiated sales. This in turn was picked up by other Exchanges and the computer systems actually started a panic selling spree.

Advertising

- Advertising is taking advantage of computers, particularly in the mail shot, 'junk mail' to many of us. The mail merge feature of the word-processing and Desktop Publishing, DTP, programs, has introduced the automation of bulk mail addressing.

Accountancy

- The use of spreadsheets has introduced an automation capability to accountancy.
- The spreadsheet can also be used as a modelling tool for simple forecasting, and the use of the 'what if' feature can assist in the development of strategy and business planning.

Management

- Specialist software exists to assist management in the decision-making process.

Project management

- Project management software is available to assist in the management of different types of projects.
- This software will program in events, sequences, etc., and will warn of over-runs or conflicts between events.

Group working

- Many tasks involve group working. The information must be available to more than one person, hence the development of group working through the use of networking.

- The network allows the sharing of information and resources, thus speeding up processing time and production of documentation in relation to the projects.

Office automation

- Numerous areas within an office now have automated features, such as:
    - Customer administration.
    - Company calendars.
    - Production of in-house publications.
    - Company contacts and address book.
- E-mail is a fast and cost-effective method of communications. With suitable hardware and applications installed, text and graphics can be transmissed quickly and easily.

Computer systems in industry

The car industry has seen over the last ten years, completely new systems of work introduced. The manufacture of a motor vehicle is extensively an automated process, where large areas of the car plant are manned by but a few personnel, mainly technicians in attendance of the robots that actually assemble the car body and shell.

Advantages

There are many advantages to be gained by the use of computer control robotic systems:

- **Reliability**: The system carries out, repeatedly, the same actions without fatigue.
- **Accuracy**: The same actions, no matter how often done, are consistently accurate.
- **Re-programming**: All systems can be re-programmed quickly and easily from one focal point.

- **Staff training**: With manual handling and assembly by staff, staff must be retrained when changes are introduced. A consequence of robotic assembly and of re-programming is that the need for staff training is minimal and therefore reduces the likelihood of error in the assembly of the product.

Disadvantages

- Loss of employment opportunities
- The introduction of robotic assembly lines saw a major reduction in numerous car plant work forces.

Take note

The banking industry has also seen the impact of the computers affect their manpower situation enormously. With the introduction of automated systems, less and less personnel are required.

Computers in education

When computers were first introduced into schools, the BBC commissioned a computer system that was known as the Acorn.

The Acorn, in its early days was quite far-sighted, however, it required its own hardware and specially written software. Cross-platform compatibility did not exist. The Acorn can still be found in many schools but is now in decline, with the introduction of Windows-based systems. The Acorn was available to the public but due to the limited quantities sold, costs of the system, including software, were high.

In 1997, the government decided that all schools would have up-to-date systems as soon as possible. In addition, and as part and parcel of the government initiative, the 'schoolnet' was introduced. The idea was to link schools via, and to give access, to the Internet.

Educational software

With the introduction of the PC into schools, the availability of educational software has increased and its cost has been correspondingly reduced.

The software available ranges from that of basic applications for use in primary schools, to more advanced applications for high schools.

There is one particular application that employs multimedia. This is a Desktop Publishing package, incorporating sound, video and hyperlinks.

Advantages

- Because most educational software is either CD or network based, information can quickly and easily be recalled.
- The student can quickly and easily return to a passage, carry out the same task, or re-read the same passage for clarification.
- A student can pace his or her own study rate.
- Some applications will monitor the student's progress and test and advise if there is a problem.

Disadvantages

- The student cannot question the tutor for clarification or request assistance.
- The computer is impersonal, and offers only limited feedback to the student.

Computers for home use

The majority of home-based computer systems are multimedia systems, incorporating CD-ROM drives and sound systems.

Office software

If the home system is to be used for business then the applications should be the same as in the office, to ensure compatibility.

Home accounts

If the system is to be used to run household accounts and your bank details, including online banking, then specialist software exists to meet your requirements. Microsoft Money 2000 provides online banking, assists in tax returns to managing your shares portfolio. There are of course other applications that will also carry out the same functions.

Hobbies

This area is too large to list everything that one could do using a computer: Some uses are discussed briefly below.

If you are keen to assemble your **family history** there are packages that will assist you in this area.

By the use of the numerous CDs that are available, you can conduct **research** into a vast array of subjects and topics. Do not forget the availability of the Internet for research as well.

There exists an ever-increasing volume of CDs for home study and revision. Whether it is for GCSEs or the Open University, the computer is an excellent tool to assist with revision, and of course, the presentation of the course work.

Computers in everyday life

Computers are encountered in our everyday life to such an extent that we are sometimes not aware of their presence. Some examples are:

Supermarkets

Barcode reader

At the checkout, the barcode reader is connected to the store's computer. When the product is passed in front of the reader, the details are read and passed to the computer, which identifies the item, advises the checkout of its price and then the details are printed out on to the customer's receipt.

Stock holdings

As well as recognising the item and pricing it, the computer will also advise its stock holding section that the item has been sold.

Re-ordering

The stock holding section will have built-in, as a feature of the software, a re-order code. Once a certain level of stock is reached, the system will automatically scan to see if stock is already on-route, when it is due to arrive and what the quantity is. In the event that there is a rush for certain products, and the on-route stock quantity maybe inadequate, then a further request for stock is placed on the company warehouse for future delivery.

Stocktaking

This is also carried out much more quickly. The staff will download, to a hand-held device, the details, such as the name and code, of the stock on hand. The staff then count the items on the shelves, and enter the quantity on the device. The two figures are tallied back on the main computer, taking in to account damaged goods and write-offs.

Another method use a hand-held device, this time with a barcode reader. Each item has a stock code displayed on the front of the shelf, the reader is wiped across the code, and the quantity on the shelf is also entered. The detail is in turn downloaded at the main computer.

Pricing

As all pricing is handled at one point, the computer, changes can be implemented quickly.

Libraries

Computerisation of library holdings has now replaced most of the old methods. Computers lend themselves to this area particularly well.

The master list

The library will have a master list of all publications on its inventory. This list is in turn arranged into categories such as: crime, historical and so on.

Each item will also be listed by title, author, and date of publication, with some specialist publications having a keyword list, on which the staff may conduct searches.

The borrower

For a person to borrow a publication, that person must first be registered at the library.

The registration will include some form of identification, usually a number, which identifies the borrower, along with that person's details such as home address, etc.

Library smart card

Some libraries issue the borrower with a swipe card, which records the above details. The borrower presents the book to the library staff, who in turn passes the card through a card reader. The detail is transferred to the computer and the book details are also entered. The date for return of the book is recorded on the computer. At this stage, the system returns to that of the old system, the library staff then stamps the return date on the sheet inside the book.

Accountancy procedures

Different libraries have different procedures however; at some stage the system will run a check on all loaned publications and produce a list of those publications overdue. This list will contain the details of whom the book was loaned to, the person's address, etc., for further action.

Doctors' surgeries

More and more doctors' surgeries are using computers to store patients' details and records as well as treatment received.

These systems are bespoke systems, especially written for the task and not available from the average computer/software retailer.

This is an area where security implications are enormous. The system must protect the patients' rights of confidentiality and the information must be access protected.

Driving licences

The recently introduced driving licence is a smart card, and has given some organisations a growing concern in respect of the 'Big Brother Watching' syndrome.

The card will record the driver's details on the face of the card, as well as storing that detail, and possibly more, on a chip in the card.

Systems and applications software

Systems software

- Systems software, the operating system, is the software required to run the computer.
- Without the systems software, the applications software cannot be loaded and will not function.

- Any number of applications may run on top of the systems software, provided that it was written for that platform.

Applications software

- Applications software is platform-specific and will use various functions within the systems software to carry out instructions on its behalf.
- It is the application software that has been especially written to perform specific tasks, such as spreadsheets for financial aspects and so on.

Smart cards

Smart cards come in many shapes and forms and include bank debit cards, credit cards, supermarket loyalty cards, fuel cards and so on. The use and potential use of smart cards is endless and is only currently limited by the need for greater security measures.

The range of uses is as diverse as:

Hotel use

In hotels to replace doors keys. The card is programmed, on issue, to open the room allocated to the customer.

Bank use

For use with Bank cash machines. The card is issued to a bank customer, as is a personal identification number (PIN).

The customer inserts the card into a slot and the card is read by the system. The user is then asked to type in the PIN, which is transmitted back to a central location and checked as correct. Once confirmed correct, the user is offered a number of options, which will include the option to withdraw cash.

The bank cash machines are another form of computer network. All the banks that own machines are eventually connected to the main system, where all the customers and their details are stored.

In addition to their own machines, a majority of banks allow other bank customers to withdraw cash from their machines, via the network of interconnected systems. Be aware though, some banks offer this service for free, while others impose a surcharge.

IT and society – the Information Age

This is the age of information. Never before has information been so freely and easily accessible by so many people, to such an extent that there is almost too much available, hence the term 'information overload'.

The abundance of information has lead to the development of specialist applications, designed to sort, filter and present it in various formats.

Impact on society

The way in which information is handled has resulted in a massive loss of jobs in administration, for example in payroll staff.

The computer is more accurate and is extremely fast when compared to a human carrying out the same or similar tasks.

Everything is required and expected to be instant resulting in an increase of stress related problems.

Medical
Medical technologies have benefited with faster and more accurate testing, scanning devices and monitoring equipment.

Weather forecasting
Computers, along with satellite communications and radar have greatly improved the accuracy of weather forecasting.

The information society
The availability of information has created an information profession. These are the people who spend a large portion of their working day processing information. The information may be as a result of filling a tax return, the census form, the driving licence application, the electoral roll and an application for a bank loan, to name but a few sources of information.

The computer vs. man

There are undoubtedly situations where a computer system, either as a computer on a desktop or controlling a robotic device, can carry out functions better than a person does.

Occasions when this may be appropriate are:

- The same repeated tasks.
- Actions that require accuracy and speed.
- Rapid processing of large quantities of information.
- Hazardous operations involving nuclear materials, deep-water operations and suchlike.

There are also occasions when man is the better choice for a certain task, such as:

- When the task is a one-off. The time spent programming a computer would prove non-cost-effective.
- When the information relating to the task is free-flowing and the computer would either have to be re-programmed or to have as part of its programming a learning function. Again most likely non-cost-effective.
- Situations when interpretation on the ground is vital. The computer cannot see or hear, at this point in time, to assimilate the data.

- A situation develops where no programming has foreseen the circumstances or likelihood of such an event.

Care of the computer system

Cleanliness is next to godliness, and that is equally true in relation to the use of computers.

- Keep all liquids away from the systems components. Tea, coffee or whatever spilt over the keyboard will spoil your day as well as ruining the keyboard.

- Because the system creates static electricity, dust will gather and penetrate in to the tiniest of locations. For example; erratic mouse control usually indicates a build-up of dirt inside the case. Follow the manufacturer's instructions and clean it regularly.

- Do not expose or subject the system to excessive heat or likewise excessive cold.

- Store all disks in containers and ensure that there are no magnetic devices in the vicinity of the disks or the computer system.

- When you have finished with the computer do not simply switch it off. There is a shutdown procedure that should be adhered to. If the system fails for whatever reason, the only way to resolve the problem may be to switch off the computer without following the shutdown procedure. Refer to the operating system handbook for more details.

Elementary fault finding

Warning, if you do not feel confident in any way to tackle the following, stop and seek assistance. Do not struggle, you may place yourself in danger or compound the situation and make it worse.

- Check the obvious first, are all the on/off switches in the on position?

- Before moving and adjusting any power cables, ensure that the mains supply is switched off.

- If the system fails to respond when first switched on, ensure that that the power cable to the computer, and the monitor cables, are fully located in their sockets at the back of the computer.

- Now switch the power back on at the source and attempt to restart the computer.

- If the above fails, switch off the supply and plug in another electrical item, at the wall socket, that you know is functioning. This will help to eliminate doubts regarding the power socket on the wall.

- If the problem cannot be resolved after carrying out the above actions, seek professional assistance.

Repeated problems

In the event that a problem recurs over a period of time, make a note of the error message that may appear. Note the circumstances and what you did that caused the error or problem to happen. This will assist the support staff and will, hopefully, save time in solving the problem.

Tip

Always have an up-to-date Emergency Repair Disk (ERD) to hand. This will assist if the system fails to start-up correctly.

Computer crashes

If your computer crashes, all may not be lost.

1 Press the [Ctrl] + [Alt] + [Del] keys simultaneously.

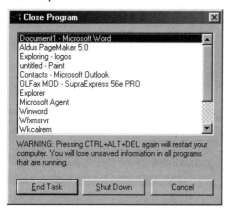

2 The Close program dialog box will open. If you are lucky, it will indicate what the problem is, highlighting the name of the offending program and adding a comment like: 'is not responding'.

3 Press the End Task button.

4 Sometimes another dialog box appears,and this may tell you that the program is busy. Press the End Task button again. This may solve the problem.

Be careful of continually pressing the **[Ctrl]** + **[Alt]** + **[Del]** keys, as this will most likely cause the computer to restart completely.

Health and safety

A problem with computer systems is the abundance of cables that connect their various items.

Ensure that cables are kept tidy and are not likely to cause accidents, for example people tripping over them and perhaps pulling the item off the desk, compounding the problem.

In the work place, it is the employer's responsibility to provide a safe working environment. Likewise it is the home user's responsibility to ensure that the home environment is also safe.

In the office environment, the employer should ensure that the correct office furniture is purchased and installed. For instance:

- Desks with cable management systems should be purchased for all workstations.
- Printer stands should allow stacking and also permit the correct paper feed.
- Some dot matrix printers, particularly the larger machines, can be very noisy. If necessary the printer should be placed inside a noise-reducing cabinet.
- During printing, laser printers will, over time, extrude fine particles of toner. The printer should not be placed where particles can be blown over people working nearby.

Mains power points

Never overload the mains power point. Never use the adapter units that allow more than one plug to be inserted into a socket outlet. There are appropriate means on the market, to permit the running of a number of computer items from one socket.

As most computer items have low power consumption, it is acceptable to use an extension lead. Keep this as short as possible and cut it to length. Do not coil it up if it is too long.

Always ensure that the appropriate fuse is in the plug. Most when purchased, will have a 13-amp fuse installed. That is too high a fuse for the average computer item.

If in doubt, seek professional advice.

Security, copyright and the law

Software copyright

Programs are usually covered by copyright. You are personally liable if you contravene the copyright of the software.

You break the law if you:

- Copy the software and distribute the copies.
- Lend the software to friends to install the software on their computers.

You may make a copy of the software solely as a safeguard, in the event that the original disk becomes damaged.

Licences held

You may only load the software on the number of computers that you hold licences for.

Security

You must afford the original disks and any legally held copies the same level of security.

You must retain all copies of licences for all software used, and maintain a list of where and on what computers the software is loaded.

Freeware

This is software that is freely available, such as demonstration disks, or some educational programs. Read the licences, to ensure that you are not inadvertently contravening any agreements.

Shareware

Software that is made freely available for a limited time, to enable you to decide whether or not you wish to buy it. If you decide that you wish to continue using the software after the trial period, you will be required to register the product and pay a fee.

You must delete the software at the end of the trial period if you are not interested in it, otherwise you will be liable to pay the producers for the product.

Software on the Internet

Pirated copies of software are sometimes available on the Internet. Be sure to check before downloading such software.

End User Licence Agreement

The End User Licence Agreement (EULA) is included as part of the installation program on all software.

As the installation of the software progresses, the user is prompted to agree to the terms and conditions of the EULA, or to discontinue the installation. A section of the EULA states that if you do not agree with the EULA, the user should not to continue with the installation and return the software to the supplier from whom it was purchased.

The supplier however, generally, has in his small print a clause that states that should the cellophane wrapping be removed, the product will not be accepted for any other reason than faulty disks.

Be aware. Ensure you know what you require before you buy.

Data Protection Act 1984

This was introduced to meet concerns arising from the threat which misuse of the power of computers might pose to individuals. These derive from the ability of computing systems to store vast amounts of data, to manipulate data at high speed and, with associated communications, to give access to data from locations far from the site where the data is stored.

All public and private organisations that hold data about individuals or companies on computer systems must register this fact with the Data Registrar, giving the purpose for which the data is held. Data held can only be used for the purpose specified.

Data users must register:

● what data they hold

● how they use it

● how it is obtained

Individuals can obtain a copy of the data held about themselves, and data users must disclose it if requested.

An extract from the Data Protection Act 1984

Schedule 1

The Data Protection Principles Part 1

1. The information to be contained in personal data shall be obtained, and personal data shall be processed, fairly and lawfully.

2. Personal data shall be held only for one or more specified and lawful purposes.

3. Personal data held for any purpose or purposes shall not be used or disclosed in any manner incompatible with that purpose or those purposes.

4. Personal data held for any purpose or purposes shall be adequate, relevant and not excessive in relation to that purpose or those purposes.

5. Personal data shall be adequate and, where necessary, kept up to date.

6. Personal data held for any purpose or purposes shall not be kept for longer than is necessary for that purpose or those purposes.

7. An individual shall be entitled –

   (a) at reasonable intervals and without undue delay or expense -

   (i) to be informed by any data user whether he holds personal data of which that individual is the subject; and

   (ii) to access any such data held by a data user; and

   (b) where appropriate, to have such data corrected or erased.

Appropriate security measures shall be taken against unauthorised access to, or alteration, disclosure or destruction of, personal data and against accidental loss or destruction of personal data.

Rights of Data Subjects – Part III

Subject to the provisions of this section, an individual shall be entitled –

   (a) to be informed by any data user whether the data held by him includes personal data of which that individual is the data subject; and

   (b) to be supplied by any data user with a copy of the information constituting any such personal data held by him;

and where any of the information referred to in paragraph (b) above is expressed in terms which are not intelligible without explanation the information shall be accompanied by an explanation of those terms.

The UK Data Protection Act 1984 is a complex document and the extracts quoted, on the preceding page, were taken from the Website listed below, and was current at the time of writing this publication.

Web site: http://www.hmso.gov.uk/acts/acts1984/1984035.htm#aofs.

A full version of the Data Act can be obtained from The Stationary Office Limited, ISBN 0 10 543584, £6.60.

Security

Computer security not only covers the aspects of theft of the computer, and its associated equipment, but the security of the data stored on the computer itself.

Data

Only legitimately held data can be stored on a computer, as covered by the Data Protection Act.

Passwords

Computer passwords must be guarded carefully, in particular that of the person afforded administrator rights on the computer system.

Copies of the passwords should be maintained and sealed in an envelope and then locked in a secure container, i.e. the company safe.

- Instructions as to who may open the envelopes should be clearly written on the outside of the envelopes.
- Any person permitted to open the envelopes should sign a document stating why, by what authority, etc. that the person is accessing the password lists.

Backup policy

As data may become damaged, lost or otherwise destroyed, there should exist a policy for creating back-up copies of all-important data.

Subject to the degree of importance attached to the data, backups may be required daily or more frequently.

The backup policy may only require the backing-up of new or recently amended data, termed **incremental backup. A full backup** occurs less frequently.

Backup storage

During the course of backing up data it is important to use a different set of tapes for each backup period. This is due to possible damage to the tape, such as tape stretch or breakage.

One copy of the backup tapes should be held on site for easy access. At least one copy of the backup tapes should be held off site as a precaution against fire of theft.

Backup procedures must be documented and clearly understood and practised by the staff responsible for creating the backups.

Equally important is that the **Backup Restore** procedures must be tried and tested. It's all well and good having a good looking document telling the staff what to do, then only to find that the system does not function.

Anti-virus protection

Viruses are becoming more and more of a problem to computer users. Viruses are, generally, small computer programs that are written to disrupt the normal operation of a computer.

Viruses cause a variety of problems, such as:

- Annoying little messages that pop-up on the screen periodically.
- The destruction of the data on the computer.

A virus hit the computer world just before Easter 1999 and caused considerable chaos within companies running e-mail.

The virus arrived via the Internet and once on a computer, would search the system for that person's e-mail address book. It would create 50 e-mail messages based on the address book, then attach itself to those e-mails and sent them through the system. On arrival at each of the 50 addressees, it started all over again.

Clearly for some systems, this created an overload and the systems crashed.

Virus intrusion

Viruses gain access to computers in many different ways, for instance:

- A floppy disk may have a virus on it. The virus transfers itself to the computer hard disk and in turn spreads to other disks.
- Documents can transfer viruses by way of macros contained within them. The viruses will transfer to the computer and spread.
- The Internet is an obvious source of viruses coming in a number of different ways such as downloading files and data.

Virus protection

All systems should employ some form of anti-virus protection, not just anti-virus software, but also company policy as to who may load programs, to what disk may be used and how they should be transported.

Power failure

Security also comes in the form of protection against power failures or power surges.

Uninterrupted Power Supplies

There exists on the market today numerous types of Uninterrupted Power Supplies (UPS) systems. These contain powerful batteries that are on constant standby and will switch in if there is a power failure.

The batteries are not usually powerful enough to allow long continuing use of the computer system, but have sufficient power to give the system adequate time to perform an orderly shut-down without losing any data.

UPS systems have specialist software working in conjunction with the power supply designed to sense a power problem.

Anti-surge protection

Power supply systems are often not running at the correct voltage, etc., due to the strain on the systems or to adverse weather conditions.

These conditions create power surges, increases and fall in the output, which if powerful enough could cause data corruption. Sufficiently powerful surges may actually cause some systems to re-boot, particular in times of storms.

UPS systems can provide considerable protection, by the way of built-in circuitry, and reduce the likelihood of data loss.

Home users can also benefit from such protection by purchasing smaller protective devices, rather than a full-blown UPS system, which can be quite costly.

Hardware, software and ergonomics

Hardware and software

Hardware is the term used to describe a component part or sub-assembly of a computer system. For example:

- the monitor
- the computer case.
- the keyboard.

Software is the term used to describe a program that is run on a computer, for example:

- Windows 98 Operating system.
- Microsoft Office Suite 97.
- Adobe PhotoShop 5.

Types of memory

Random Access Memory (RAM)

RAM is a non-permanent memory system. For RAM to function the computer system must be up and running and functioning correctly.

The operating system and application are loaded in to RAM, as is the information that is currently being processed.

RAM can be written to, that is when information is placed into the memory, and can be read from, that is when information can be retrieved from the memory.

When the computer is shutdown, any data that was in RAM is lost. Once the system is switched off, that data cannot be recovered.

RAM is known by a number of different names, e.g. memory, internal storage.

Read Only Memory (ROM)

As the name suggests ROM can only be used to retrieve information. ROM comes in many forms and can be found burnt into a chip that resides inside the computer.

The chip that comes immediately to mind is the one that contains the start-up instructions for the computer. This is also referred to as the BIOS or CMOS.

- The BIOS or CMOS contains the basic instructions required by the computer on start-up, including information such as what hard drives and other devices are installed, and the instructions to enable it to carry out the POST test before handing the system over to the operating system.

A CD-ROM is also a ROM device.

A floppy disk can be set to a read only state by moving the slide button to expose an aperture. This will prevent the disk being written to until such time that the slide switch is adjusted again to close the aperture.

The purpose of backup

The purpose of backing up information is to ensure that in the event of either:

- an equipment failure, resulting in the loss or damage to data
- the physical destruction of the data by fire
- the actual theft of the data

that the organisation can continue to function by having a second copy of the data available.

A point of fact

Following the bombing of the World Trade Center in New York, some years ago, it was some considerable time before access to the buildings was permitted.

A number of companies, working out of the centre, had backup plans and procedures in place. However, only a small percentage of these stored their backup data off-site and therefore could immediately access that data. The remaining companies did not have access to their data for weeks and in some cases months.

It was estimated, 12 months after the event that some 40% of those companies had gone out of business as a direct consequence of poor backup policy and procedures.

Procedures

There are numerous procedures for backing up data, however, no matter how good the procedures may look on paper, they must function in practice.

Run the backup procedures and the restore element to ensure the data is actually restored.

Input and output devices

Input devices, as the name suggest, input data, instructions and so on into the computer. Examples of input devices are:

- The keyboard
- A scanner

Output devices display the result of the computation. Examples of output devices are:

- The monitor
- A printer

Printers

There are a wide range of printers available for use with computers. The printers are varied in the type and purpose that they are intended for.

Printers are listed under three main headings:

- Laser printers.
- Inkjet printers
- Dot matrix printers.

There are other types, but these tend to be for more specialist use and are not covered here.

All three types of printer are available in either black and white or colour.

Laser printers

Laser printers are generally more expensive and use toner, not ink, to produce the image.

Colour laser printer prices are falling, but compared to the inkjet colour printers, are still extremely expensive.

There are other considerations to be taken in to account other than just the purchase price:

- Toner is expensive.
- Replacement drums are expensive.

- The printing time is longer and slower.
- Most current Laser colour printers have a maximum resolution of 600 x 600, and this is often too low to produce very high quality graphics.

The final printed product, unlike that of the inkjet, is stable and will not run if it comes in contact with moisture.

Inkjet printers

Inkjet printers are quite cheap when compared to laser printers. They use an inkjet to produce the printed document. There are limitations with the ink. Should it be exposed to moisture, the ink will run and if exposed to prolonged sunshine, will fade.

The high majority of inkjet printers are usually a dual inkjet system; that is to say, colour is almost always built-in as standard.

Apart from price, other considerations are:

- What is the end product and what it is intended to convey? Will it include high-end quality graphics and photography?
- Inkjet printers are available with many different resolutions. Some of which are quite low, while others are higher.
- High-resolution printers are a must if it is intended to print photographic images.
- Will special paper be required to produce the imagery on, and how will this look with the everyday paper used in the document.
- Some ink cartridges contain multiple colour inks, which can means that you are throwing away unused ink in these. Others have individual ink cartridges for each colour ink.

Dot matrix printers

The dot matrix printer was once a very common printer however, with the fall in prices of both the inkjet and laser printers, it has declined in use and popularity. They are not often seen in the average office of today.

Dot matrix printers are available in colour as well as black and white.

The print is made up of a series on small dots, from a set of pins, which first must punch onto a ribbon and then impact on to the paper.

There are two sizes for the print head, 9-pin and 24-pin. 9-pin print quality is often poor.

Health and Safety considerations

The European Union issued a series of publications, which became known as the 'six pack'. One of the publications specifically dealt with computer workstation ergonomics and the following areas were addressed:

- Display screens
- Keyboards.
- Work desk/surface.
- Work chair.
- Space requirements.
- Lighting.
- Reflections and glare.
- Noise.
- Heat.
- Humidity.
- Computer/user interface.

All the above items will, in some way or another, have an impact on the working environment of the user. For instance:

- Glare from the monitor screen or from a glossy desktop.

- A strong light behind the monitor, i.e. windows.

- A chair that is not adjustable or does not meet the safety standards laid down in the regulations.

- Cramped and restraining working space.

- Poor lighting conditions that reflect on to the monitor screen.

- The monitor set either too high or, most commonly, too low.

Breaks

The user must take short breaks if involved with prolonged work involving the display screen. The break does not necessarily mean leaving the location of work, but a change of activity away from the display screen.

Eye Tests

Regulation 5 of the Health and Safety (Display Screens Equipment) Regulations 1992 gives the user or those about to become users the opportunity to have an appropriate eye and eyesight test as soon as practicable after request and at regular intervals.

- Special corrective appliances are to be provided by the employer for users where normal ones cannot be used.

- The costs of the tests and special corrective appliances are to be met by the employer of the user.

- The term 'special appliance' will be those prescribed to meet vision defects at the viewing distance – anti-glare screens are not special corrective appliances.

Further regulations

There are a number of further regulations that the employer and casual user should be aware of. The regulations are not simply for guidance but are to be implemented as a matter of law.

Common sense

Most problems can be quickly overcome by the application of a common sense approach however; common sense must not override the application and enforcement of the rules and regulations that apply to the working environment, etc.

Advice

If in doubt, contact your local Health and Safety Executive (HSE) office for advice.

Information network services

A network is a group of connected computers, which can share files, printers and in some cases, applications. All information on a network is potentially shareable. The sharing of information helps to increase the productivity of personnel and of workgroups.

There is also a capital saving to be made by the sharing of printers and other devices. All in all, networks better utilise computer resources and the availability of information.

Network connections

There are a different number of systems used to connect computers, to create the network.

Networks vary in size and complexity. The number of computers on a network will vary, subject to factors such as traffic volume, workgroup design, function, style and much more.

Workgroups

'Workgroup' is another term for a network and is usually used to describe a small group of people, within a small establishment or office and often employs peer-to-peer networking.

Peer-to-peer

In peer-to-peer networking, all the people on the network usually store their files on their own computers, and give access to some, or all, of the files to other users.

This method of networking is cheap and easy to install and is often sufficient for a small office.

Printer sharing

In peer-to-peer networking it is normal to share printers. A shared printer is connected to one computer and the others on the network use that computer's resources to access the printer, thereby saving on costs.

A Local Area Network

A Local Area Network (LAN) may describe a number of computers connected together, in one room, on one floor, in one building or generally in an immediate locality.

A peer-to-peer network, in strict terms, is a LAN. However LAN systems usually employ what is known as a client/server network.

The *client* is the computer at which the user sits – the workstation. All computers are connected to the *server*, via their workstations. The server is a central computer that stores all the files used in common by the company or organisation.

Also running off the server may well be a number of other shared facilities, such as printers and modems.

Wide Area Networks

Wide Area Networks (WAN) interconnect smaller networks. These networks can be close or at a great distance to each other.

The Internet is a series of smaller networks interconnected.

Standard network topologies

All network designs stem from three basic topologies, connection structures.

Bus

The bus topology is the simplest to install and maintain. It consists of a single cable, known as a truck, backbone or segment, that connects all the computers together in a single line.

One disadvantage of the system is that if a cable fails, the complete network will crash.

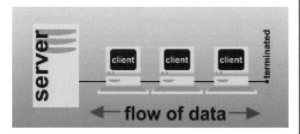

Star

The star topology connects all the computers, by individual cable runs, to a centralised component called a hub. Unlike the bus topology, if one cable fails, the network as a whole will not crash. However, one hub failing may cause a network crash.

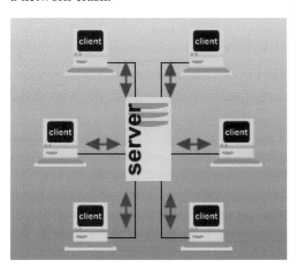

Token ring

The token ring topology connects the computers to a single circle of cable. The signal travels around the cable in one direction and passes through each computer in turn. Each computer acts as a repeater to boost the signal.

The failure of one computer may impact on the entire network and cause a crash.

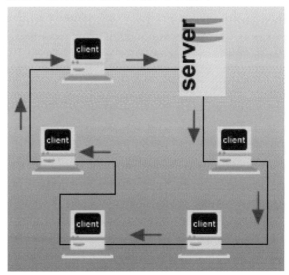

Telephone systems in computing

Telephone systems play a major part in computer networking.

Modems

A modem (*mo*dulator–*dem*odulator) is an device that coverts binary data to analogue tones and voltages that are suitable for transmission over standard dial-up or leased telephone lines.

Many modems also have a fax capability, and in addition, many now offer voice mail facilities, via the software bundled with the modem.

Most home computers now include a modem, which will allow you to connect to the Internet. If you work from home, you can, with the appropriate authorisation, connect to your company's own network. The method used is called dial-up networking.

Dial-up networking

To use dial-up networking, you must have a modem and access to a phone line or a suitable mobile telephone and its associated hardware. You must also have the necessary authority to access the respective network, usually in the form of a telephone number, an approved logon name and the correct password.

You dial the number, and subject to the software and network set-up, may be prompted to logon and provide a password. Some software packages store the logon name and password, thus speeding up the dial-up process. There are of course security implications of such a system.

The handshake

The modem, before it can start transmitting data, carries out what is known as a handshake with the distant modem. This establishes how the modems will exchange information. After the handshake, the modems are ready to pass or receive data as required.

Data compression

The transmitting modem will compress the data, then send it to the distant modem, which will decompress the data. The modems will use what is known as error control, to ensure that the data reliably reaches its destination.

Speeds

Modems have the option of using different speeds to transfer data. When communicating, modems must use the same speed. A fast modem can talk to a slow modem, but both will communicate at the slower speed.

Current Standard

The current standard for most common modems, for everyday use, is V90 56K x2. The explanation of this standard is somewhat involved and is beyond the scope of this book.

Terminology

Online

You are online when the modem has connected to another modem, and is ready to exchange information.

Offline

When the modem is not connected to another, you are offline.

Integrated Services Digital Network (ISDN)

Instead of using standard telephone lines and a standard modem, some companies use an ISDN line. ISDN transfers information four times faster than the standard modem. ISDN requires the use of a specialist modem, called a terminal adapter.

The Internet

The Internet is extremely useful in many ways, shapes and forms and is covered in more detail in Chapter 7.

E-mail

Electronic mail, e-mail, is a very popular feature of the Internet. E-mail can be exchanged with anyone around the world, provided of course that both parties have access to the Internet and have an e-mail address.

To send e-mail, you must have in addition to the above, a computer with suitable software, a modem, telephone line and an Internet Service Provider (ISP).

You can access your e-mail from anywhere in the world, simply by dialling the appropriate telephone number for their ISP, and their e-mail can be accessed using their logon name and password.

Internet browser

To access the Internet, you must have a suitable browser, which translates the Internet data in to a usable visual display on the screen.

Costs

E-mail is fast, easy, inexpensive and cuts out the use of paper, thus creating a saving of resources in one respect.

Voice over the Internet

In the not-too-distant future, greater use of the Internet will be made in the field of voice communications.

Information access

The Internet gives the user access to an abundance of information, often free, through locations far and wide, via newspapers, magazines, academic papers, government documents, television transcripts, speeches, job listings and much, much more.

Entertainment

Hundreds of games are available on the Internet, again often free of charge. Music is now also downloadable. Using the Internet, you can review current movies, theme songs and have interactive conversions around the world, sometimes with celebrities.

Discussion groups

You can join discussion groups around the world, with people who have similar interests. The discussion usually takes place mainly by text. You can ask questions and respond to questions posed by other members of the discussion group.

Online shopping

Online shopping is becoming more and more popular, as more organisations and companies become online shopping providers.

You can buy books, flowers, music CDs, pizza, stocks and shares and order your weekly grocery requirements and have them delivered to your door.

Sample paper1: Basic concepts of IT

Section 1		
1	Name three 'peripheral' items that can be attached to a PC.	1. 2. 3.
2	Name three components typically found WITHIN a PC (i.e. within the case)	1. 2. 3.
3	Which operating system (OS) came first, MS-DOS or MS Windows?	
4	What does 'GUI' (pronounced 'gooey') stand for?	
5	Name three functions of the PC's Operating System (OS)	1. 2. 3.
6	Name three types of application software typically found on a PC.	1. 2. 3.
7	What is the difference between memory and data storage media on a computer?	
8	Which is bigger, a terabyte or megabyte?	Terabyte/ Megabyte
Section 2		
9	Name one advantage and one disadvantage of the use of computer systems in industry.	
10	Cash dispenser points or 'hole in the wall' machines are more accurately known as 'ATM's'. What does ATM stand for?	
11	When computers were first introduced into schools a specially designed computer system commissioned by the BBC was used. What was the name of this system?	
12	Name two current uses of the 'Smart Card' in everyday life.	

	Section 3	
13	Name two occasions where it is considered that a computer is more appropriate to a given task than a human; and two where the human is a more appropriate choice than a computer.	
14	Give two fundamental rules when considering the care of your computer.	
15	When your computer crashes there are three keys which when pressed simultaneously may assist you in discovering the nature of the fault and allow you to shut down your computer in a controlled manner. Which keys are they?	
16	Name a possible Health and Safety issue associated with dot-matrix printers, and how this issue can be overcome.	
	Section 4	
17	Under what circumstances are users allowed to make copies of copyrighted software?	
18	What is the difference between 'freeware' and 'shareware'?	
19	Under the Data Protection Act of 1984 data users must register three pieces of information pertaining to their data. What are these three pieces of information?	
20	Name three aspects of security that must be addressed to ensure the safety of the data on your computer system.	1. 2. 3.
	Section 5	
21	Which of the following can be classified as hardware and which as software?	
	Computer Monitor	Software/Hardware
	MS Windows operating system	Software/Hardware
	Microsoft Office	Software/Hardware
	Mouse	Software/Hardware
	Floppy Disk	Software/Hardware

22	Which of the following statements are true:	
	Random Access Memory (RAM) will store data after the PC has been switched off	True/False
	RAM may be referred to as memory or internal storage	True/False
	ROM stands for Read Once Memory	True/False
	The ROM chip that holds a computer's start-up instructions is called the BIOS or CMOS	True/False
24	Name three common types of printers	1. 2. 3.
25	Which ONE of the following is a likely consequence of increasing the RAM on a PC?	
	You can store more files and folders on the PC	True/False
	The graphics on your monitor will be clearer	True/False
	Your PC will process and run quicker	True/False
	You will be protected against certain viruses	True/False
26	Name FIVE factors associated with working on a PC that have Health and Safety considerations associated with them.	1. 2. 3. 4. 5.
Section 6		
27	Give two reasons why you would want to network a number of PCs in an office.	1. 2.
28	Is the Internet an example of a LAN or a WAN?	LAN/WAN
29	Which ONE of these is NOT a network topology:	
	Shuttle	True/False
	Token Ring	True/False
	Bus	True/False
	Star	True/False
30	Which transfers data the quickest, modems over a telephone line, or a terminal adapter over an ISDN line?	
31	What does the 'E' in 'E-mail' stand for?	
32	Name two uses for the Internet.	

2 Using the computer

Using the computer

System start up

Chapter 1 gave you a basic introduction to the computer hardware. We now move on and take a look at how we get the system up and running, what it is doing during this phase and what the display should look like. Finally, there is a section on the mouse and common fuctionality aspects across applications.

Before you switch on the system always check that there is not a floppy disk in the drive unit. We will return later to why there should not, in most cases, be a disk in the drive when the system starts. Now cast your mind back to the previous lesson and you will recall that the system on/off switch is normally located on the front panel of the main unit. Switch it on.

A power unit built into the computer supplies all the components with power, and you will most likely hear the fan whirr and maybe hear the hard disk drive start to spin as well.

The POST test routine

At this stage the computer carries out a self-test, to determine that everything that should be there is present and functioning. This is known as the <u>POST routine</u> (Power On Self Test) and is stored in a permanent memory area in the system.

During this phase the computer checks that various systems are functioning and will also detect any errors. If the POST discovers a problem, for instance with the floppy drive, it will return an error message, e.g. 'Floppy Disk Drive Failure'.

Numerous errors can be detected by the POST routine, but successful completion of the test does not guarantee that your system is actually free of all errors and problems. On completion of the POST routine, we will assume that the system is fully functional.

The system then loads the routines that are essential to the operation of the computer into the memory. The operating system (OS), Windows 95/98, Windows NT or any other OS is loaded as required. The special files adapt the OS to the hardware requirements.

Finally the Windows interface is loaded and the Desktop appears.

The Desktop display

Think of the computer Desktop as being similar to an office desk and how you arrange the various items that you often find on a desk, such as the documents that you are reading or writing, your telephone, file trays, pens and pencils and so on.

As desktops are configurable to your requirements and preferences, there is no such thing as a standard display. There are, however, certain items that most people retain on their Desktop.

The Desktop display is made up of a number of areas and items.

- **The Background** may be a plain colour, or may be made up of patterns and/or images. These patterns and images are referred to as the wallpaper and a number are pre-packaged in Windows 95/98 operating system.

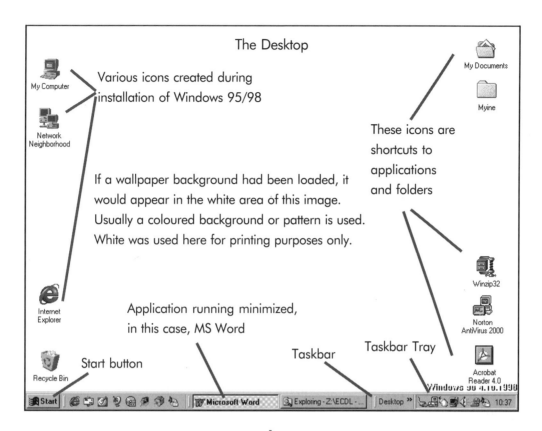

The Desktop

Various icons created during installation of Windows 95/98

My Computer

Network Neighborhood

These icons are shortcuts to applications and folders

My Documents

Myine

If a wallpaper background had been loaded, it would appear in the white area of this image. Usually a coloured background or pattern is used. White was used here for printing purposes only.

Internet Explorer

Application running minimized, in this case, MS Word

Winzip32

Norton AntiVirus 2000

Taskbar Tray

Taskbar

Start button

Recycle Bin

Acrobat Reader 4.0

Windows 98 4.10.1998

You can, once you master the system, create your own backgrounds if you so desire.

- It is from the **Taskbar** that you will generally select and start the applications you wish to use. The Taskbar is usually located along the bottom area of the screen, and has a number of regions that are independent of each other.

- At the extreme left edge of the Taskbar is the **Start button**. This has the word Start on it, and the Microsoft Flying Window logo.

Move the cursor over the Start button and pause. A Tool Tip will pop up.

The Start menu

Click once on the Start button and a pop-up menu will appear.

This is divided into three regions.

The lower region will, in most cases, have only one option available and this is the **Shut Down** command, used to shut down the system.

The middle region has seven options. The top four of these have right-facing arrows, to the right of the items. These indicate that there are secondary menus, and by moving the cursor over the item, a further menu will open. This type of system is known as a cascading menu.

Move your cursor over the option **Programs**.

The secondary menu will open and you may find that there are more right arrows by some of its items.

Do not start any of the applications at this stage. Move the cursor back over the main Start menu and the Programs menu will close.

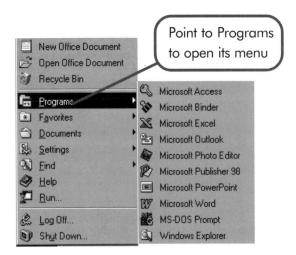

Point to Programs to open its menu

The upper region of the main menu is customisable – you can insert or remove items.

Ensure that the Taskbar is still visible and look to the extreme right-hand side. What you will see is subject to how the computer has been set up, however, there is usually at least one item in this region, and it is the clock.

Move the cursor over the clock, pause and the date will be displayed in the area above the clock.

Other items may well be displayed on the Taskbar and this again will depend on the operating system version and computer setup.

Once an application is open, its name will appear on the Taskbar. If you have two running simultaneously, both names will appear on the Taskbar. It is from here that you can switch between applications. Click once on the application name to bring it up on the screen.

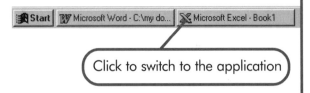

Click to switch to the application

Elsewhere on the Desktop are a number of icons. This again is subject to how the computer has been set up and personalised. Where the icons appear is irrelevant to its operation. In general, one would expect to see the following:

A small image of a computer with the label 'My Computer'.

An image of two computers connected together and the words 'Network Neighborhood'.

An image of a waste bin. This is the Recycle Bin and its name appears below the image.

Other icons may well be on the Desktop but we will end our brief tour at this point.

Starting applications

It's now time to run an application. Move the cursor over the **Start** button and click once. Move up to **Programs,** pause and a cascade menu will open. Move to the right and select .

Microsoft Word will open and the user is ready to either edit an existing document or start a new document altogether.

System shut down

You should never simply switch off the computer using the on/off switch. There is a set procedure for closing down, and the computer itself will tell you when it is safe to switch off.

Restarting the computer

You may sometimes need to shut down the computer and restart it. For instance, if you install new software, for the operating system to recognise the presence of the application, it is often necessary to restart the system.

The **Shut Down Windows** dialog box has an option to restart the computer. Simply select the **Restart** option and click on the **Yes** button, and the computer will shut down and then automatically restart.

Basic steps

1 Ensure all programs have been closed down, in this case, Word.

2 Click the Start button.

3 Select Shut Down from the pop-up menu. A dialog box will open.

4 Select Shut down the computer or Restart the computer as required.

5 Click Yes to confirm the action.

6 The system carries out a series of checks and saves any changes that you may have made to the Desktop, etc.

7 On shut-down, you will then see the message '*It is now safe to switch off your computer*'. Switch off the computer and any peripherals that are connected to it.

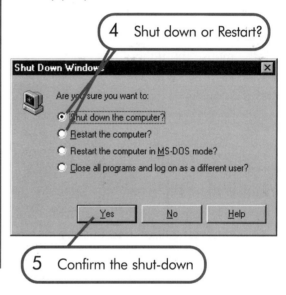

4 Shut down or Restart?

5 Confirm the shut-down

Using the mouse

The mouse is essentially a pointing device and is extremely important because many Windows applications rely heavily on the mouse to initiate actions or functions. This short section will introduce you to a number of mouse actions and the terminology used in association with the mouse throughout this course.

Types of mouse

There are different types of computer pointing devices available, but basically all devices have the following:

- **Roller Ball**. Built into the body of the mouse is a heavy roller ball, which responds to your movements of the mouse by moving the mouse pointer in the vertical and horizontal plains on the screen.

- **Buttons**. There are always at least two buttons, located on top and to the front of the mouse body.

The left button is generally the most used. This is used to select, highlight or in Drag and Drop operations. Generally, when directed to select or highlight an item, it is the left button that is used and is expressed as 'left-click' or simply 'click'.

The right button has recently been given more functionality and acquired an increased importance within Windows applications. The most common result of using of the right mouse button is to bring up a context or pop-up menu. When directed to use the right mouse button, the term generally used is 'right-click'.

Shortcut keys

There are certain actions that when carried out using the mouse can actually slow you down. For instance if you are typing text with both hands on the keyboard, and decide to save your work. To do this requires you to remove a hand from the keyboard and place it on the mouse, then move the mouse pointer up to the Standard toolbar, and then click the Save icon.

This all takes time. Consider the same situation, but this time you keep both hands on the keyboard and you use the keyboard shortcut Ctrl+S. Simultaneously press the Control (Ctrl) and the letter 'S' keys and the item that you are working on is saved. Much quicker, with both hands still at the keyboard.

Common shortcut keys

The really good thing about shortcut keys is that a majority of them are available to you irrespective of the application you are using. The shortcut, Ctrl+S, will save any work in Word, Excel, Access and many more applications.

The 'Save' shortcut combinations uses the Control key. You should be aware that there are other shortcuts, that use combinations of Shift, Control and Alt(ernative) keys. To learn more of these keys, use the online Help.

- **Abbreviations**. Control is abbreviated to Ctrl, Delete is Del and Escape is Esc.
- **Applying the shortcut**. In this book, the shortcut combination is written as Ctrl+S for Save. The plus (+) sign is only shown to indicate that you must press the indicated combination simultaneously. You do not have to press the plus key as well.

Listed below are some of the most common shortcut key combinations and we suggest that you memorise and use them when appropriate. You will be occasionally reminded to use the appropriate shortcut key method.

The list is not exhaustive and you should be aware that applications will have their own unique shortcut keys, which apply only to them. Do remember that common functions, such as Copy and Paste, are common to all Windows based applications.

For further information and lists of shortcut keys, use the online Help for each application.

Shortcut	Action	Shortcut	Action
Ctrl+S	Save current work	**Ctrl+X**	Cut selection to Clipboard
Ctrl+Z	Undo last action	**Ctrl+C**	Copy selected text/image
Ctrl+V	Paste Clipboard contents	**Ctrl+A**	Select entire document
Ctrl+Right Arrow	Move one word to the right	**Ctrl+Left Arrow**	Move one word to the left
End	Move to end of line	**Home**	Move to start of line
Ctrl+End	Move to end of document	**Ctrl+Home**	Move to start of document

Cut, Copy and Paste

Throughout this book you will often encounter the terms cut, copy, paste and Clipboard. So what are we talking about and how does it work? Listed below are a series of short explanations on each item and how the computer deals with each action.

With a sound understanding of these, you will develop a greater understanding of how the computer carries out relatively simple commands, which will increase your productivity, afford you considerable flexibility and reduce the sometimes repetitive tasks.

Clipboard

The Clipboard is a reserved area of computer memory, which cannot be used for any other purpose, that stores data, which originates from the Cut and Copy commands.

The Clipboard can normally only store one section of data/image at any time. For instance, if you cut a section of text and move it, then later cut a different section of text, the previously Cut text is over-written and lost. The situation changes somewhat with Office 2000, which extends the Clipboard so that it can hold up to a dozen separate items of data.

The Clipboard contents can be reused repeatedly, if required, it is not lost until such time that it is either over-written or the computer is switched off.

The commands

In any Windows application, the Cut, Copy and Paste commands can be found as items on the Edit menu and as buttons in the Standard toolbar.

Cut

The Cut action is used to remove a section of selected text, data or image from one location in a document, retains it in memory, ready to be placed in a different location of the same document, or in a different document or application.

Copy

Copy functions in a similar manner as the Cut command, except it does not remove the selected text, it only copies it. Whatever was copied, is retained in memory, and can be placed in another location within the same document, or in a different document or application.

Paste

The Paste command instructs the computer to look in the Clipboard and then to copy, whatever is found, to the cursor location within the current document.

File management

File management is just what the name implies, a means of filing or storing, in a logical and orderly manner all the documents, spreadsheets, databases and images that one creates on the computer. There is no requirement to differentiate between a Word document or an Excel spreadsheet, or any other such item, because in file management terms they are all the same and known as *files*.

Imagine having no system or management of all the files already on the computer; that is even before you start saving anything. Clearly we would spend more time looking for files than actually using them.

Included within the Windows operating system is a program especially designed to assist in file management. It is called Windows Explorer and it is this that we shall investigate.

Most computers only have one hard disk drive and this is referred to as the 'C:' drive, or root directory. Don't concern yourself too much at this stage about remembering all the names and alternatives. We will return to it in more detail later.

Think of the C: drive as a large filing cabinet that has a number of drawers. Within these drawers are a number of folders. 'Folders' is the same term used by Explorer and these folders serve the same purpose as those in the filing cabinet with one exception; the folders in Explorer are electronic folders.

You can do most things with the computer folder that you can with those in a real cabinet.

You can move the folder from one drawer to another. You can insert documents (files) into the folders and likewise you can remove items. If you so decide, you could throw the folder away for good, by deleting it.

You can copy a file, so that you have two identical files, but be careful though this could lead to confusion, and Windows will not allow you to do this in some instances.

Exploring Windows Explorer

Okay, it's now time to take a look at Windows Explorer. Move the cursor over the Taskbar and then click on the Start button once.

The Start menu will pop up. Move the cursor up to **Programs** and another menu will open the right. Remember that a right-facing arrow on a menu means that there is a further menu.

Windows Explorer is usually situated in the lower area of the Programs menu. Click once on Windows Explorer and after a short while Explorer will open. The screen should look similar to the one shown here. The main areas that are of interest to us at the moment have been labelled.

Look first at the All Folders pane that fills the left-hand side of the window. At the very top of this is an icon that represents the Desktop. Imagine that you are sitting at a conventional desk and all your various items and equipment are placed on the desktop. The principle is the same here, the Desktop is the visual focal point of the computer.

Windows Explorer

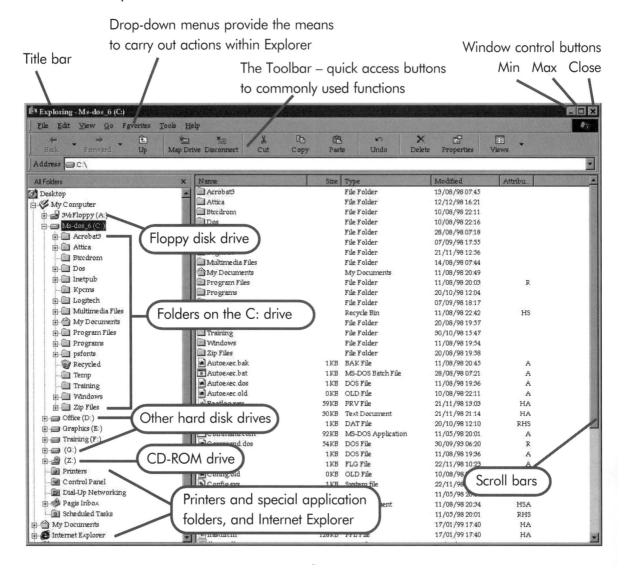

Title bar

Drop-down menus provide the means to carry out actions within Explorer

The Toolbar – quick access buttons to commonly used functions

Window control buttons
Min Max Close

Floppy disk drive

Folders on the C: drive

Other hard disk drives

CD-ROM drive

Printers and special application folders, and Internet Explorer

Scroll bars

You will see that the system is laid out in a hierarchy.

- The highest level is the Desktop.
- The second level down after the Desktop is My Computer, with other items below.
- You will also see that a number of the items shown have a + adjacent to them, to the left. Clicking once on the + sign will open a branch below that item.

Return to the top of the window and you will see a number of drive units.

- The first drive listed is the 3½" floppy (A:). The letter A identifies it as the A: drive.
- Below the floppy drive is the first hard drive, C. In the example the drive also has a name, MS-dos_6 which is followed by (C:).

All storage units are assigned letters to identify each one.

- The letters A and B are reserved for the floppy drives, even though only one floppy is usually fitted in most computers today.

- Below the floppy drive is the C drive, the only hard disk drive in most computers.

- The CD-ROM drive and any other types of unit are also assigned drive letters. If your computer is connected to a network, letters will be assigned to identify the various network connections and drives.

- As the alphabet has 26 letters, so you can assign up to 26 letters to drives.

Folders

Folder names

Windows 95 introduced long file names to the Windows based PC. Prior to the arrival of Windows 95, MS-DOS rules applied and one could use no more than 8 letters in a file name.

With the long file name rules and conventions, you can use up to 256 characters, including hyphens and spaces when naming folders.

There are a number of characters, such as the colon and full stop, that are reserved for the operating system, which means we cannot use them. Windows will usually prompt you if you do attempt to use them and will give you the opportunity to change the name.

Folder structures

Folders' names should be unambiguous and relate to their content. For instance, if you deal with invoices, a first level folder could be named *INVOICES IN* and another folder called *INVOICES OUT*.

Within each folder there could be a subfolder for each financial quarter, perhaps called *INVOICES 1-98*, *INVOICES 2-98*.

The optimum name should contain a maximum of 15 characters. Long names only cause confusion and consume time and space.

Naming files

The rules and conventions for file naming are much the same as for naming folders. You can use upper and lower case letters as well as hyphens and spaces and up to 256 characters.

The notable exception when naming files is the use of the extension. This consists of a full stop followed by a group of three letters and comes at the end of the file name. The letters indicate what type of file it is.

In this example you will see that there are two files, each with a different extension. The first, *6Test.doc*, is a Word document, indicated by the extension *.doc*.

The second, *7Test.xls*, is an Excel spreadsheet indicated by the extension *.xls*.

Opening folders

Sometimes you will have to open several subfolders to locate a file. In this example I am looking for the file *Basic.dll*. To reach the file I first have to open three folders.

We now are looking at the folder called *Logitech*. This is on the C drive and has a + sign to its left. I click once on the + sign.

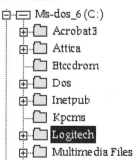

Note the + sign next to some of the folders. This indicates that there are subfolders within them.

In this example note that the + sign has changed to a – sign. We now see that there is a folder within *Logitech*, called *Mouse*, and it too has a + sign next to it. A click on the + sign will open the folder.

In this example the *Mouse* folder has been opened to reveal a further three folders.

Note the absence of any + or - signs adjacent to any of the three folders.

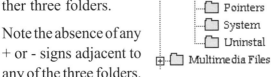

In this example the folder called *System* has been opened. In the window on the right you can see the files that are stored in the *System* folder.

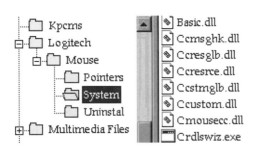

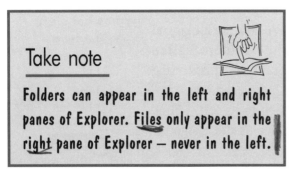

Take note

Folders can appear in the left and right panes of Explorer. Files only appear in the right pane of Explorer – never in the left.

Creating folders

You can create folders as required. Folders can be created within folders, and are referred to as subfolders.

For this exercise we will create a number of folders, using the names listed in the sequences outlined below.

Basic steps

1   Run Windows Explorer and click once on the C: drive.

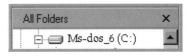

2   Open the File menu, point to New and select Folder.

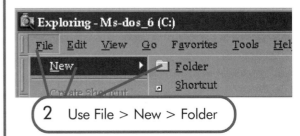

2   Use File > New > Folder

3   Type in the name *0Student*, the 0 is actually a zero not a letter O.

4   When you finish typing, press [Enter]. This tells the computer that it should now carry out the instruction, in this case, apply the new file name.

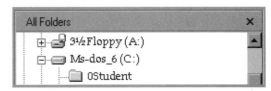

5 Now press the F5 key, at the top of the keyboard to refresh the screen display. The folder will now appear at the top of the C: drive listings.

❑ That's it. You have just created your first folder. However, we are not going to stop at just one folder. We require a number of folders to complete this exercise, so carry on as outlined below, and remember to read each instruction carefully.

Tip

If you make a mistake while typing in the file name and have not yet pressed [Enter], you can erase the error with [Backspace].

If you have pressed [Enter] and then realise that the name is incorrect, click on the file name, then press [F2] which will highlight the name so that you can overtype it.

Creating additional folders

Create another folder, following the sequence already described. Select the C: drive in the left pane first, so that the new folder is created at that level, and call this new folder *1Student*, use the figure '1' not the letter 'I'.

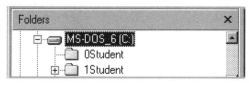

We still require another folder. This one is to be placed within the folder you have just created, *1Student*. This will be a subfolder.

Basic steps

1 Click on the folder *1Student*.

2 Select File > New > Folder.

3 The new folder will appear in the right pane. Name this folder *Exercise*.

4 When you pressed [Enter], a '+' sign appeared adjacent to the folder *1Student*. Click once on the '+' sign and *Exercise* will appear below *1Student*.

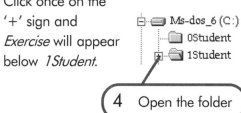

5 The '+' sign will change to a '-' sign. Click on the '-' sign and *Exercise* will no longer be visible.

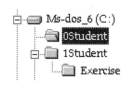

Creating files

At this stage we have created three folders, which are empty. We will now create a number of files and place them in the new folders. In this exercise we will create the files without actually opening any applications.

Basic steps

1 Select the folder *0Student*.

2 Move up to the menu bar and select File.

3 Point to New, then select Microsoft Word Document.

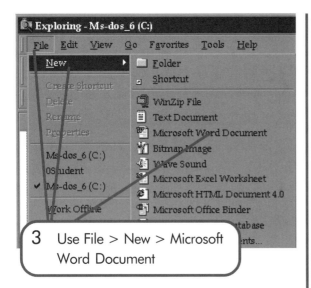

3 Use File > New > Microsoft Word Document

4 Look in the right pane and you will see a new file, called *New Microsoft Word Document*. It may have an extension .doc.

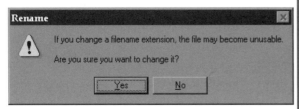

5 Note that the file name is highlighted ready for you to type in the name for the file. As soon as you start typing, you will overwrite the name in the box.

6 Enter the name *2Test.doc* – do not include any spaces. If you do not type in the .doc at the end of the name the following dialog box will appear:

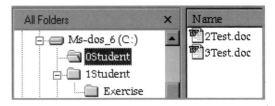

7 Should this occur, click No, and you will be returned to Explorer. Retype the name, with the .doc, and press [Enter].

To continue with this exercise we require a number of additional files. Carry on, follow the instructions and create the files, with the names given, in the stated folders.

In the folder *0Student*, create another Microsoft Word Document, and call it *3Test.doc*.

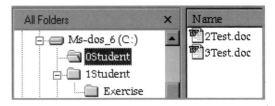

We are now going to create two spreadsheet files. Follow the procedure as above, but in this instance select Microsoft Excel Worksheet. Before you type in the name, note that the extension, now reads *.xls*. This will identify the file as an Excel worksheet.

In the folder *1Student*, create the files *4Test.xls* and *5Test.xls* – **remember** not to insert any spaces in the names.

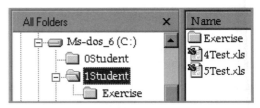

Finally, create one Word and one Excel file (named *6Test.doc* and *7Test.xls*) in the folder *Exercise*. Remember that this is a subfolder within *1Student*.

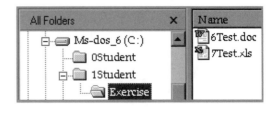

That's it. We have all the folders and files needed to enable us to move onto the next phase of the exercise, which is, to copy and move files between folders.

Copying and moving files

The Copy command allows you to copy a file and place the copy in a different location. As is often the case with Windows, there are a number of ways to do this. For this exercise, we will use the pop-up menu. Pop-up menus are available within most applications, and apply to specific areas within each application.

Basic steps

1 In the left pane of Explorer, click on the '+' sign adjacent to the folder *1Student* to expand it and reveal its subfolder *Exercise*. We will need access to this folder shortly.

2 Select the folder *0Student* and move the cursor over the file *2Test.doc*.

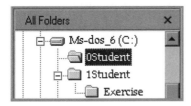

Take note

You cannot copy a file to a folder that already contains a file with the same name. If you attempt to, you will be prompted and asked if you wish to overwrite the existing file. If in doubt click No on the prompt, investigate the File and then decide what course of action to carry out.

---

3 DO NOT select the file, but right-click once over it – a menu will pop up.

4 Take a moment to investigate the options, but note that your menu may differ from this, depending on your PC's configuration.

Use Cut to move items. The Cut command will remove the file, or folder, from its current location and store it in temporary memory. It can then be Pasted into its new location.

Copy stores a copy of the file or folder in memory, ready for use in a different location.

Paste completes the Copy or Cut command and inserts the file in its new location. Paste does not appear in the menu that pops up from a file.

5 Point to the file *2Test.doc*, in the folder *0Student*. Right-click and select Copy.

6 Move across to the left pane and point to the folder *1Student*. Right-click on it and select Paste from the pop-up menu.

❑ At this point in time you will not see the result of the Copy command because Explorer is still looking at the *0Student* folder.

7 Click on the folder *1Student* to select it. Look in the right pane of Explorer and you will see that there is now an additional file, *2Test.doc* present, in the folder.

8 Open the folder *0Student* and you will see that it is now empty.

Tip

The Cut, Copy and Paste commands were introduced on page 56.

Alternative method

We are now going to use another method of moving files and folders. This is known as 'Drag and Drop'.

Basic steps

1 Move the cursor over the folder *Exercise*. Click once on the left button but *DO NOT* release the button. Keep holding it down.

2 Move the mouse, keeping the left button pressed, up to the folder *0Student*. This will become highlighted as the cursor moves over it.

3 Once the folder is highlighted release the mouse button.

4 The folder *Exercise* will now appear in the right pane and a '+' sign will appear next to *0Student* and disappear from *1Student*.

The Edit menu

The actions carried out above introduced you to the pop-up menu, the Toolbar and the Drag and Drop methods. There remains another method and it is available via the Edit menu.

Left-click once on Edit and you will find the Cut, Copy and Paste commands are available from this point also.

Deleting files

You have already deleted one file earlier in the exercise. However it is necessary to explain how Windows 95/98 actually deletes items, because it is not quite as straightforward as first appears.

Windows reserves a portion of hard disk, usually about 10%, for use by the **Recycle Bin**. When you select an item and then press the Delete key, the file is actually moved to the Recycle Bin. It is not deleted immediately.

● If an item was accidentally deleted, it could be recovered from the Recycle Bin, provided the Bin has not been 'emptied'.

● To restore a file, open the Recycle Bin, highlight the file, and select **File > Restore**. The file will be restored back to its original location.

● To empty the Recycle Bin, open the Bin, select **File > Empty Recycle Bin**, and click **Yes** when prompted. After this stage, there is no recovery – the item is gone forever.

Multiple file selection

It is possible to copy, move or delete a group of files rather than handling files individually.

If the files are listed one after the other, simply select the file at the top of the list, press and hold down **[Shift]**, then select the last file in the list. All the files in the group will be highlighted. Double-check that you have selected only those files that you wish to delete.

If the files are not in a contiuous block, select the first file, press and hold down **[Control]**, then individually select each file. Should you inadvertently make an incorrect selection, keep **[Control]** down and click once more on the incorrectly selected file to deselect it.

The highlighted files can then be cut, copied or deleted as a group, using the same methods as for individual files.

Renaming files

There may come a time when you will want to change a file name. There are several ways to do this – we will use Explorer.

Basic steps

1 In Explorer, open the folder *1Student*. In the right pane you will see four files.

2 Right-click once over the name area of the file *4Test.xls* to get the pop-up menu.

3 Select Rename. The file name will become highlighted.

4 Type in the new name *Exel.xls*. You must remember to type in the extension (.xls) or you will be prompted for a response from the operating system.

An alternative method

You could rename a file by using the command **File > Rename**, or by pressing **[F2]**. In both cases, you must select the file first.

Saving files

When saving files you will have the option of where, or more accurately, on which storage device you store the file. In most cases, it will be either the hard disk, usually the C: drive or the floppy disk A: drive.

Of course other storage devices are available and are being used more and more. However, for the sake of simplicity, we will assume, at this stage, that only the A: and C: drives are available to you.

You will recall that earlier in the book the subject of creating folders and managing files was discussed, along with a number of recommendations and suggestions as to how you can structure your filing system.

- Initially when saving a file, either the **Save** option is selected from the **File** menu, or by clicking on the **Save** icon on the Standard Toolbar.

- When a file is saved for the first time, the Save As dialog box will open. This is because the system recognises the fact that the file does not currently have a file name.

- Once a file has a name, subsequent changes are saved to the same file name.

If at any time you should decide that you need to save the file using a different name, then the **Save As** option should be selected. You then simply allocate the file a different name, and straightaway what you have is actually a copy of the orginal file.

This option of saving the same file under a different name is extremely useful and permits you to modify either file to suit your requirements, while retaining a copy of the original.

The Save As dialog box

Shown below is the **Save As** dialog box and it is within this that you select where the file will be stored and allocate it a name.

The selected storage device, in this instance the 3½" floppy disk

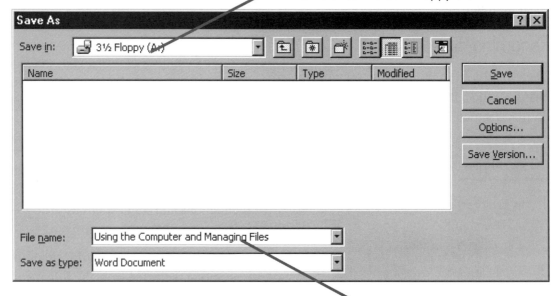

The File name box

Path

The term 'path' is used to identify the route to, or to express it in another way, the location of a file. Let's assume that we have just saved a file, using the name *Sales*, in a folder called *August* and that folder is on the *A:* drive. Using the Path method of description it would appear as *A:\August\Sales*. This is a quicker and simpler method of describing the file's location.

Disk drives

Floppy disks and hard disks consist of platters, coated with a magnetic surface. It is this magnetic material that is the storage medium and the data is stored by rearranging the magnetic pattern on the disk.

Damage and misuse of disks can result in data loss. Floppy disks in particular are susceptible to damage simply by being left too close to items that have a magnetic field. Do not bend or touch the disk inside the plastic casing.

Disks must be formatted before they can be used.

Formatting disks

What is formatting? To enable the computer to store information on a disk, in an orderly and logical manner, some form of structure is required. Formatting creates this structure on the disk. Without going too deep into it at this stage, formatting creates sectors on the disk and each sector becomes addressable.

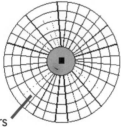

Sectors

The size of the sectors depends upon the disk size, and is not easily changed once set. Basically the larger the disk, the larger the sector.

When you save a file to disk, the file may well be smaller, or for that matter greater, than the sector size on the disk. Let us assume that the file to be saved is greater than the sector size. The file is saved to disk and fills up one sector, the remaining part of the file is placed in another sector. If this portion of the file does

Take note

If you format a disk with data on it, that data is lost and cannot be recovered. Always check the disk content before formatting.

not fill the sector, the remaining area of this sector cannot be used for saving any other files. It effectively becomes wasted space.

To keep track of where all the individual pieces of file are stored, a particular area on the disk is reserved, and it is known as the File Allocation Table, FAT for short.

File fragmentation

Now imagine that you had originally saved a file to disk, then deleted that file. The FAT takes this in to account and when you next save a file, this space is available and may be used. Because this space is almost certainly spaced out around the disk, file fragmentation occurs. What this means is that the file is not saved as one long continuous file but rather sections of the file fill up any space available, irrespective of where on the disk the space is.

Over a period of time, fragmentation can become a problem and slow down the time it takes to find and open programs and files. To assist in overcoming this problem, Windows includes a number of tools, and we will return to the subject of tools later.

Basic steps

1 Place the floppy disk into the disk drive – the metal shutter end goes in first, and the label should be uppermost.

2 Minimise any open windows so that you can see the Desk-top. Double-click on the My Computer icon.

3 Once open, right-click over the 3½" Floppy (A:) and select Format from the pop-up menu.

4 The Format dialog box will open and it is here that you can set your format options.

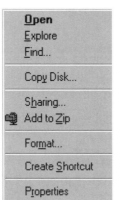

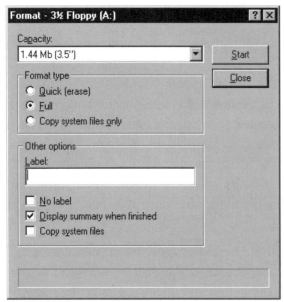

5 The Capacity will indicate the disk type, in the instance 1.44 Mb(3.5").

6 In the Format type area select *Full*.

7 You can, if you wish, type in a Label.

8 Ensure that the Display summary when finished checkbox is ticked.

9 Click Start. You can see the progress made by checking the Formatting progress bar at the bottom of the dialog box.

10 The Format Results dialog box gives you a full status report on the disk when the formatting is complete. Click Close.

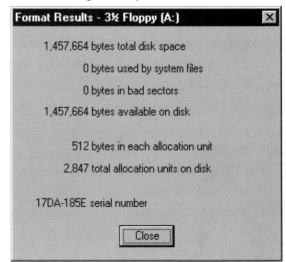

11 Back at My Computer, double-click on the 3½" Floppy (A) and its window will open. This is empty because you have just formatted the disk. Any data that was on the disk has now been lost.

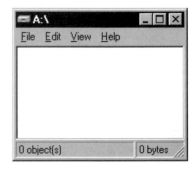

Backups of data

The expression 'Backup' means that you make copies of your important data in case a disaster occurs and the original data is corrupted, or is destroyed in some way or another.

There are a number of different, and some complex, methods of backing up data. The hardware involved could be as simple as a floppy disk however, for large quantities of data other methods are used.

On networks, the hard disk drives can be connected in a manner known as mirroring. What this means is that when data is saved, the information is saved simultaneously to two or more hard disks. In the event of a drive failure, the other drives will continue to function and data is not lost. A drive failure occurs when either the drive develops a fault, or a poor cable connection occurs.

Another method, used in conjunction with the above, is daily backups to a tape drive. A different tape is used each day and copies are stored off-site for additional security, for instance in the event of a fire.

Companies who have vast quantities of data will sometimes take their backup systems to the extent of actually having empty offices with duplicated computer systems running in parallel to the operational in-use system.

Creating backup files

We are not going to go to the extent of duplicating computer systems however, we are going to make backup copies of a number of files.

These files, because they are not large, will be stored on a floppy disk. Remember the standard floppy disk can only hold a maximum of 1.44 MB of data.

Basic steps

1 Open Windows Explorer.

2 Insert a floppy disk in to the disk drive.

3 Right-click on the folder *1Student*.

4 The pop-up menu will open. Point to the Send To command, and from its submenu select $3^1/_2$ Floppy (A).

5 A dialog box will open and you will see a visual display of the files being copied to the floppy drive.

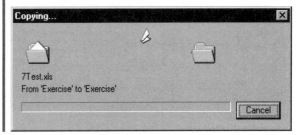

6   Now double-click on the 3½ Floppy (A:) and you will see the folder, *1Student*, has been copied to the floppy disk.

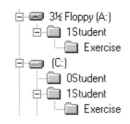

Identifying file details

Once you have made copies of your important data, you must remember to change the backup copies each time you amend or change the master files.

How do you do this? When you save a file, not only is your data saved but this additional information is also saved:

● The file name and extension.

● The file size.

● The file type.

● The date and time the file was modified.

Name	Size	Type	Modified
6Test.doc	11KB	Microsoft Word D...	17/Nov/96 00:00
7Test.xls	14KB	Microsoft Excel ...	17/Nov/96 00:00

Not only does the above information assist in keeping track of backups, but it will also assist you when you are searching for a file. If you have forgotten where you stored a file, or you just remember that you last amended it on a certain date, these details will speed up your search. More on this later.

Backup software

Windows has, as part of the operating system, a backup software package, which is fairly elementary but quite adequate, in most cases for home and small office use.

To access the backup software, open Windows Explorer and right-click over the drive on which the files are stored that you wish to backup. Select **Properties** from the pop-up menu and when the Properties dialog box opens, select **Tools**.

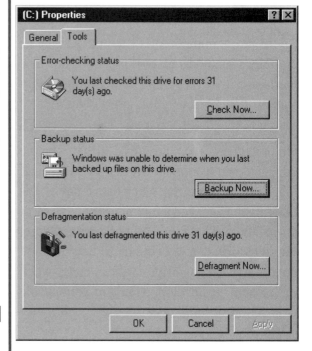

The backup application is located in the central area of the dialog box.

It is recommended that you read the online Help section on backups before attempting to backup any data, so that you have a better understanding of the application, which may initially appear somewhat confusing.

Third party products

If you have a requirement to backup large volumes of data, the backup application in the Windows operating systems may not be adequate. You like most business users will probably require a third party specialist product.

The term 'third party product' means an application or utility produced by a company or organization other then the operating system vendor. The product is not supplied as a part of the operating system, but must be purchased separately and then loaded on to the computer in the same manner as any other application.

Most of these products will employ a compression method. What this does is to 'squeeze' the data, which makes the file smaller and it then takes up less space on the storage medium used. However, there are drawbacks to this method, mostly in that it takes quite a long time to backup large quantities of data, and it is not always easy to recover a single file rather than whole blocks of data.

Winzip

A well known and often quoted product, that is extremely handy for the home user, is Winzip. This product is given away for free on most computer magazines. There are one or two limitations of the free version of the product, however, it is still a very useful utility to have for home and small office use. Winzip is not designed for large-quantity data backup.

Caring for floppy disks

Never leave disks exposed to direct sunlight

Never expose disks to magnetic or electrical fields

Do not bend the disk

Store disks at room temperature

Do not open the shutter and touch the disk directly

Selecting printers

The computer is a tool to produce letters, spreadsheets, databases and much more. The end products of most of these are frequently required to be printed out for distribution and so on. To this end a printer is installed and connected to the computer.

More than one printer can be installed on a computer, though there is only one connection port, known as LPT1, for the printer. Additional ports can be installed if required.

Methods of connecting printers

There are a number of ways that one could connect additional printers to the computer using switch boxes, or what is becoming the norm, using the USB ports available with Windows 98. Refer to your computer manual for further details.

Another method of connecting to a different printer is through a network. The printer is connected directly to a network and can be set up in such a manner that anyone can use it, or a password list can authorise access to the printer.

Yet another connection could be used where another computer is on the network, and its printer is 'shared'. What this means is that the printer is set up by the operating system to be available to anyone on the network.

Networked printer

Shared printer

When more than one printer is installed on a computer, one is designated the default printer. What this means is that printing will always be carried out by this printer unless the setup is specifically changed (see below). If you look in the *Printers* folder, the default printer is indicated by a tick next to its icon.

A document can be sent to the printer using two different methods.

The first is by clicking once on the printer icon on the Toolbar. This will send the whole file to the default printer, using the current settings.

The printing of single pages in covered later in the book.

The Print dialog box

The other method of printing is to open the **File** menu and select **Print**. This will open up a dialog box, shown overleaf, where you may change the printer selection, or the number of copies to be printed and other factors.

To select a different printer, click on the down arrow at the end of the printer name slot. A drop down-list will appear, click once on the printer that you require and the list will close; that particular printer is now selected.

When the drop-down list closes, you are ready to print. Left-click on the OK button and the document is sent to the printer.

The dialog box will close and you are returned to whichever application you were using.

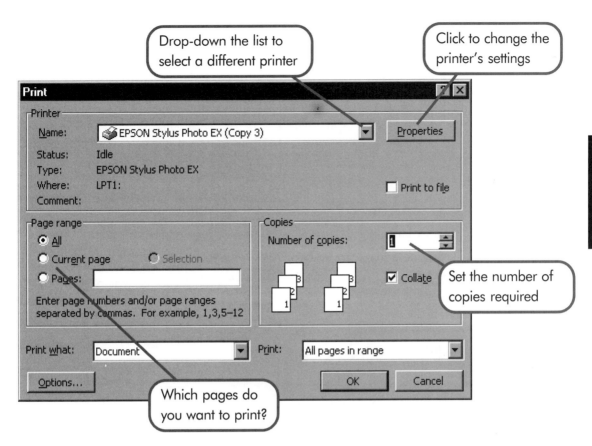

Drop-down the list to select a different printer

Click to change the printer's settings

Set the number of copies required

Which pages do you want to print?

Printing selected pages

There will be times when you have a multi-page document, but do not want to print it all.

To print just one page, place the cursor on that page before you use **File > Print** and when the dialog box opens, select *Current page* from the Page range section.

If you decide that you do not require the complete document to be printed, say for example, you have amended a number of pages, you can specify which pages are to be printed. For example, to print pages 2, 4, 5, 6 and 8, type 2,4-6,8 into the *Pages* slot. Click **OK** to print the selected range.

Printing multiple copies

To print more than one copy of your document select **File > Print** to open the dialogue box. Move the cursor over to the **Copies** section and click the up arrow next to *Number of copies* to set the number required.

Changing printer properties

Most modern printers will display a **Properties** button on the Print dialog box. Clicking this will open a further dialog box from which you may make adjustments to the quality of the printing, select specialist paper, if you are using a colour printer, and change the printer resolution. We are not going to make any adjustments at this time, but you should be aware of this facility.

Online Help

The Help functions can be accessed in two ways.

- Either click the **Start** button on the Taskbar and select **Help**,
- or from within Windows Explorer open the **Help** menu and select **Help topics**.

Either method will take you to the same window, where you can find help in several ways. Here's how to use the Index.

Basic steps

1 Select the Index tab.

2 Type into the slot a 'keyword' a word which describes the feature for which you want Help.

3 As you start typing, the pane below will scroll through the index to match the letters that you are typing.

4 Select a topic from the list.

5 Click Display.

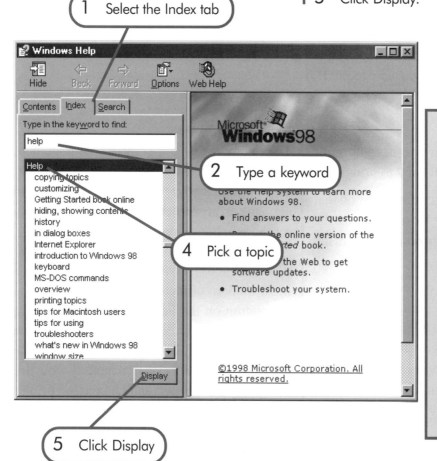

1 Select the Index tab

2 Type a keyword

4 Pick a topic

5 Click Display

Tip

If you can't find what you want in the Index, try typing one or more keywords into the Search tab. The routine here will search through the text — not just the titles — of all the pages in the Help system to find matching words.

❑ If there is only one Help page available on the topic, it will be displayed in the right-hand pane. If there are several pages the Topics Found dialog box will open.

6 Select a subject and click Display.

7 The dialog box will close and the selected Help topic will be displayed.

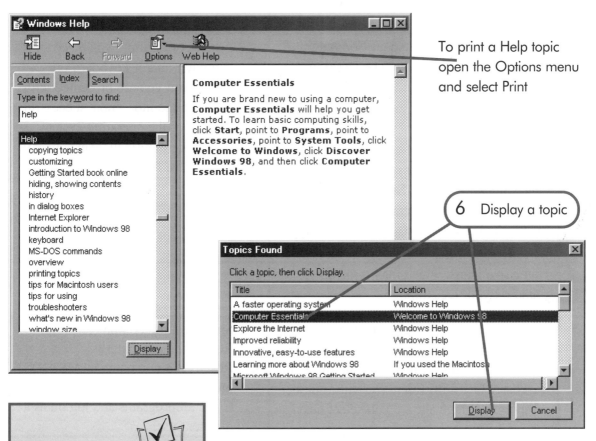

To print a Help topic open the Options menu and select Print

6 Display a topic

Tip

Experiment with the Help facility to familiarise yourself with Microsoft names, and lists of various actions and commands. Switch to the Contents and Search tabs and explore their possibilities.

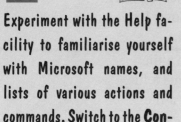

Take note

Windows' online Help is not dissimilar to that of applications such as Word or Access, though these have more flexibility, or in the case of Access more interactivity with the application. Experiment and you will learn considerably from the Help system.

Sample paper 2: Using the computer

1	When switched on, the computer runs a self-test routine sometimes called a 'POST' routine. What does 'POST' stand for?	
2	When referring to a Personal Computer, what is usually meant by 'The Desktop'?	1. A piece of furniture you place your computer and/or keyboard on. 2. The screen you are presented with on your monitor upon successful loading of the operating system. 3. The background wallpaper you may have on your computer monitor.
3	When clicking on the **Start** button on the Taskbar, you are presented with a pop-up menu. Name two options or commands typically found within that pop-up menu.	1. 2.
4	Name two icons, which may typically be found on your Desktop.	1. 2.
5	When switching off your computer there is a set procedure you should follow. First you should click the 'Start' button on your Taskbar, which will present you with a number of options. Which should you select next?	1. Shutdown the computer? 2. Restart the computer? 3. Restart the computer in MS-DOS mode? 4. Close all programs and log on as a different user.
6	What is the name of the program specifically designed to assist you with File Management on your Personal Computer.	1. File Manager. 2. Internet Explorer. 3. Windows Explorer. 4. Excel.
7	Which of these can you NOT do using the Windows file management system?	1. Move a file. 2. Rename a file. 3. Copy a file. 4. Delete a file. 5. Re-size a file.
8	The buttons, at the top right of a window, control the window itself. What does the 'X' button enable you to do?	

9	Which letter is normally used to represent the floppy drive on a PC?	
10	What does the '+' sign next to a folder indicate.	1. The folder is 'open'. 2. The folder is 'closed'. 3. The folder has subfolders within it. 4. There are no subfolders within it.
11	When deleting a file within Windows 95/98 the system temporarily stores the file on a reserved portion of the hard disk. What is this area known as?	
12	When examining a file using Windows Explorer you can see certain information about the file. File name and type are two things, name a further two.	1. 2.
13	Why do floppy and hard disk drives have to be formatted?	
14	The FAT keeps track of where information on a disk is stored. What does FAT stand for?	
15	What happens to data stored on a disk if that disk is then formatted?	
16	Name three factors, which may damage a disk.	1. 2. 3.
17	Making copies of data to use in case the original data is lost is known as what?	
18	What is the most common connection port for a printer called?	
19	What symbol next to a printer indicates that it is the default printer?	
20	When you choose to print a document via the **File** menu you are presented with a **Print** dialog box which allows you to set options. Selecting the printer to use, and which pages to print are two, name another option.	

3 Word processing

Introducing Microsoft Word

Word is the word processing application included in the Microsoft Office suite. You will recall from Chapter 2 that any document, produced by a computer is in electronic form. As such, we can move, copy or delete various sections of the document easily. Images can be inserted, as can tables and columns.

Starting Word

You can start Word a number of different ways. If Word is installed as part of the Office suite, a shortcut bar is also installed, and you can start the applications from it. We, however, will use the Start button method.

Locate the Taskbar and click the Start button. Move the cursor up to the Programs area of the menu. A second menu will open out to the right, locate Microsoft Word and click on it.

Below is an example of Word's main window, showing the key areas and features. There are a number of items and controls not shown and these will be identified and discussed later.

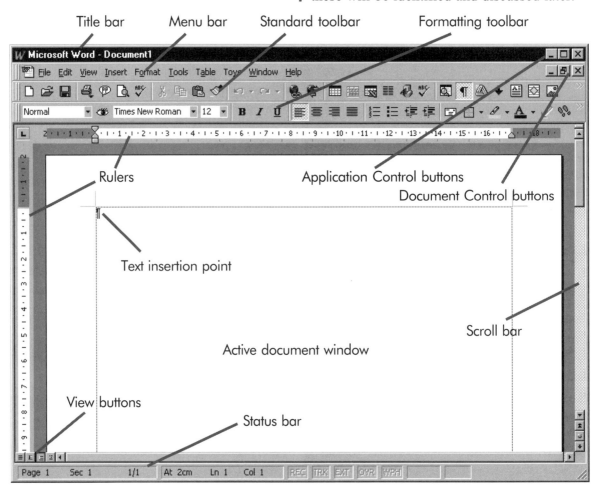

Title bar   Menu bar   Standard toolbar   Formatting toolbar

Rulers

Application Control buttons

Document Control buttons

Text insertion point

Scroll bar

Active document window

View buttons

Status bar

Menus and toolbars

Microsoft applications can be customised by their users, so you may find that some of the examples in this book do not match exactly what you see on your screen. Do not concern yourself because we will only use the standard menus and toolbar commands when telling you how to carry out a particular procedure.

The Menu bar

This is the uppermost bar located immediately below the Title bar. It is from the Menu bar that most commands and functions are located. In the example shown below the Format drop-down menu is shown open, listing all the standard default formatting options available.

There are several different ways to access commands and functions in Word, as in all Windows applications.

Menu Bar

Standard Toolbar

The Standard toolbar

The Standard toolbar gives you one click access to the commands and functions that are most commonly used in Word. As you move the cursor over the icons, a Tool Tip will appear to identify the purpose of the respective icon. The icons are grouped together on the toolbar in accordance to their functions.

Starting at the left of the toolbar, the first group on icons relates to opening a new blank document, opening an existing document and saving a document.

You will often find yourself using the third group of icons. The icon with the scissors image is the Cut icon, followed by the Copy and Paste icons. For more on Cut, Copy and Paste, please refer back to page 56.

The Formatting toolbar

It is from the Formatting toolbar that most text based formatting can be carried out.

As already mentioned, there are a number of ways that you can access various commands, and if you look at the drop-down menu in the Menu Bar example, you will see that the Formatting toolbar duplicates a number of the Format menu options.

Formatting Toolbar

Viewing a document

When Word starts up, a new blank document is displayed, and if you check the Title Bar you will see that Word has given the document a default name. If it is the first document opened, default name will be Document1. The number at the end of the word 'Document' will increase as you open subsequent new documents, until you actually save the document.

There are four ways that you can view the document: Normal, Online Layout, Page Layout and Outline.

To understand the how the different views display text, I suggest that you open a document that has text in it. When the document is open, select **View** on the menu bar and select each of the above options, in turn, to seen the manner in which the page and text is displayed.

You will, in time, find the best View to suit your methods and way of working, however for the duration of this course please use the Page Layout view.

The examples shown in the exercises that are used in this course are all in Page Layout view.

Opening documents

We will use the toolbar icons to open and save documents, though you can carry out the same functions by selecting New, Open, or Save from the File menu. The icons are:

☐ Open a blank new document

☞ Open an existing document

🖫 Save a document.

Entering text

Open a blank new document and type in the text shown below. Save the document to the 3½ Floppy (A:) disk, and call it 'Colliery'.

The Colliery

The news had just leaked out that the Pit was to close. Pop had never known any other work, except of course when he was sent to France during the First World War. Pop, as man and boy, from the age of fourteen had worked this pit, and now it was all to end.

The closure program was to be formally announced later that afternoon, even so, the news swept around the colliery in no time at all. Even the men at the coal-face knew the news before they even came up from underground. They questioned the man at the gate guard as they stepped out of the cage, "is it true, are they really closing us down?" they asked. Just the look on his face was sufficient to confirm their worst fears.

Some four hundred men worked the colliery, and a high percentage of them were in their late forties and early fifties. Even though some of the men would move to other collieries, the future looked bleak for the majority of the men.

Remember

● Press **[Enter]** twice to insert a new line after each title and paragraph.

● Do **not** press **[Enter]** when you reach the end of a line. Word will automatically wrap the text to the next line.

● Insert two spaces after each full stop, one space between each word and after a comma.

Formatting text

- We are going to format the heading, so must first select it. Place the cursor in the margin to the left of the line, and it will change to an arrowhead. Click and the heading will be highlighted. This is a good way to select an entire line.

- Move to the Formatting toolbar, and click the down arrow to the right of the text size box. Select 14 and Word will change the highlighted text to that size.

- With the text still highlighted, press **[Shift]** and **[F3]** keys together. This shortcut will change the text to all capitals.

- Highlight '*fourteen*' in the first paragraph, by double-clicking in the middle of the word. Select *I* the Italic icon, on the Formatting toolbar, to change the word to italic.

- Save the changes to the document. Use the **Save** icon on the Standard toolbar.

Time for more text. Enter the new paragraphs (on the right) as given, including the mistakes, the spell check it.!

Spell checking

Dependent on how Word is configured, you may see a red wavy line below some words. This indicates that Word has not recognised them.

adressing

To spell check the document, select the ABC icon on the Standard toolbar. The **Spelling and Grammar** dialog box will open.

After the shift change, and when the men had washed and showered, the shift assembled in the canteen. One of the Deputies caled for order and the Manager walked in. The canteen fell silent and the men waited forlornly for the formal announcement of the closure.

The Manager, Jack Harkins, not used to adressing such a large audience, cleared his throat and started to speak. "I'm sure that you have all heard, at least something to the effect, that the colliery is to close. Gentlemen, I am afraid that the rumour is true, and the colliery will close in four months time".

The men, even though they were expecting the whorst, groaned loudly. They turned to their pals and the noise in the canteen rose from a deady silence to such a level that the Manager could not be heard, and he had to bang on the table to regain the men's attention.

The suspect word is indicated in green

The buttons are self-explanatory

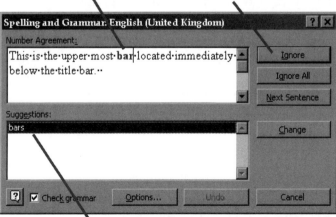

Word offers its suggestions

Formatting the layout

Change the margins of the document as follows:

- Use **File > Page Setup** to open this dialog box. Click the **Margins** tab.
- Change the Top and Bottom margins to 3 cm and the Left and Right margins to 2.5 cm.
- Ensure the **Apply To** option is set to *Whole document*. If not, use the drop-down arrow and select it from the list.
- Click the **OK** button, and the changes will take place.

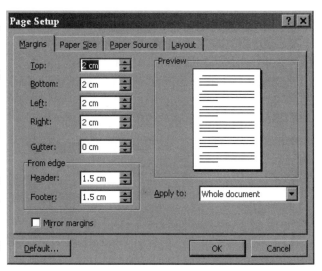

Further text formatting

- Highlight the heading of the text and move the cursor to the Formatting toolbar.
- Click ≡ the **Centre** icon, the heading text will now move to the centre of the page.
- Click **U** the **Underline** icon on the For-matting toolbar and the text will be under-lined.

Save the changes by clicking 🖫 the Save icon.

Enter the additional text, given on the right, exactly as shown, then spell and grammar check the document again.

Justified text

At the moment the document is formatted *Left Justified*. What this means is that the text on the left of the page is lined up on the left margin, while the right margin is ragged.

We will now change the document formatting to *Full Justified*. What this means is that the application will adjust the text. The text closest

The talk in the pubs and clubs that evening was only of the forthcoming closure. Wives had joined their husbands, all hoping that someone else knew a little more than they did, only to find that there was no further news.

A number of the young men thought that they would be better off leaving the industry alto-gether, the question was, where else was there to go? The general consensus of opinion was that the closure would be the death of the valley.

The Manager waited until there was silence, he then told the men that the majority of the equipment underground, that could bt used elsewhere, would be removed. This meant that there would be a requirement, after the mine had formally closed, for a limited work force to remain ot remove the equipment. The re-sponse from the men was utter silence. The shock of the closure, and its speed of implmentation, was still working its way home for most.

to the right margin will now line up and the ragged edge will disappear.

- Highlight all the text, except for the heading.

- Click ▥ the **Full Justification** button on the Formatting toolbar.

- The text will adjust and you will see the difference, mainly in the right margin area, which will be lined up vertically.

- Save the changes to the document.

Moving text

Some of the text is clearly in the wrong place within the general story and has to be moved.

- Place the cursor at the beginning of the last paragraph starting '*The Manager waited until there...*'. Drag the cursor to the right and down to include the full stop after the word '*...most*'. All of the paragraph should now be highlighted.

- Click ✂ the **Cut** icon on the Standard toolbar. The selected text will disappear.

- Move the cursor and click to place the insertion point directly below the fifth paragraph, then press **[Enter]** once to insert an additional line.

- Click 📋 the **Paste** icon on the Standard toolbar, and the text will appear at the insertion point.

Tip

To select a whole paragraph quickly, click three times anywhere within it.

- Make any adjustments necessary, ensure the space above and below the inserted paragraph is consistent.

- Save the document changes.

Indenting text

- Place the cursor to the left of the first word of the first paragraph, starting '*The news had just...*'

- Press **[Tab]** and the first line of text will move to the right. This is 'first line indentation'.

- Now select the whole paragraph starting '*The Manager waited until...*'

- Move the cursor up to the Formatting toolbar and click ⬌ the **Increase Indent** icon. The paragraph will adjust and move to the right.

- Spell and Grammar check the document.

- Save the changes to the document and then close it.

Hyphenation

The following is an extract from the online Help, which gives considerable information about Word's hyphenation feature.

To give your documents a polished and professional look, use the hyphenation feature. For example, hyphenate text to eliminate gaps or 'rivers of white' in justified text or to maintain even line lengths in narrow columns.

You can hyphenate text automatically or manually. If you hyphenate manually, Word searches the document for words to hyphenate and then asks you whether to include a hyphen and where to position it.

For even more control over hyphenation, you can use optional hyphens and nonbreaking hyphens. Use an optional hyphen to control where a word or phrase (such as 'AutoFormat') breaks if it falls at the end of a line (for example, 'Auto-Format'). Use a nonbreaking hyphen to prevent a hyphenated word or phrase (such as 'MS-DOS') from breaking if it falls at the end of a line.

Hyphenate text automatically

On the **Tools** menu, point to **Language**, and then click **Hyphenation**. Select the **Automatically hyphenate document** check box.

In the **Hyphenation zone** box, enter the amount of space to leave between the end of the last word in a line and the right margin.

To reduce the number of hyphens, make the hyphenation zone wider. To reduce the raggedness of the right margin, make the hyphenation zone narrower.

In the **Limit consecutive hyphens to** box, enter the number of consecutive lines that can be hyphenated.

If the **Hyphenation** command does not appear on the **Language** submenu, you need to install the hyphenation tool.

Further assistance

Refer to the online Help for more information, particularly if you wish to manually control hyphenation, though most users will generally accept the default settings for hyphenation.

Create a new document

Open a new blank document save this document as Word2, on the 3½ Floppy (A) drive.

Type in the following text, exactly as shown below and remember to save the document, calling it *Word2*, as you progress.

Six months after the colliery had closed, and all the equipment that was worth removing had gone, the demolition started. Reinforced retaining walls were built at the shatf bottom. The wals were there to stop the in-fill spilling out into the galleries. Ton upon ton of rock and gravel was poured down the shaft until it was full, and finally a plug was set in at the top of the shaft.

Mid-way through March a short service was held at the pit head, to remember men and boys lost in accidents over the long years that the mine had been worked. Pop Jones, Alun Davis and Jim Walker stood together, each thinking back to when the number four gallery had flooded. The speed and rush of water was such that they, even though they were some considerable distance from the source, were swept off their feet. In all the cofusion and chaos they lost sight of their pal Peter Dillion. It was not for some time after the evnet that Peter was found dead, trapped between two drams that had overturned.

Eventually the winding gear and superstructure was dismantled. The filling of the shaft seemed to most to be the end of the colliery, but in actual fact it was the removal of the winding gears and towers that really brought home the fact that the pit was no more.

Carry out a Spell and Grammar check and then save the document.

Copying and moving text

Examine the new document and you will see that it does not flow or follow in a logical order.

- Place the cursor to the left of '*Eventually*', at the start of the last paragraph. Hold the left button down and drag it right and down to highlight the complete paragraph.
- Click ✄ the **Cut** icon.
- Now place the cursor after the last word, '*shaft*', of the first paragraph and press **[Enter]** twice to insert two additional blank lines. Leave the cursor at this position.
- Click 📋 the **Paste** icon and the text will be inserted between the two existing paragraphs.
- Carry out any formatting required, such as deleting the double line spacing between the paragraphs.
- Do not close the document.

Copying between documents

We require a number of blank new lines in the document. Place the cursor after '*overturned*', the last word of the last paragraph and press **[Enter]** to insert ten blank lines.

Enter the following text:

Any resemblance to actual events, or to persons living or dead, is purely coincidental.

We are now going to copy text from this document, *Word2*, to the *Colliery* document.

- Highlight the text, from '*Any resemblance…*' to '*…purely coincidental.*' and then click the Copy icon.

- Re-save the document, but do not close it.
- Open the document *Colliery* and place the cursor at the end of the last paragraph. Press **[Enter]** five times to insert five new lines.
- Click the Paste icon and the text from *Word2* will be copied over to this document. Save the changes to this document.
- Close *Word2* but keep *Colliery* open, because we require it for the next exercise.

Inserting a file

We are now going to combine two separate documents and produce one new document. This procedure is extremely useful if two people have been working on a project and each has produced a separate document.

The end product will result in the two individual files remaining intact, with an entirely new document being produced.

- Place the cursor at the end of the paragraph ending '*death of the valley.*' and press **[Enter]** twice to insert two new blank lines.
- Open the **Insert** menu and select **File…** At the **Insert File** dialog box select *3½ Floppy (A:)* in the **Look In** slot.
- Select *Word2.doc* from the list, then press the **OK** button.
- The file *Word2.doc* is inserted into the current document, as an integral part of it.
- We are going to save the document with a different name. Select **File > Save As** and a dialog box will open. Save the document as *Word3.doc* on the floppy disk.

You will now have three documents: the original document; the source of the additional text; the document produced after text insertion.

Deleting text

There is now a duplicate paragraph in the *Colliery* document. Locate the first instance of the paragraph:

"Any resemblance to actual events, or to persons living or dead, is purely coincidental."

● Highlight the paragraph and press **[Delete]**. (If you delete the wrong one, by mistake, use **Edit** > **Undo** to restore it.)

● Save the changes.

Re-formatting the heading text

With the Word3 document still open, select the heading '*The Colliery*'. We are going to change the format of the heading as follows:

● Click on the Bold icon on the Formatting toolbar.

● Click on the drop-down arrow to the right of the Font box and select the font name *Arial*.

● Save the changes to the document.

Fonts

Word offers you an assortment of fonts to use in your documents. Each font has a specific **typeface**, which determines the appearance of the characters. These are identified by names such as Arial, Courier and Times New Roman.

Each font also has a **size**, which is specified in points. One point is equal to 1/72 of an inch, so a 72 point font would measure 1 inch from the bottom of its lowest hanging character (g, y) to the top of its largest letter (T, I).

Fonts are classified as *proportional* or *non-proportional*. A proportional font such as Times New Roman, will use more space on the paper for the letter "w", than it does for the letter "I". A non-proportional font such as Courier uses the same amount of space on the paper for every character.

Here are some examples of fonts and sizes:

This line is in Times New Roman, size 12.

This line is in Times New Roman, size 16.

`This line is in Courier, size 12.`

This line is in Helvetica, size 12.

THIS LINE IS IN ALGERIAN, SIZE 12.

This line is in Lucida Handwriting, size 12.

Printing documents

The time has come to print the documents. We require one copy of each of these files. Open each in turn and print all their pages. (Refer to page 73, if necessary.)

Compare each document, starting with *Colliery.doc*. Find the section where you inserted the file and compare it with the document *Word3.doc*. Confirm that the file inserted is the same as the document *Word2.doc*.

Take note

Printed copies of documents are known as "Hard Copies". Keep all copies of the print outs for future reference.

Headers and Footers

The Headers and Footers function is a particularly useful feature of Word, and is a means of producing the same text, or image, on each page without repeated retyping or insertions. If you require each page to be numbered, it is through the use of Footers that this is achieved.

Inserting file names

Frequently people produce documents and do not use them for some time. You may well have a paper copy of the document, but may not recall what the saved document was called. Headers and Footers provide a means of indicating the file name. You can save the name, along with the name of the person who created the file and the date it was last modified.

To enter text or imagery in the Headers and Footers follow the example below:

- Open the document that you want headers and footers in, in this instance *Colliery.doc*.
- Open the **View** menu and select **Header and Footer**.

The active document will adjust its position on the screen, moving up to the top of the document and you will see a broken line box.

It is within here that the header or footer items will appear. In addition, another toolbar will appear, either roughly at the centre of your screen or underneath another toolbar.

Move the cursor over each of the icons on the toolbar and a Tool Tip will appear indicating what that icon's function is.

You can select text and change its font style and size, in the usual manner, in the Header or Footer. If necessary change the font size to 10.

- Type your name in the Header area.
- Click ▦ the **Switch Between Header and Footer** icon to change to the Footer area.
- Change the font size to 8 and then type in *Colliery.doc* and press the spacebar once.
- Click ▦ the **Insert Page Number Icon**.
- Click the **Close** button.

If you cannot see the Header and Footer, open the **View** menu and select **Page Layout**. Move to the top of the document and you will see the Header text, dimmed; move to the bottom and you will see the Footer, also dimmed.

Header area

Header

Header and Footer toolbar

Switch between Header and Footer

Header and Footer

Insert AutoText ▾ | Close

Insert Page Number

Insert Number of Pages

Format Page Number

Insert Time

Insert Date

Find and Replace

The Find and Replace feature of Word is extremely powerful and can speed up changes or amendments to documents immensely.

● Open the **Edit** menu and select **Replace**. The **Find and Replace** box will open. In the **Find what** slot type in what you wish to find and change. Press **[Tab]** to go to the **Replace with** slot and type in the new word. In the example, we are about to replace '*box*' with '*window*'.

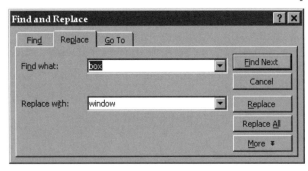

● Click the **Find Next** button. Word will search the document and will highlight the first occurrence of '*box*' and moves the document to enable you to see the word.

● If this occurrence of the word is one that you wish to change, click the **Replace** button. Word will replace '*box*' with '*window*' and move on to look for the next occurrence. This will continue until Word cannot find another occurrence of the word, or you end the search by clicking on the **Cancel** button.

● Alternatively, if you are satisfied that you can safely change all occurrences of the word '*box*', click the **Replace All** button.

Paragraph numbers

If it is not already in use, open the document 'Colliery.doc'.

● Select the first two paragraphs at the start of the document.

● On the Formatting toolbar, select ▦ the **Paragraph Numbering** icon.

Word will automatically insert paragraph numbers adjacent to the two selected paragraphs. Close the document but **DO NOT** save the changes. We do not require the paragraph numbering.

If you know, before you actually start typing a document, that paragraph numbering is a requirement, you can start paragraph numbering immediately by just clicking on the icon, and then start typing. Word will insert paragraph numbers as you progress. There are limitations with this feature, experiment to find out how best you can use it.

Creating tables

Tables are an extremely useful feature of Word, and with the latest version of Word, the options available in the design and use of tables have increased tremendously. When it is particularly important to maintain good control over the alignment and positioning of one area of text with another section of text, use a table. Also consider using a table without any borders or inside lines.

You can design the table yourself, with different border styles, the use of colour and such-like. Word also has some predefined table layouts. These can be found in the **Autoformat** option in the **Insert Table** dialog box.

- To create a table, open a New blank document and save as 'Temp.doc'.
- Open the **Table** menu and select **Insert Table** to open the **Insert Table** dialog box.

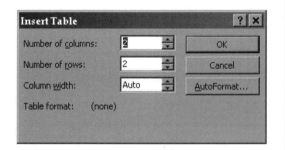

It is here that you can set the number of columns and rows for the table, and if desired, select one of the predefined table layouts.

- Change the number of columns to three and the rows to four, using the up/down arrows. **Do not** select any **Autoformat** options at this time – just click the **OK** button.

The table will appear on screen with three columns and four rows, all the same size. This cann be adjusted as required. Here's how to merge two cells into one. Any block of cells can be merged in this way.

- Place the cursor in the second column of the first row, click and drag the cursor to the right through into the third column, highlighting the two cells.
- Release the mouse button. Open the **Table** menu and select **Merge Cells**. Word will join the two cells together into one large cell. Click anywhere in the table to remove the highlight from this new cell. This is how your table should look:

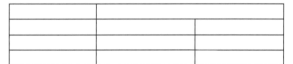

- Select the merged cell and click the Bold and Centre text icons.

Entering text in tables

- Place the cursor in the first cell, of the first row and type 'REGION' in capitals. Select the word and click the Bold icon.
- Press [Tab] to move the cursor into the next cell. Type 'TEMPERATURES', again all in capital letters. Note that the text is in the centre of the cell and is emboldened.
- Using [Tab], move to the second column of the second row and type in 'Mid-Summer'. Press [Tab] once more to move to the third column. Type in 'Mid-Winter'.

- Still using **[Tab]**, move along to the next row and type in '*North*'.
- Move to the next column, which now appears under the heading of *Mid-Summer*. Type in '*85*'.

  Follow the example below and enter the remaining text as shown:

REGION	TEMPERATURES	
	Mid-Summer	Mid-Winter
North	85	56
West	92	61

Changing the cell width in tables

Ensure that the cursor is placed in the table. The first column is a little wider than necessary, move the cursor over the outside left line of the table. The cursor will change to a double headed arrow with small vertical lines. Once the cursor has changed, keep the left button pressed; drag the line in the required direction, in this case to the right. When the table looks satisfactory, release the mouse.

Inserting columns and rows

To insert additional columns and rows, place the cursor where the additional column or row is required. Open the **Table** menu and select the appropriate **Insert** command. (Experiment inserting rows and columns at a later date.)

Deleting columns and rows

Highlight the column or row that you wish to delete then select **Delete Row** or **Delete Column**, as appropriate, from the **Table** menu.

Lines and borders

Lines and borders can be changed by placing the cursor anywhere in the table, then opening the **Format** menu and selecting **Borders and Shading**.

Create a second table

We need another table, for use later in the Mail Merge section. Proceed as follows:

- Open a new blank document.
- Change the page layout to Landscape. Open the **File** menu and select **Page Setup**. At the **Page Setup** dialog box open the **Paper Size** tab and choose *Landscape* in **Orientation**, to give a page that is wide rather than deep.
- Now click on the **OK** button.

Title	LastName	Company	Address1	Address2	City	PostalCode
Mr	Jones	Jones Heating Contractors	5 Marylebone Road	Bolton	Lancs	B19 8YH
Mr	Bryon	Lington Heating Controls Limited	12 High Street	Logton	Lincs	LM8 3HJ
Mr	Collins	Collins and Son Heating Contractors	56 Bridge Street	Middletown	Notts	NH32 4AG
Mrs	Kaye	Kaye's Engineering and Heating	98 Benton Road	Longparish	York	YM6 6JK

- Create a table, which has seven columns and five rows. **Do not** apply any Auto-Formatting to the table.

- You will find however that when the table was inserted into the document that all the columns were of equal size. We will adjust the column widths later, simply type in the sample data given above.

Now adjust the column widths until you can fit all the text in the columns as shown on page 92. Ensure the cursor is placed in the table, so that you can view the column widths. Place the cursor over the vertical lines of the columns and when it changes to a double arrow, drag the line in the appropriate direction to match the text formatting as seen in the table above.

Once all formatting has been completed, save the document as: *Data Source Information*.

Print a copy of the document and keep it safe as you will require it later when working through the Mail Merge section.

Take note

[Tab] is used to move from cell to cell within the table. If you wish to indent text — the normal function of [Tab] — you must use the key combination of [Control] and [Tab] together.

Page breaks

You will have noticed that Word senses when it has reached the end of the page, and inserts an additional page as required.

There will be occasions when you will require text to appear on a new, or the next, page. To achieve this, there are a number of different ways. The simplest and easiest way is the Quick Key method. Open *Word3.doc*.

- Place the cursor at the end of the text where you want the new page to start from, press **[Control]** and **[Enter]** at the same time and Word will insert a *Forced Page Break*.

- To try out this feature, place the cursor in the blank line above the paragraph starting 'Six months after the colliery had closed....'

- Press **[Control]** and **[Enter]** simultaneously and release immediately. Word will force the text on to the next page. When you are in Normal View note the broken line indicating where the Page Break is.

··Page Break··

If you find that you have placed the Page Break in the wrong place, or simply wish to remove it, place the cursor to the left of the Page Break symbol and press **[Delete]**.

There are other types of Breaks that are available within Word however, we will not cover them here. Experiment on your own later by investigating the options available from Insert command on the Menu Bar.

Save the changes to the document and close it.

Using tabulation

Tabulation is a method of lining up text and numbers in vertical columns or evenly spaced text on horizontal lines. By default, Word tabs are set at ½ inch intervals, but you can adjust the setting as required. Open a new document.

Enter the text as shown below, insert one Tab before the words 'Chapter' and after the chapter number and again before the page numbers.

Section 1
    Chapter 1 The first chapter of eight 4
    Chapter 2 The second, a short chapter 8
    Chapter 3 The third chapter   25
    Chapter 4 The fourth chapter   35
Section 2
    Chapter 5 The fifth chapter   56
    Chapter 6 The sixth chapter   68
    Chapter 7 The seventh chapter   88
    Chapter 8 The eighth and last chapter 118

Save this document as *Tabulation.doc*.

Word has a number of tab types, which you can apply to suit your own requirements:

L	The default tab is left justified
⊥	Centre justified
⌐	Right justified
⊥	Decimal aligned tab

Tabulation options

To change the tab settings, ensure that the Ruler is visible. If it is not, open the **View** menu and select **Ruler**. Located in the top left-hand corner of the Ruler is a small square with a symbol indicating the type of tab currently selected. The example below indicates a left justified tab is selected.

To change the tab, click the symbol and it will change to centre tab, and each subsequent click will change the setting to right justified, decimal aligned, then back to left justified.

Changing tabulation settings

If it is not already open, open the document *Tabulation.doc*, and make the Ruler visible.

- Open the **Edit** menu and select **Select All** so that the whole text is highlighted.

- Select the left justified symbol on the Ruler. Click on the Ruler at the 2.5cm position. A faint symbol will appear, indicating a left justified tab has been set. The text will now adjust the first tab position to 2.5cm.

- Ensure that all the text is still selected, and that the tab is still set to left justified. Click on the Ruler at 6cm. The tab is set and the text will move along to align at 6cm.

- Click twice on the tab symbol to select a right justified tab. Click on the Ruler at the 12.5cm to insert a right justified tab there. The text is moved along to align under the 12.5 location. Note that the numbers have aligned in number order alignment. Had you not selected the right justified tab but left it as a left justified tab, the numbers would not have aligned correctly, as shown in the example opposite.

Save the changes to the document.

Your document *Tabulation* should now match the example shown opposite.

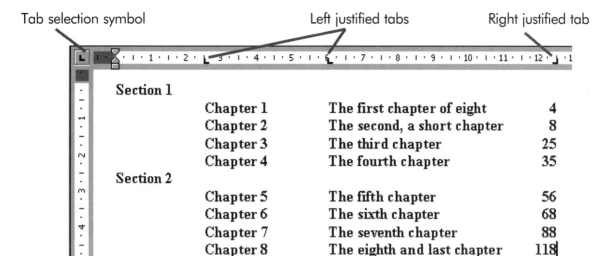

Tab selection symbol   Left justified tabs   Right justified tab

Section 1

	Chapter 1	The first chapter of eight	4
	Chapter 2	The second, a short chapter	8
	Chapter 3	The third chapter	25
	Chapter 4	The fourth chapter	35

Section 2

	Chapter 5	The fifth chapter	56
	Chapter 6	The sixth chapter	68
	Chapter 7	The seventh chapter	88
	Chapter 8	The eighth and last chapter	118

Decimal aligned tabulations

Decimal tabs are used to align columns of figures that include decimal places. Open a new blank document.

● Create a list as shown below. Insert one tab after each item before the price:

Chocolate mix	£1.45
Flour	£1.65
Sugar	£0.99
Eggs	£1.25
Milk	£0.65
Baking tin	£12.45

● Save the document as *Decimal.doc*.
● Now select all the text and numbers.
● Change to the decimal tab on the Ruler.
● Click on the Ruler at the 4.5 position. The figures will now align on the decimal point.

Chocolate mix	£1.45
Flour	£1.65
Sugar	£0.99
Eggs	£1.25
Milk	£0.65
Baking tin	£12.45

● Save the document changes and close it.

Changing line spacing

When producing draft copies of fairly long and complex documents it is common practice to use double spacing. This leaves room for hand written amendments to be inserted.

Open a new blank document and type in:

> Goals
> The individual shall have a sound knowledge of how a word processing application can be used. He or she shall be able to understand and accomplish normal everyday operations; editing or creating new documents.

Save the document as *Double.doc*, then:

● Select all the text, including the heading.
● Open the **Format** menu and select **Paragraph** and the **Paragraph Formatting** dialog box will open.
● In the **Spacing** section, select *Double* for **Line spacing**, then click **OK**.
● Save the changes and close.

If you know beforehand that you want a document in double-spacing, you can set this selection before typing any text.

Inserting graphics

A graphic, whether it's a photograph or a clip art image, will add impact to a document and enhance its appearance. Use imagery to draw attention to the subject matter, but use it with care as too much may distract the reader.

In the following exercise, we are going to create a simple 'no smoking' sign.

- Open a new blank document and save it as *Sign.doc*.

- Open the **File** menu and select **Page Setup**. At the **Page Setup** dialog box, select the **Paper Size** tab, then choose *Landscape* in **Orientation**.

The page orientation will change to Landscape, so that the longest edge of the paper is now at the top, not the side. This orientation is ideal for making most signs.

- Change the Font style to Arial and the size to 72. Right-click anywhere on the document and select Font to open the Font dialog box. Click the down-arrow by the **Color** slot and select *Red*. Click on the **OK** button to close the dialog box and make the changes.

- The text will look better if it is centred on the page. Click ≣ the Centre icon on the Formatting toolbar, then press **[Enter]** once.

- Type in the words 'No Smoking' and press **[Enter]**. The text is large and coloured red. Of course you will have to print out the document on a colour printer to have the colour effect.

- Open the **Insert** menu, point to **Picture** and select **Clip Art**. The Clip Gallery window will open. Ensure that the Clip Art tab at the top has been selected.

- Select *Signs* from the **Categories** list. Find and highlight the smoking cigarette image or an appropriate alternative, then click the **Insert** button.

- The image will appear on the page, probably not quite where you want it and its size may also require some adjustment.

- Right-click over the image and from the pop-up menu select **Format Object**. When the Format Object dialog box opens, ensure that the **Size** tab is selected.

- Locate the **Scale** section of the Size box and ensure that the **Lock aspect ratio** and **Relative to original picture size** tick boxes are ticked as shown below. You should be aware that these figures will not necessarily match what you have on your screen.

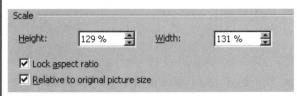

- When you change the size figures you will only have to make one change to either the **Height** or **Width** boxes, not both. This is because Word, with the two boxes ticked, will automatically maintain the proportions relevant to its original size.

- This next adjustment is a judgement call on your part. Increase or decrease, if necessary, the size of the image until it occupies the lower central area of the page.

Finally we should now check the overall layout of the poster, the positioning of each element in relation to each other and general presentation.

To do this, we must first change the page view so that you can see the full-page size, and we can do that using the Zoom control.

- Left-click over the drop-down arrow located to the right of the **Zoom** control on the Standard toolbar.

- Select *Whole Page* from the Zoom drop-down list.

- Move the cursor over the image once more and when cursor changes to a four-headed arrow, left-click and hold the button down.

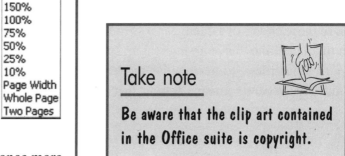

- Drag the image to the centre of the page below the text 'No Smoking'. When the image is in place, release the mouse button. Your sign should resemble the example shown below.

- Save the document changes and close.

Inserting images is as simple as that. Obviously Word offers more options and features when working with imagery and you should experiment later.

Take note

Be aware that the clip art contained in the Office suite is copyright.

Mail merge

One of the many features of Microsoft Word is Mail Merge. Mail Merge is designed to assist the user who has to produce numerous similar letters to send to many clients. Each letter will contain very much the same content, with minor changes, though each letter is personalised in its salutation and address details.

Imagine having a database of several hundred clients, and you wish to inform just one hundred of those clients of a change in a specification to an item they have an interest in. In the days of typewriters, to personalise the letters would have meant someone typing them all out separately. No longer – read on.

Mail Merge will produce bulk letters, using two previously prepared documents. Word uses particular names in the merge process, so it is important to remember these names and exactly what they are.

The Form Letter

This is the skeleton of the letter that contains the common information each client will receive. One advantage of a Form Letter is that should you later have to amend it, you only have one document to change. You can build-up a set of Form Letters for different uses.

It is not strictly necessary to create the Form Letter first; you will decide in time your preferred method of working.

The Data Source

This is the document that contains the personal details of the clients, including their names, how you will address each and of course, the addresses. Data Sources, like the Form Letter, are reusable. You can produce a Data Source in Word or use another application as the source.

To use names and addresses of contacts in your Outlook Contact List, as a data source, with the Mail Merge in Word, first add your Outlook Address Book to your user profile.

- Open Word and click **Mail Merge** on the **Tools** menu.
- Click **Get Data**, and then click **Use Address Book**. Select *Outlook Address Book*.

For powerful sorting and searching capabilities, use Access or Excel to edit longer lists of data.

When you consider that you are most likely already using other lists or applications for data, it is worth spending a little time investigating if these sources can be utilised. After all, that's one reason for using a computer; to store and reuse information without duplication.

The Main Document

It is from the Form Letter and the Data Source, that the Main Document is produced. This is the document that you will send to the clients after the Mail Merge has been completed.

Creating the components

We will use Word to create the various components necessary for the following exercise, and will start by creating the Form Letter.

Creating the Form Letter

- First open a new blank document, and save it as 'Form Let1.doc'.
- We will use the standard business layout for the Form Letter. To save time and space, we have omitted our company details, logo, etc. which would usually appear above the Ref. and client address.

Follow the example shown below:

- Once you have completed the Form Letter, save the document.
- With the document still open, drop-down the **Tools** menu and select **Mail Merge**. The **Mail Merge Helper** dialog box will appear.

Ref: JAW/ct

Date (Read the *Take note* below)

Dear

PRICE REDUCTIONS ON ALL HIGH EFFICIENCY PUMPS

This is to advise you that we have once again reduced the cost price of our low energy, high efficiency water pumps.

As a valued client, we thought that you should be amongst the first to be advised of the price reduction. Furthermore, with your customer discounts applied, this will add up to a substantial saving to you.

We look forward to receiving your orders, which will receive our prompt attention.

Yours sincerely

John A Worthington

Take note

An example of a fuller business style letter is included to the rear of this booklet for guidance.

Leave a blank line after the Ref section, then insert an automatic date entry as follows: Open the Insert menu and select Date and Time. At the dialog box select the format '12 March 1999'. Tick the Update automatically box. This will ensure that each time the Form Letter is used, Word will insert the current date.

Note that when the **Merge Mail Helper** dialog box first opens you only have the one option available and that is the **Create** button. The other options buttons, **Data source** and **Merge the data with the document** will only become active as you progress through the mail merge process. This is to ensure that the process is completed in a logical order and that you do not overlook an important step.

- Click once on the **Create** button and a further box will open. At this, select **Form Letters** and the box shown below will open.

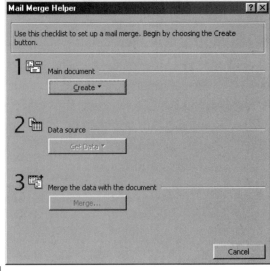

We have already produced the Form Letter, and it is open. Select Active Window.

Creating the Data Source

When you are returned to the Mail Merge Helper dialog box you will see that the **Get Data** button has become active.

- Click the **Get Data** button to drop down its menu and select **Create Data Source** to open this dialog box.

You will see that Word has already inserted a number of common **Fields**. You can remove any that are not wanted or add new fields if required. We will use some of the fields provided by Word for this exercise. Select each of these fields individually and when highlighted, click the **Remove Field Name** button: *Country*, *HomePhone* and *WorkPhone*.

- Once the unwanted fields have been removed, click the **OK** button. You will be prompted to save the Data Source, even though you have not entered any data yet.

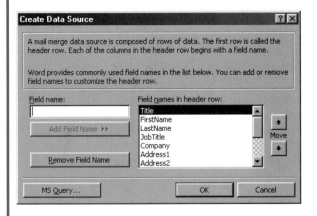

Select **Yes** and save it as *Data Source1*.

- When the Data Source has been saved, a further box will open offering you a choice of **Edit Data Source** or **Edit Main Document**. Select **Edit Data Source**.

The **Data Form** dialog box will open. This is where we will fill in our client's details. Use the information contained in the document that you created earlier and saved as *Data Source Information*.

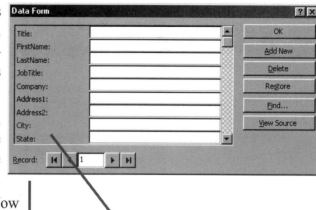

- When you reach the last field for a client, click the **Add New** button. Continue entering the clients' details until all have been entered, then click the **OK** button.

You are now returned to the Form Letter. Now look for the Merge Toolbar, it should appear adjacent to the Formatting Toolbar.

You will note that only nine fields are available, as the others were deleted.

Inserting the Merge Fields

We need to insert the address fields and the salutation fields in the appropriate places in the Form Letter.

Merge to new document

- On the Form Letter, place the cursor at the end of the Date line and press **[Enter]** twice.

- Locate the button **Insert Merge Field** and click on it to open its drop-down list.

- From the list, select the *Company* field. The field should now appear in the Form Letter as <<Company>>.

- Move down one line at a time, by pressing **[Enter]** and insert the four remaining address fields, each on its own line. When all fields have been entered, ensure there is a blank line between the address block and the salutation.

- On the Form Letter, place the cursor after the salutation starting 'Dear'. Insert a single space after it, or the words will run into each other.

- Click the **Insert Merge Field** button, and select the field *Title*, then the field *LastName*. These fields are to appear on the same line one after the other.

DO NOT enter spaces between field names, i.e. Title and LastName. The mail merge process will insert spaces as appropriate.

Once the necessary fields have been inserted, the top of Form Letter should look like this.

Ref: JAW/ct

Date

<<Company>>
<<Address1>>
<<Address2>>
<<City>>
<<PostalCode>>

Dear <<Title>><<LastName>>

We are now at the stage to carry out the actual merge. On the Mail Merge toolbar click the **Merge to New Document** button.

The completed merge

On releasing the Merge button, the box will close and the merge process will take place. Word has now produced a four-page document. This is, in fact, four different letters separated by page breaks between each letter.

This is the final product – the merged document. Save as *Merge* and close each document.

This was a simple merge involving only four records in the Data Source, and therefore this merge was easy to carry out, without any complications. To carry out a merge task accessing hundreds of records in the Data Source is more complex. You will have to select the clients that have an interest in the subject of the Form Letter. There will almost always be fields in the records that are surplus to requirement.

This section should be practised a number of times to gain confidence in using the facility.

Use the online Help to learn more of Mail Merge and how you can carry out more complex Mail Merge tasks.

Take note

You can also merge by using the menu option Tools > Mail Merge. The Merge dialog box will open and the default option is to Merge to a new document. Accept this option and click on the Merge button.

Using templates

A template is a pre-defined document that can be used time and time again. You can create templates of your own design and content. Word also comes with a series of templates already defined, which can be modified to suit your own specifications and requirements.

Good instances of templates would be:

- A document that has a company letterhead, with a logo at the top, while the remainder of the document is blank, ready for any text, etc. to be inserted.

- Forms, such as an order form that has certain standard text entries plus blank spaces, which the user would fill in.

A template is saved with a different extension. Instead of 'doc', templates use the extension 'dot' to denote that it is different from the everyday document, e.g. *Elegant Fax.dot*.

Open a template

To open a template you use a slightly different procedure, from that used for opening a standard document. Templates are stored in their own individual folders, one for each application.

To use templates follow this procedure:

- Select **File > New** to open the **New** dialog box. Click on the **Letters and Faxes** tab.

You will see a number of items – some are template documents and others are 'wizards'. We will return to the subject of Wizards later. Remember that Templates are identified by the 'dot' extension after the document name.

The templates are grouped into folders

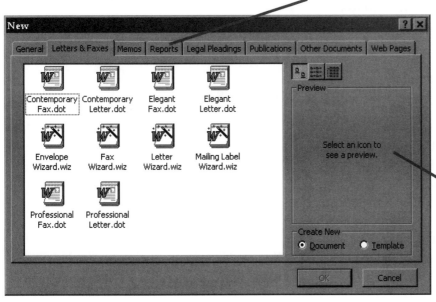

Some templates have previews to give you an idea of how they look

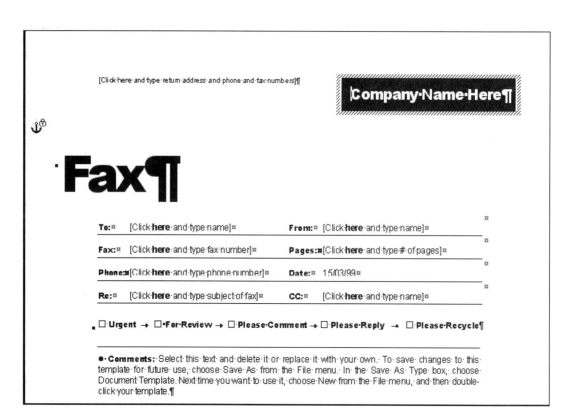

[Click·here·and·type·return·address·and·phone·and·fax·numbers]¶

Company·Name·Here¶

Fax¶

To:¤ [Click·**here**·and·type·name]¤   From:¤ [Click·**here**·and·type·name]¤

Fax:¤ [Click·**here**·and·type·fax·number]¤   Pages:¤[Click·**here**·and·type·#·of·pages]¤

Phone:¤[Click·**here**·and·type·phone·number]¤   Date:¤ 15/03/99¤

Re:¤ [Click·**here**·and·type·subject·of·fax]¤   CC:¤ [Click·**here**·and·type·name]¤

□·**Urgent** → □·**For·Review** → □·**Please·Comment** → □·**Please·Reply** → □·**Please·Recycle**¶

●·**Comments:** Select·this·text·and·delete·it·or·replace·it·with·your·own.·To·save·changes·to·this· template·for·future·use,·choose·Save·As·from·the·File·menu.·In·the·Save·As·Type·box,·choose· Document·Template.·Next·time·you·want·to·use·it,·choose·New·from·the·File·menu,·and·then·double- click·your·template.¶

Using a template

Select the template *Professional Fax* either by clicking on it, then clicking **OK**, or by double-clicking on it.

When the template opens, you will see that a number of the items in the document require further action by you. See the example above.

Complete the instructions given on the template and fill in your own details as required.

When a template is opened for use, Word changes it to a standard document, thus preserving the template for further use. When you save the document Word will automatically assign a 'doc' extension to it.

You can modify the template permanently, i.e. insert your company name, address and telephone details and then resave the template under a different name, remember the 'dot' extension. The next time that you wish to use the Template, a high percentage of the detail is already complete.

Templates are extremely useful and can save you some considerable effort and over a period of time you will find more and more uses for templates.

Wizards

A Wizard is an automated process that creates documents, using a number of preformatted styles and layouts. It asks questions and uses the answers to automatically lay out and format a document, such as a newsletter or resume.

Wizards can be identified by the extension, wiz, which appears after the wizard name, e.g. *Fax Wizard.wiz*.

Styles

A Style is a named set of format settings that can be accessed from the Formatting toolbar. A Style can specify a font type and the size. In addition it may also specify indentation, line spacing and justification.

Applying a Style is a lot faster than manually applying individual Formatting adjustments to sections of text and assures consistency.

Word has several predefined Styles, and you can also create your own. Word predefines Styles as either paragraph or character:

Paragraph Styles are applied to entire paragraphs and may include all of the formatting elements listed above. Every paragraph, in a Word document, automatically has the default style, *Normal*, applied to it. This Style is based on your default selection of font and size.

Character Styles are applied to any section of text and can include formatting such as font type and size, underlining, embolden and so on. If you apply a character Style such as boldface to a section of text that is already formatted as italic, the text will then appear as both bold and italic.

Applying a Style

First select the text to be styled.

- To apply a Style to more than one paragraph, select them all.
- To apply a Style to only one paragraph, place the cursor anywhere inside it.
- To assign a character style, select the text you want the style to be applied to.

Now carry out the following:

- Click on the Style drop-down arrow on the Formatting toolbar. A list of Styles will appear, with the name in the Style's font.
- Select the required Style by clicking on its name. The Style will then be applied to the specified text.

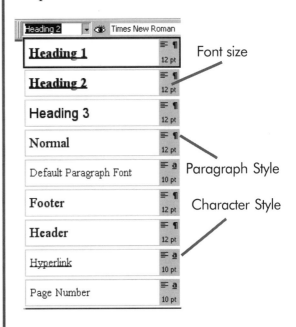

To remove a Style

Select the text and from the Style drop-down list select *Default Paragraph Font* or *Normal* as appropriate to your requirements.

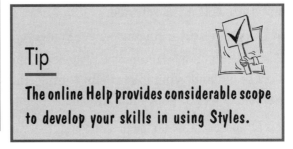

Tip

The online Help provides considerable scope to develop your skills in using Styles.

Integrating with other applications

Information stored within a Word document can very easily be copied or linked to any of the other applications in Microsoft Office.

Charts or data can be inserted in a Word document, an Excel worksheet or a PowerPoint presentation, and vice versa.

To exchange data between Word and Excel

To analyse the data from a Word table in Excel, you can copy and paste the data to a new Excel workbook. You can also import worksheet data into Word.

When you become proficient in using Excel, you could create a 'PivotTable' to analyse data from a Word table, just as you could from a data source such as an Access database.

Practice

It will only be possible to practise the following if you have already completed the module on Excel, so you might want to leave this for now and return to it later.

- Open the Word document *Data Source Information* and highlight the complete table.
- Open the **Edit** menu and select **Copy**.
- Open Excel with a new workbook.
- Ensure cell A1 is selected.
- Open the **Edit** menu and select **Paste**.

The table contents will now be pasted into the workbook and you may then format the worksheet to suit your requirements.

It is almost certain that the pasted version of the table will require some reformatting once within the worksheet. In particular cell lengths will require some adjustment to display long entries or field names.

You should, in time, learn how to use software integration to your advantage and reduce duplication in time and effort. Creating a table in Excel, which already exists in Word, or vis-a-visa, is wasteful. In the example above you copied the table, but you could have easily created a special link between the two applications, which will permit the table in Excel to be automatically updated when changes are made to the source table in Word.

Take note

The on-line Help system in Word is almost identical in style, appearance and operation to that of Excel (and all Microsoft applications). See page 137 if you need help with Help.

Sample paper 3: Word-processing

1	Explain how to highlight a section of text.	
2	Explain how you would insert the © symbol in a document.	
3	List two of the Views available to the user in Word.	1. 2.
4	Name the three parts of a mail merge.	1. 2. 3.
5	What is a template?	
6	List the two methods that can be used to re-size an image in a document.	1. 2.
7	Which item must be visible for setting or changing tabulations?	
8	You have just opened a new document, what is the first thing that you should do now?	
9	You have completed a document and require three copies of it printed. Explain briefly the sequence of events necessary to print three copies of the document.	

4 Spreadsheets

What is a spreadsheet?

A spreadsheet is a tool for managing numbers and calculations. It is made up of columns and rows in which you record data or write formulas to perform calculations on it. Excel does not use the term 'spreadsheet'; instead it uses 'worksheet' (a single page), contained in a 'workbook' which may have up to 16 sheets.

Excel enables you to perform a wide variety of functions including sorting and selecting from lists. Automatic calculations mean that you will always have up-to-date results in your spreadsheet. Excel includes a feature that will produce charts from numeric data.

Excel also has a linking feature that allows you to enter data in one location and use it in other documents, which will be updated from source automatically. This speeds up and improves productivity, while reducing the likelihood of any errors being introduced by rekeying.

Excel allows you to experiment with the design and layout on the screen before actually printing the final product.

Below is an example of a simple spreadsheet.

The example is extremely simple in design and appearance. The calculations performed by it simply total up the sales figures, down by region and across by month.

Calculation operators

Operators specify the type of calculation that you want to perform on the elements of a formula. Excel includes four different types of operators: arithmetic, comparison, text, and reference.

Arithmetic operators perform basic mathematical operations such as addition, subtraction, division or multiplication; combine numbers; and produce numeric results.

There are specific rules when entering formulas in spreadsheets. Should you find that your results are not what you expected, first check how the formula was entered. If you have not used mathematics for sometime, this is an area where practice should make perfect.

If you combine several operators in a single formula, Excel performs the operations in the order shown in the following table.

Region	Jan	Feb	Mar	Area Totals
		Quarterly Sales		
North East	50,985.00	45,987.00	48,755.00	145,727.00
North West	47,800.00	47,855.00	47,522.00	143,177.00
South East	51,200.00	46,585.00	52,456.00	150,241.00
South West	49,125.00	52,100.00	47,800.00	149,025.00
Monthly Totals	199,110.00	192,527.00	196,533.00	588,170.00

Operator	Description
: (colon) , (comma)	Reference operators
–	Negation (as in - 1)
%	Per cent
^	Exponentiation
* and /	Multiplication and division
+ and –	Addition and subtraction
&	Concatenation (connect strings of text)
= < > <= >= <>	Comparison

If a formula contains operators with the same precedence, e.g. both multiplication and division – Excel evaluates them from left to right. To change the order of evaluation, enclose the part to be calculated first in curved brackets.

The following produces two different results if the rules described above are not applied, i.e.

$(2+2)*3 = 12 \Rightarrow 2+2=4$, then $4 * 3 = 12$

$2+2*3 = 8 \Rightarrow 2 * 3 = 6$, then $6+2 = 8$.

Actual use of operators will be discussed later in the course.

Consult the online Help system for more information and examples of how to apply the various operators.

Starting Excel

In common with many Windows applications, you can start Excel a number of different ways. Here is one method. It is assumed that the computer has been switched on and that Windows is fully up and running normally.

● Click on the **Start** button to open its pop-up menu.

● Point to **Programs**. A further menu will open to the right. Click on **Microsoft Excel**.

Excel will open, and display a screen similar to that shown below.

4: Spreadsheets

Standard toolbar Formatting toolbar Column header Control buttons

Menu bar Formula bar Top 3 for Excel
Lower 3 for worksheet

Active cell

Row number Worksheet number Scroll bars

Starting a new workbook

In Excel, a workbook is the file in which you work and store your data. Because each workbook can contain many worksheets, you can organise various kinds of related information in a single file.

Use worksheets to list and analyse data. You can enter and edit data on several sheets simultaneously and perform calculations based on data from multiple sheets. When you create a chart, you can place the chart on the worksheet with its data or on a separate chart sheet.

The names of the sheets appear on tabs at the bottom of the workbook window. To move from sheet to sheet, click the sheet tabs. The name of the active sheet is bold.

Excel opens with a new blank workbook. For this section of the course we will close this workbook and open another new workbook.

This reason for doing this is to see where and how you can start a new workbook.

Basic steps

1 Close the blank workbook by clicking ☒ the Close button in the workbook controls.

2 If prompted to save the workbook, click the NO button.

3 Select File > New and the New dialog box will open.

4 Ensure that the General tab is selected.

5 Click on the Workbook icon.

6 Now click the OK button. A new workbook will now open, with the cursor in cell A1.

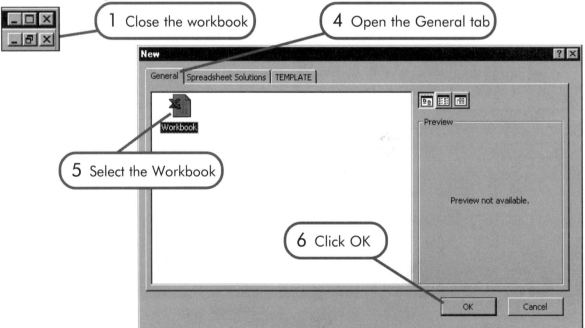

1 Close the workbook

4 Open the General tab

5 Select the Workbook

6 Click OK

The number of sheets in the new workbook depends upon the default settings. You can change these to suit yourself.

● To change the default number, select **Tools > Options** and then the **General** tab. In the **Sheets in new workbook** area set the number and click **OK**. No changes will occur until you next open a new workbook.

Saving the workbook

We will now start entering text and figures in our worksheet. However, before we actually start we will save the workbook.

Basic steps

1   Select File > Save and the Save As dialog box will open.

2   Select a folder or disk to save the workbook in – in this instance select the 3½ Floppy (A:)

3   Click in the File name slot and type in the name *ECDL1*.

4   Click the Save button.

Take note

Excel set the following maxima:

32,000 characters in a cell

65,536 rows by 256 columns per worksheet

16 worksheets in a workbook

16 Undo actions.

Working with worksheets

There are a number of points worth mentioning before we actually start work.

Naming worksheets

By default, Excel names the worksheets as *Sheet 1, Sheet 2* and so on. It is often more practical to identify sheets by names rather than numbers and Excel allows you to do this.

● Double-click over the name tab and when it is highlighted, type in the name, then click on the worksheet to effect the change.

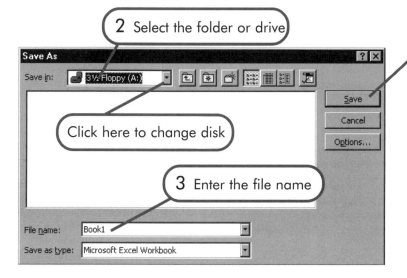

2 Select the folder or drive

Click here to change disk

3 Enter the file name

4 Click Save

Take note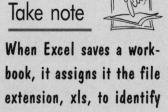

When Excel saves a workbook, it assigns it the file extension, xls, to identify it as an Excel workbook.

Inserting worksheets

To insert an additional worksheet, select the last one in the workbook and from the menu bar select **Insert > Worksheet.**

Excel will allows you to place the new sheet in front of the selected one. For instances, if you select sheet 2 and then insert a new worksheet, it will appear between sheets 1 and 2.

The new sheet will be assigned the next sequential number. If there were six sheets in the workbook, the new sheet will be sheet 7. This will occur irrespective of where you insert it.

Moving worksheets

To move the position of a worksheet within a workbook, select the worksheet name tab and drag the sheet to the required location.

Moving within a worksheet

There are a number of methods that you can use to move the cursor from one cell to the next within a worksheet. The most common are:

Tab key

To move from one cell to the next, horizontally within the worksheet, press [**Tab**].

Shift-Tab keys:

Press [**Shift**] and [**Tab**] to move the cursor back to the previously selected cell.

The arrow keys

The four arrow keys will move the cursor in the direction of the selected key.

Mouse

Left-click in the required cell.

Entering data

Left-click in cell A1, which then becomes the active cell. The active cell is the one surrounded by a thick rectangle.

- Type the following text, then press **[Enter]**:
  QUARTERLY SALES FOR AUTUMN 1998

- Move to cell B3 enter '*October*'.

- Look closely at the active cell, particularly the lower right corner, where you will see a small square.

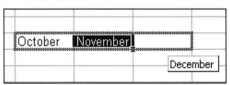

Drag on this point

- Place the mouse cursor over the square and the cursor will change its shape to a thin black cross when correctly placed over the small black square.

- With the cursor indicating a thin black cross, press and hold the left mouse button and carefully drag the cursor to the right, over the two cells C3 and D3.

October	November	
		December

As you drag, you will see that Excel has recognised that you have entered a calendar month name. Because you are dragging the cursor to the right, Excel assumes that you require the following months, *November* and *December*, entered in the selected cells. This feature is called **AutoFill**. If you had dragged the cursor to the left, Excel would have inserted *September*.

Excel has a number of similar features, and you should investigate these features at a later date by going to the menu bar and selecting **Tools > Options > Customs Lists**. You can also create your own requirements within the Custom Lists. We will be using a number of these features in due course.

Continue to enter the following detail in the cells as indicated below, using Capital letters:

Cell location	Detail
A4	FOOTWEAR
A5	CLOTHING
A6	TOILETRIES
A7	MISC

	A	B	C	D
1	QUARTERLY SALES FOR AUTUMN 1998			
2				
3		October	November	December
4	FOOTWEAR			
5	CLOTHING			
6	TOILETRIES			
7	MISC			

Text may appear to run into adjacent cells

You may find that some of the text appears to have run into the adjacent cell. In actual fact the text remains in its respective cells. We will rectify the appearance of the display shortly.

Adjusting column widths

There are a number of ways to display the text correctly but we will investigate only one option at this stage. Do not carry out any actions yet, read the following first, then make the necessary adjustments.

- Point to the column headers, just between the headers A and B. The cursor will change to a double-headed arrow.

 ← Drag to resize

- Left-click and drag the cursor to the right until you are satisfied with the positioning.

A quicker method, is to start as described above, and when the cursor changes to a double-headed arrow, double-click on the left button. Excel will automatically open out the column to the correct width.

If you adjust the width at this stage, you will not achieve the desired results. This is because there is a longer piece of text already in cell A1 and Excel will open the column to accommodate that text. The width will be excessive. To overcome this problem, we will first carry out some formatting to the text in cell A1.

- Place the cursor over the cell A1. It should resemble a fat white cross.
- Press the left button and select the cell A1.
- With the button held down, drag the cursor to the right and select the cells A1 to D1 inclusive, then release the button.

- With all four cells selected, click ⊞ **Merge and Centre** on the Formatting toolbar.

The cells will merge and the text become centred within the four. You will hardly notice any change, in respect of the text placement, but you will see that the four cells are enclosed in a bold rectangle without any highlight.

We can now adjust the width of column A.

Point to the line between the headers A and B, as described previously and double-click on the left button when the cursor changes its shape. The column will be widened to accommodate the text contained in cells A4 to A7.

	A	B	C	D
1	QUARTERLY SALES FOR AUTUMN 1998			
2				
3		October	November	December
4	FOOTWEAR			
5	CLOTHING			
6	TOILETRIES			
7	MISC			

Before column width adjusted

	A	B	C	D
1	QUARTERLY SALES FOR AUTUMN 1998			
2				
3		October	November	December
4	FOOTWEAR			
5	CLOTHING			
6	TOILETRIES			
7	MISC			

After column width adjusted

Continue to enter the data as shown below:

Cell	October	November	December
B4	3980	3285	4120
B5	5740	5566	5990
B6	2541	3500	2654
B7	1500	1750	1458

This is what your worksheet should now look like after all the above data has been entered:

	A	B	C	D
1	QUARTERLY SALES FOR AUTUMN 1998			
2				
3		October	November	December
4	FOOTWEAR	3980	3285	4120
5	CLOTHING	5740	5566	5990
6	TOILETRIES	2541	3500	2654
7	MISC	1500	1750	1458

Formatting figures

When entering data into cells Excel will align text to the left and numbers to the right.

There is still considerable formatting to be carried out on the figures yet. The figures as they stand could mean anything, when in actual fact they are monetary sums. We will format them to show only whole currency, that is to say, not any denomination less than £1.

Here is a quick way to format all twelve cells together, rather than having to apply the formatting to individual cells.

Basic steps

1 Select the cells containing the sales figures. Click on cell B4, and drag the cursor down and to the right until all the cells B4 to D7 are highlighted, then release the button.

2 Right-click over the highlighted area.

3 At the pop-up menu, select Format Cells.

4 The Format Cells dialog box will open. Ensure that the Number tab is selected.

5 Select *Currency* from the Category list.

6 We will not be showing value less than £1. Click the down arrow next to the Decimal places slot to set this to 0.

7 Drop down the Symbol list and select *None*. We do not require the £ sign displayed in these cells at this time.

8 Click OK and the format will be applied.

The area will still be highlighted. To clear this, click in a blank cell.

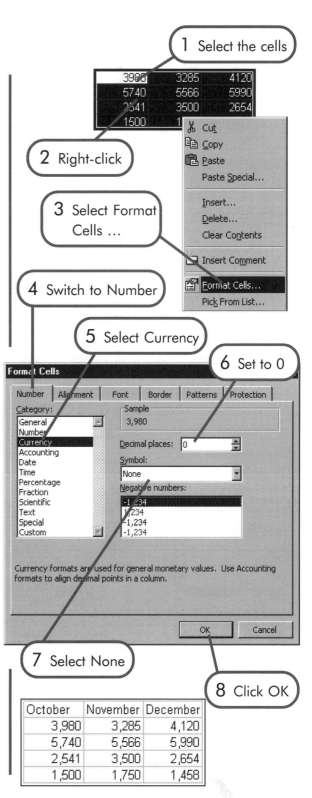

1 Select the cells

2 Right-click

3 Select Format Cells …

4 Switch to Number

5 Select Currency

6 Set to 0

7 Select None

8 Click OK

October	November	December
3,980	3,285	4,120
5,740	5,566	5,990
2,541	3,500	2,654
1,500	1,750	1,458

Font styles and sizes

The title of this worksheet, in its current format, is not very eye-catching. We will increase the font size and add a little colour to it to make it more attractive. Naturally you will need a colour printer to gain the full effect of colour.

Basic steps

1 Click onto the cell A1 to select it.

2 Open the Format menu and select Cells.

Or

3 Right-click on the cell and select Format Cells from the pop-up menu.

✂	Cu<u>t</u>
📋	<u>C</u>opy
📋	<u>P</u>aste
	Paste <u>S</u>pecial...
	<u>I</u>nsert...
	<u>D</u>elete...
	Clear Co<u>n</u>tents
📝	Insert Co<u>m</u>ment
📑	<u>F</u>ormat Cells...
	Pic<u>k</u> From List...

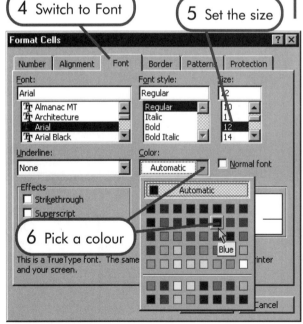

4 Switch to Font

5 Set the size

6 Pick a colour

4 At the Format Cells dialog box, select the Font tab. The current settings are highlighted. We are going to set the size to 12 and the colour to blue.

5 Using the scroll bars if necessary, find and click on the figure 12 in the Font size list.

6 Click on the arrow next to the Color slot. A palette will appear. Select blue, and the palette will close automatically.

7 Click the OK button.

As you will see, the text is too large for the cell. We will rectify this problem in a moment.

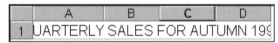

	A	B	C	D
1	UARTERLY SALES FOR AUTUMN 199			

We will now change the font size back to 10, but this time we will do it in a different way.

Basic steps

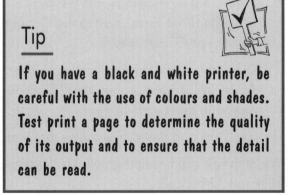

1 Select the title cell, A1.

2 In the Formula bar, click at one end of the text and drag to the other to select it all.

> ## Tip
>
> If you have a black and white printer, be careful with the use of colours and shades. Test print a page to determine the quality of its output and to ensure that the detail can be read.

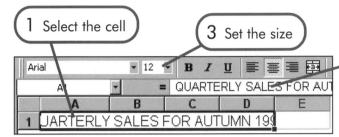

3 Click the Font size down arrow in the toolbar, and select 10.

4 Click on any part of the worksheet to activate the change. You will now be able to see all of the title text.

We are now going to format the text *October* through to *December*, to make it stand out from the rest.

Basic steps

1 Click onto cell B3, October, then drag across to highlight C3 and D3.

2 Click the Bold and then the Center icons on the Formatting toolbar.

3 Adjust the columns widths to compensate for the change in the text, i.e. bold occupies more space.

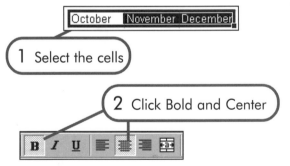

Your worksheet should now look like the example shown below. Note how the names of the months stand out now that they have had the Bold format applied.

	A	B	C	D
1	**QUARTERLY SALES FOR AUTUMN 1998**			
2				
3		October	November	December
4	FOOTWEAR	3,980	3,285	4,120
5	CLOTHING	5,740	5,566	5,990
6	TOILETRIES	2,541	3,500	2,654
7	MISC	1,500	1,750	1,458

Close this workbook, making sure that you save any changes. We will return to this workbook later in the course.

Creating a second workbook

Create another workbook, saving it as *ECDL2*, on the floppy disk. Enter the data, and format it, as shown here.

	A	B	C	D	E
1		**QUARTERLY SALES FOR WINTER 1999**			
2					
3		January	February	March	
4	FOOTWEAR	2,976	2,367	2,989	
5	CLOTHING	4,356	2,340	3,452	
6	TOILETRIES	2,350	2,956	2,870	
7	MISC	1,300	1,456	1,299	

- The title, QUARTERLY SALES FOR WINTER 1999, goes in cell B1, but should be Merged and Centered across B1 to E1.

- For the months, enter 'January' and use AutoFill to write the others.

- The width of column will need adjusting to accommodate the descriptions.

4: Spreadsheets

119

Entering formulas

In the new sheet, add the following text – these will be the headings for our formulas.

> In cell E3, enter: *Quarterly Sales*
>
> In cell A9, enter: *Total*
>
> In cell A10, enter: *Monthly Sales*

Adjust the column widths to accommodate the newly entered text.

We will shortly enter the formula that will add together the sales for the months January to March, and display the result in cell E4. **Do not type anything yet** – just read the explanations.

When entered the formula will appear in the Formula bar as follows:

> =SUM(B4:D4)

Before we enter the formula, let's see how it is made up and the meaning of its components.

The syntax – the structure – of a function begins with the name, followed by its arguments, separated by commas and all enclosed in parenthesis (). If the function starts a formula, you need an equal sign '=' before the name:

> =SUM(B4:D4)

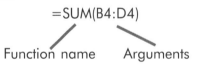

Function name   Arguments

The SUM function adds given values or the values in cells, or in ranges of cells.

The details contained within the parentheses are known as arguments and identify the cells that the calculation is to be based upon.

The formula =SUM(B4:D4) means: display the total of the values in cells B4, C4 and D4.

How to enter the formula

Click into the cell E4 and type in the equal (=) sign followed by the word 'SUM' and the opening parenthesis. **Do not** leave any spaces when entering the formula details.

- The formula should appear like this: **=Sum(**

- Click into cell B4 and drag the cursor over to cell D4. As you drag, a broken outline appears around the cells. The detail in cell E4 also reflects the movement of the cursor and inserts the cell references into this cell.

- When the three cells, B4, C4 and D4 have been selected, release the button. Your worksheet should look like this:

SUM		X ✓ =	=sum(B4:D4	
	A	B	C	D	E
1		QUARTERLY SALES FOR WINTER 1999			
2					
3		January	February	March	Quarterly Sales
4	FOOTWEAR	2,976	2,367	2,989	=sum(B4:D4
5	CLOTHING	4,356	2,340	3,452	
6	TOILETRIES	2,350	2,956	2,870	
7	MISC	1,300	1,456	1,299	
8					
9	Total				
10	Monthly Sales				

- Type in the closing parenthesis to complete the formula and press **[Enter]**. The formula appears in cell E4 and in the Formula bar like this: **=Sum(B4:D4)**

Take note

Formula names and cell identifiers in formulas are not case sensitive – you may use uppercase, lowercase or mixed.

- Re-select cell E4, move the cursor to the lower right corner of the cell and when the cursor changes to a thin black cross, left-click and drag the cursor down to cell E10 and then release the button. This action copies the formula down to the other cells and adjusts it accordingly.

Select cells E5, E6 and E7 in turn and you will see that Excel has adjusted the cell references relevant to each cell as it copied the formula.

E10		▾	=	=SUM(B10:D10)	
	A	B	C	D	E
1		QUARTERLY SALES FOR WINTER 1999			
2					
3		January	February	March	Quarterly Sales
4	FOOTWEAR	2,976	2,367	2,989	8,332
5	CLOTHING	4,356	2,340	3,452	10,148
6	TOILETRIES	2,350	2,956	2,870	8,176
7	MISC	1,300	1,456	1,299	4,055
8					0
9	Total				0
10	Monthly Sales				0

The example now shows all the calculations completed. There is a small problem however. Cells E8 and E9 display zero (0) values and their presence is an unnecessary distraction.

- Click into cell E8 and drag down to include cell E9 in the selection.
- Press **[Delete]** and the cells will be cleared.

The worksheet is not complete. The formula for the *Monthly Sales* has yet to be entered.

- Select the cell B10 and type in the formula: =Sum(B4:B7), then press **[Enter]**.
- Point to the lower right corner of the cell. When the cursor changes to a thin black cross, drag it to the right to select cells C10 and D10. Release the button and the formulas will be copied into the cells, and the totals calculated and displayed.

Notice that as you dragged the cursor to the right, the zero value in cell E10 was changing to reflect the increase in totals. Your worksheet should resemble the example shown below.

	A	B	C	D	E
1		QUARTERLY SALES FOR WINTER 1999			
2					
3		January	February	March	Quarterly Sales
4	FOOTWEAR	2,976	2,367	2,989	8,332
5	CLOTHING	4,356	2,340	3,452	10,148
6	TOILETRIES	2,350	2,956	2,870	8,176
7	MISC	1,300	1,456	1,299	4,055
8					
9	Total				
10	Monthly Sales	10,982	9,119	10,610	30,711

Save any changes to the worksheet and then close it by selecting **File > Close**.

Practical exercise

Re-open the worksheet *ECDL1*.

Select **File** and, provided that you have not opened many other worksheets since last working on it, you will find *ECDL1* in the lower area of the **File** drop-down menu. If *ECDL1* is shown in the list, click on it and it will open.

The aim is now to apply to this **all** the additional text and formatting that was applied to the worksheet *ECDL2*. Enter the new text and the formulas, complete with formatting, and carry out any adjustments if necessary.

When you have completed all the additions and adjustments to ECDL1, Save the changes. The worksheet should resemble that shown below.

	A	B	C	D	E
1		QUARTERLY SALES FOR AUTUMN 1998			
2					
3		October	November	December	Quarterly Sales
4	FOOTWEAR	3,980	3,285	4,120	11,385
5	CLOTHING	5,740	5,566	5,990	17,296
6	TOILETRIES	2,541	3,500	2,654	8,695
7	MISC	1,500	1,750	1,458	4,708
8					
9	Total				
10	Monthly Sales	13,761	14,101	14,222	42,084

Inserting rows and columns

At some stage you may need to insert a new row or column in a worksheet. Inserting rows and columns is quite simple.

Basic steps

1 Open *ECDL1*. Move to row 7, and right-click on the row number. The row will be selected and a pop-up menu will appear.

2 Select Insert. The worksheet will roll down one row and a new row 7 will appear. The old row 7 will be re-numbered as row 8.

3 Select cell E7. Notice that the Formula bar is empty. When a row is inserted, formulas in the old row are not copied over.

4 Point to the lower right corner of cell E6, and drag it down to cell E7. Release the button. Select E7 again and you will see that it now contains a copy of the formula.

In row 7, enter the following new details:

Cell A7, HOSIERY
Cell B7, 1256
Cell C7, 1045
Cell D7, 1145

Note that as you enter the *Hosiery* figures, the *quarterly sales* in E7 is updated automatically.

Inserting columns

We will now insert a new column in the ECDL1 worksheet. The new column will be used to display an Average Sales figure and is to be located between the column for December and the Quarterly Sales figures.

1 Right-click on the row number

	A	October	November	December	Quarterly Sales
1	QUARTERLY SALES FOR AUTUMN 1998				
2					
3		October	November	December	Quarterly Sales
4	FOOTWEAR	3,980	3,285	4,120	11,385
5	CLOTHING	5,740	5,566	5,990	17,296
6	TOILETRIES	2,541	3,500	2,654	8,695
7	MISC	1,500	1,750	1,458	4,708

Cut
Copy
Paste
Paste Special...
Insert
Delete
Clear Contents
Format Cells...
Row Height...
Hide
Unhide

| 10 | | 13,761 | 14,101 | 14,222 | 42,084 |

2 Select Insert

E7 = =SUM(B7:D7)

	A	B	C	D	E
1	QUARTERLY SALES FOR AUTUMN 1998				
2					
3		October	November	December	Quarterly Sales
4	FOOTWEAR	3,980	3,285	4,120	11,385
5	CLOTHING	5,740	5,566	5,990	17,296
6	TOILETRIES	2,541	3,500	2,654	8,695
7					0
8	MISC	1,500	1,750	1,458	4,708
9					
11				14,222	42,084

4 Copy in the formula

Note that when a new column is inserted, the selected column and all those to its right will be moved one column to the right.

- The new column is to be inserted between the current columns D and E. Right-click in the header area of column E.

- Select **Insert** from the pop-up menu. Excel will insert a new column E and move the old one to the right, making it column F.

Place the cursor on cell E3 and type in: 'Average Sales', then press **[Enter]**. Format the new column title to match the others.

The formula that we will create will calculate the average monthly sales for each line of goods. It will be placed in cells E4 to E8.

- Select cell E4 and type in:
  =AVERAGE(B4:D4)

The AVERAGE function will add the contents of the cells, then divide by the number of cells. In this case:

(3980 + 3285 + 4120)/ 3 = 3795

- Use the drag method to copy the formula down to cell E11. Note that as you copy it down to each cell Excel carries out the calculation and displays the result in the appropriate cell.

- Highlight cells E9 and E10 and clear the cell contents by pressing **[Delete]**.

The completed sheet should look like this:

	A	B	C	D	E	F
1	QUARTERLY SALES FOR AUTUMN 1998					
2						
3		October	November	December	Average Sales	Quarterly Sales
4	FOOTWEAR	3,980	3,285	4,120	3,795	11,385
5	CLOTHING	5,740	5,566	5,990	5,765	17,296
6	TOILETRIES	2,541	3,500	2,654	2,898	8,695
7	HOSIERY	1,256	1,045	1,145	1,149	3,446
8	MISC	1,500	1,750	1,458	1,569	4,708
9						
10	Total					
11	Monthly Sales	15,017	15,146	15,367	15,177	45,530

Reformatting currency cells

It was decided when we first created the worksheets that we would not display any decimal places for any currency of a value of less than one pound. In other words no pence would be shown. Obviously this is somewhat unrealistic, so we will re-format the worksheet to show any pence that may be included in any calculations. We will also re-format the cells to display the pound (£) sign.

- Select the block of cells from B4 to F11, then right-click on the area and select **Format Cells** from the pop-up menu.

- At the **Format Cells** dialog box, ensure the **Number** tab is open, then select *Currency*.

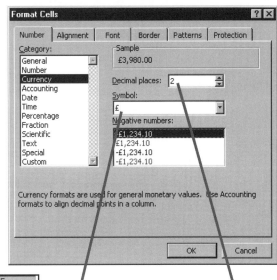

Set the Decimal places to 2

Set the Symbol to £

The currency figures after reformatting

	A	B	C	D	E	F
1	QUARTERLY SALES FOR AUTUMN 1998					
2						
3		October	November	December	Average Sales	Quarterly Sales
4	FOOTWEAR	£3,980.00	£3,285.00	£4,120.00	£3,795.00	£11,385.00
5	CLOTHING	£5,740.00	£5,566.00	£5,990.00	£5,765.33	£17,296.00
6	TOILETRIES	£2,541.00	£3,500.00	£2,654.00	£2,898.33	£8,695.00
7	HOSIERY	£1,256.00	£1,045.00	£1,145.00	£1,148.67	£3,446.00
8	MISC	£1,500.00	£1,750.00	£1,458.00	£1,569.33	£4,708.00
9						
10	Total					
11	Monthly Sales	£15,017.00	£15,146.00	########	£15,176.67	£45,530.00

The reformatting may result in some cells not displaying correctly, as the new format may need more space than is available. The problem can be solved by adjusting the cell width.

Sorting data

There will be occasions where you may wish to present the data in a different order, for instance you may wish to display the sales data in ECDL1 in ascending order.

Basic steps

1   Highlight the block A4 to D8.

	A	B	C	D	E
1	QUARTERLY SALES FOR AUTUMN 1998				
2					
3		October	November	December	Average Sales
4	FOOTWEAR	£3,980.00	£3,285.00	£4,120.00	£3,795.00
5	CLOTHING	£5,740.00	£5,566.00	£5,990.00	£5,765.33
6	TOILETRIES	£2,541.00	£3,500.00	£2,654.00	£2,898.33
7	HOSIERY	£1,256.00	£1,045.00	£1,145.00	£1,148.67
8	MISC'	£1,500.00	£1,750.00	£1,458.00	£1,569.33
9					
10	Total				
11	Monthly Sales	£15,017.00	£15,146.00	£15,367.00	£15,176.67

2   Click ![Sort Ascending] the Sort Ascending button. The highlighted area will re-arrange to display the data as shown in the example below.

	A	B	C	D	E
1	QUARTERLY SALES FOR AUTUMN 1998				
2					
3		October	November	December	Average Sales
4	CLOTHING	£5,740.00	£5,566.00	£5,990.00	£5,765.33
5	FOOTWEAR	£3,980.00	£3,285.00	£4,120.00	£3,795.00
6	HOSIERY	£1,256.00	£1,045.00	£1,145.00	£1,148.67
7	MISC'	£1,500.00	£1,750.00	£1,458.00	£1,569.33
8	TOILETRIES	£2,541.00	£3,500.00	£2,654.00	£2,898.33
9					
10	Total				
11	Monthly Sales	£15,017.00	£15,146.00	£15,367.00	£15,176.67

3   Click in a blank cell to remove the highlight.

All the corresponding cells will automatically re-calculate their respective values in relation to the changes brought about by the Sort.

Copying data

Data and formulas can be easily copied from one worksheet to another. This is done by using the Copy and Paste features found in Excel. We are going to copy a row and a column.

Ensure that both ECDL1 and ECDL2 worksheets are open. There are a number of ways that you can move from one worksheet to the other. We will use the method described below.

● Ensure that the ECDL1 worksheet is active, i.e. the one that you can see. To confirm this, check the name in the title bar.

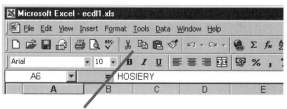

Cut, Copy and Paste buttons

● Open the **Window** menu. In the lower section there are the file names of the two open worksheets.

The one with the tick alongside is the active worksheet.

We are going to copy the Hosiery row and the Average Sales column from ECDL1 to ECDL2.

Before we start, move to ECDL2, select the cells A4 to D7 and carry out a Sort Ascending on them. This will bring both of the workbooks in to a common presentation of data. If this is not done, the copied data, when pasted in, will not correspond to the correct data.

- Re-select workbook ECDL1.

Pasting a row

- Select row 6 and copy it, either by using the right-click menu option or by selecting **Edit > Copy**.

- Change to ECDL2 and select row 6 using the right-click menu option **Insert Copied Cells**.

Note that row 6 has carried over the formatting of row 6 in ECDL1, including the Average Sales figures in cell E6. The Quarterly Sales figure for Hosiery is now in cell F6.

Copying the row from one workbook to another has resulted in our worksheet displaying various figures in the wrong columns and this must be corrected before we proceed.

- Click in cell E6 and press **[Delete]** to re-move the cell contents.

- Select cell F6, point to its lower edge and when the cursor changes to an arrow drag it into the empty cell E6. Release the button and the data will be transferred across.

Copying columns

When we created the workbook ECDL2 we placed the worksheet title, '*Quarterly Sales for Winter 1999*', in cell B1, whereas when we created the workbook ECDL1 the worksheet title was placed in cell A1.

The reason for changing the location was to highlight a problem often encountered when copying between workbooks or worksheets.

If you encounter difficulties when attempting to copy columns, re-check the overall layout of the worksheets – you will often find that there is a difference in the general layout of such items as titles, etc.

We will not be able to insert a new column because of the different locations of our title, but we can overcome this quite simply.

- Ensure that ECDL2 is the active worksheet.

- Select the cell B1, then right-click on it and select **Cut** from the pop-up menu. A dashed outline will now appear around the cell.

- Point to an area below the data and select an empty cell, e.g. A20. Right-click on it and from the pop-up menu select **Paste**. The title will now be moved to its temporary location.

We can now proceed and start copying the column from one workbook to another.

- Ensure that ECDL1 is the active worksheet.

- Select column E and using either the right-click or **Edit > Copy** method, copy it.

- Switch to ECDL2.

- Select column E, right-click on it and from the pop-up menu select **Insert Copied Cells**.

Take note

If you use Paste to copy in cells, the data will overwrite any existing data in the target cells.

The original column E will move to the right and become column F while the *Average Sales* figures column will now become column E.

We now want to move the title back up to the top of the worksheet, above the data. Select the title cell, Cut it from its current location and Paste it into cell A1.

There will now be some inconsistency in the overall formatting and appearance in the ECDL2 worksheet. Reformat as required for an overall consistency and in line with that of the workbook ECDL1.

Save the changes to the worksheet.

Tip

Remember to periodically save any changes to the workbook. Use the Toolbar Save button 💾 or the shortcut [Ctrl] and [S].

Review

This may have seemed a somewhat long and protracted method to insert data from one worksheet to another. However, consider the following facts:

- Our worksheets are on the small size and contain little data in comparison with that of Company/Corporate worksheets, which could, and do contain numerous columns and rows, so Copy and Paste would certainly save time.

- Most errors, if they are to occur, will happen as the user is typing in data. Copy and Paste facilities reduce the likelihood of error.

The exercises just completed, involved moving columns and rows. You should be aware that you can copy blocks of data as well as complete columns and rows.

The procedure is simple.

- Highlight the required range, right-click on the highlighted area and select **Copy** from the pop-up menu.

- Right-click over the appropriate cell, where you wish the copied data to appear, and from the pop-up menu select **Paste**. The text will appear in the appropriate cells.

Take note

A workbook may have several sheets. If you are not sure of which sheet you are on, check the lower left corner of the workbook and the worksheet numbers appear there. To change from one sheet to another, simply click once on the sheet that you require.

Charts

'*A picture paints a thousand words*', and Excel gives you charts and graphs to help give figures more meaning. Charts make it easier to spot trends, highlight important changes and compare individual figures. Charts in reports and presentations will display numbers to your audience in a format that is easy to understand.

When you create a chart, each row or column of data on the worksheet makes up a *data series*. Each individual value within a row or column is called a *data point*.

The chart can include row and column headings. These are used as category labels and legend text. If the range does not include headings, Excel creates default headings.

You can either embed a chart in the worksheet you are currently working with, or create it on a chart sheet. When you want the chart and the worksheet data viewed or printed together, you should use an embedded chart.

A chart sheet is a separate worksheet in the workbook that contains only the chart. If you want to use the chart by itself (for example, in a presentation) you should use a chart sheet. Both kinds of chart are linked to the worksheet data and updated automatically if the data is changed.

The Chart Wizard

The Chart Wizard assists you in creating a chart by leading you through a series of dialog boxes that allow you to choose options. You can quickly learn the essentials of creating a chart using the Chart Wizard.

Basic steps

1 Open the worksheet ECDL1. Drag to select the range containing the data to be included in the chart – in this case, A3 to D8.

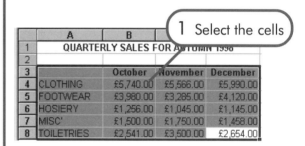

1 Select the cells

2 Click 📚 the Chart Wizard icon.

3 For the Chart type, select Pie, with the 3D Chart sub-type.

4 Click the Next button.

3 Choose Pie, 3D

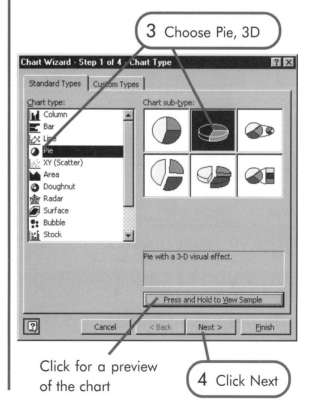

Click for a preview of the chart

4 Click Next

5 Set the Series in option to *Rows*.

6 Click the Next button.

7 At the next stage, ensure that the Title tab is selected and type in '*Quarterly Sales Autumn 1998*'.

8 Click on Data Labels and select Show label and percent.

9 Click Next.

10 The next window will offer you two options as to where the chart should reside. Select: As new sheet.

11 Click Finish.

Use the Legends tab if you want to turn the legend off or reposition it – the default Placement is to the Right

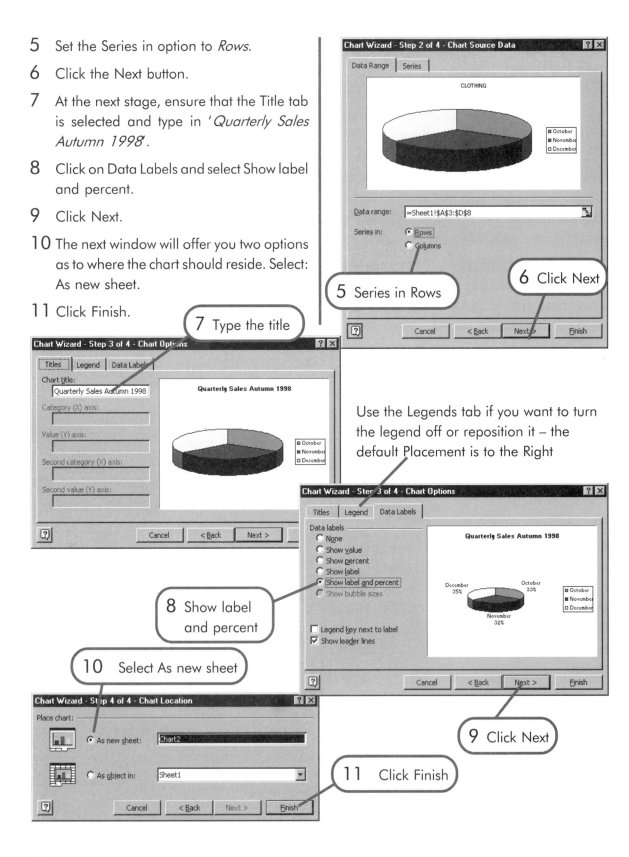

That completes the chart building process using a Wizard. The chart should now appear as shown below.

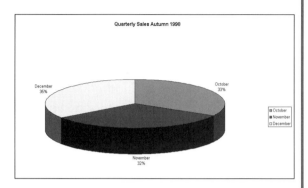

Creating a second chart

We are now going to create a second chart, this time using the ECDL2 worksheet. Close ECDL1 and save any changes if prompted.

This time we want all the figures except the *Average Sales* to be included in the chart. Open ECDL2 and follow the procedures below:

● Click into cell A3 and drag down to cell D8 to highlight this area. Release the button.

● Press **[Control]** and keep it pressed. Click on cell F3 and drag down to cell F8.

This will highlight the data within this range while retaining the previously highlighted data.

	A	B	C	D	E	F
1	QUARTERLY SALES FOR WINTER 1999					
2						
3		January	February	March	Average Sales	Quarterly Sales
4	CLOTHING	£4,356.00	£2,340.00	£3,452.00	£3,382.67	£10,148.00
5	FOOTWEAR	£2,976.00	£2,367.00	£2,989.00	£2,777.33	£8,332.00
6	HOSIERY	£1,256.00	£1,045.00	£1,145.00	£1,148.67	£3,446.00
7	MISC	£1,300.00	£1,456.00	£1,299.00	£1,351.67	£4,055.00
8	TOILETRIES	£2,350.00	£2,956.00	£2,870.00	£2,725.33	£8,176.00

The method is used to select scattered blocks and can be extremely useful when working with large worksheets.

Basic steps

1 Click 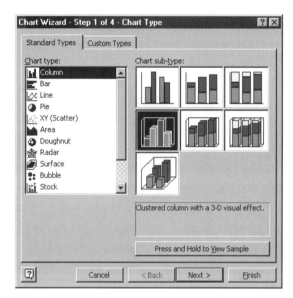 the Chart Wizard icon.

2 At the first step, ensure the Standard Types tab is open. From Chart Type, select *Column* and from the Chart sub-type, click on the first image on the second row.

3 Click the Next button.

4 At Step 2, select the Series in *Rows* option and click the Next Button.

5 At Step 3, make the following selections.

On the Titles tab, type the Chart Title: 'Quarterly Sales Winter 1999'.

On the Legend tab, tick Show Legend and select *Right* for the Placement.

On the Data Labels tab, select None, click the Next button.

6 At Step 4, Chart Location, select the option: As object in – the adjacent slot should show *Sheet 1*. Click the Finish button.

129

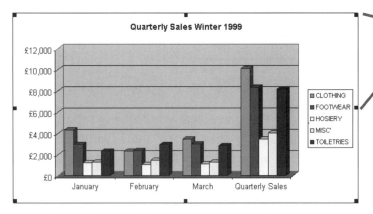

Handles

The components of the chart – the grid, axes, title, legend, etc., can be selected individually for moving, resizing or formatting

The Chart Wizard will now close and the chart will appear on the current sheet.

Moving a chart

You may find that the chart is not placed where you want it and it may be covering your data.

When the chart appears on the worksheet it should already be selected. You can confirm this by the presence of a dark outline, with 'handles' at the corners and mid-sides. Once the chart has been selected, it can be moved around the sheet or resized as required.

To move the chart, select it, then point up to the chart line until the cursor changes to a single arrow. When it does, click and drag in the direction that you wish to move the chart. The cursor will again change its shape, this time to a four-headed arrow pointer. ✛

To resize a chart

It is possible to change the size of the chart. Select the chart, by clicking over an area that has no detail in it.

Point to the handle at the lower right-hand corner. The cursor should change to ↘ a double-headed arrow. Press the left button and hold it down. Drag the cursor in or out to change the size. Be careful at this stage – too much adjustment in either the horizontal or vertical planes may distort the chart.

To keep the chart in proportion, while changing its size, hold down **[Shift]** while dragging the cursor. When the desired size has been achieved, release both cursor and **[Shift]**.

Re-save the worksheet and then experiment moving and sizing the chart.

Also experiment with the components of the chart. For instance right-click over the Legend and a pop-up menu will appear from which you may Format the Legend…

Save the changes.

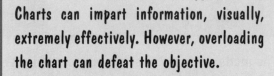

Tip

Charts can impart information, visually, extremely effectively. However, overloading the chart can defeat the objective.

Experiment with all aspects of the chart feature, to learn its versatility and which chart best suits the task and type of data.

Headers and footers

Before printing the sheet and chart we will first create a Header and Footer to contain descriptive text such as title and page numbers. Open ECDL2 and follow the steps.

Basic steps

1 Open the File menu and select Page Setup.

2 At the dialog box, click on the Header/Footer tab.

3 Click the Custom Header button.

4 At the Header dialog box, type your name in the Center section, then click OK.

5 Back at the Page Setup dialog box, select *Page 1* from the drop-down Footer list to set the page numbering style.

6 When you have done click the Print Preview button.

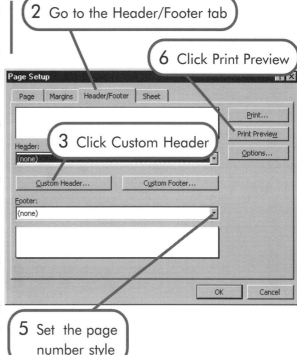

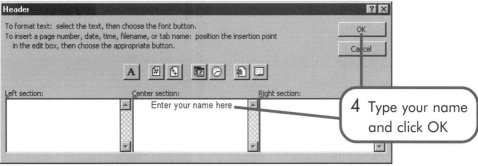

Print Preview

This shows how the sheet, and its embedded chart, will look when printed. Use it to check that the layout is satisfactory and that the page contains all the elements you want to show.

The layout should be similar to the example overleaf. If the image is rather small, click once on the Zoom button to increase the view size. Clicking on the Zoom button again will reduce the view size.

After checking, close the Print Preview window, as we are now ready to print the worksheet.

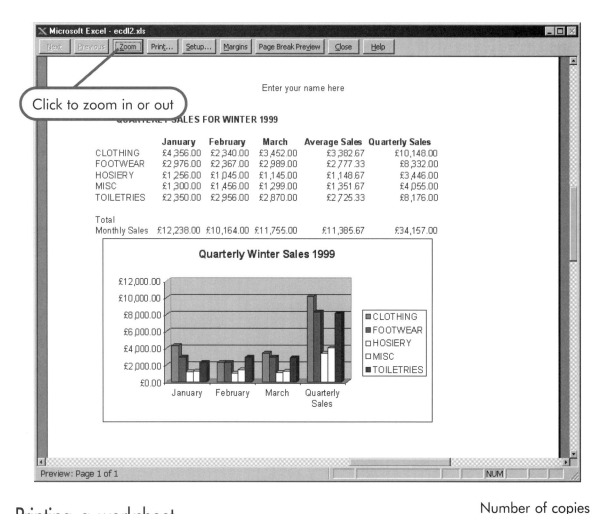

Printing a worksheet

Ensure that ECDL2.xls is open, and follow the procedures outlined below:

- Open the **File** menu and select **Print** to open the **Print** dialog box.

- Ensure that the **Active sheet(s)** option is selected.

- If more than one copy is required, set the Number of copies.

- Click the **OK** button to print the worksheet.

Experiment with the other aspects of the print output that can be altered in this dialog box.

Number of copies

Pages to print

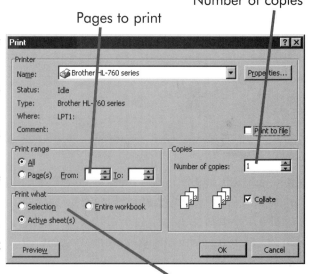

A selected block can be printed

Absolute references

When you enter cell references in a formula they are *relative* references. If you copy the formula, the cell references change relative to where the formula is copied. You saw this happening when we first entered formulas (page 120).

Absolute references do not change when used in formulas. The reference cell remains fixed because the value in that cell does not change when applied to other cells. Two examples of the use of an absolute reference are:

- Fluctuating currency exchange rates, where the rate changes after a period of time. When the rate is changed only the one figure, the absolute reference, has to be changed to reflect the overall change in holdings.

- Commission, usually awarded at a fixed rate for a given period of time. If the basic salary is increased, the commission percentage will usually remain the same, the absolute reference.

When entering an absolute reference in a cell the $ sign is used to fix the row and column identifiers, e.g. A15.

We are going to create an absolute reference in our worksheet ECDL1. The scenario is that it is company policy that each branch manager receives a 2.5% commission on sales.

Basic steps

1   Open the worksheet ECDL1.

2   In cell A13 type '*Managers*', then in A14 type '*Commission*'.

3   In cell A15 type: 2.5

4   Select cell B14 and enter the formula:
    =B11/100*A15

5   Press [Enter] and you should now have the figure 375.425, or £375.43 if the currency format has been applied to this cell.

6   Copy the formula into cells C14 and C15 and carry out any formatting necessary, i.e. format cells to display the £ sign.

4: Spreadsheets

Tip

You can also use **Mixed References** — where only the row or column is fixed. This subject is beyond the scope of this book.

4 Enter the formula

2 Type the labels

3 Enter the rate

6 Copy across

B14		=	=B11/100*A15		
	A	B	C	D	E	F
1	QUARTERLY SALES FOR AUTUMN 1998					
2						
3		October	November	December	Average Sales	Quarterly Sales
4	CLOTHING	£5,740.00	£5,566.00	£5,990.00	£5,765.33	£17,296.00
5	FOOTWEAR	£3,980.00	£3,285.00	£4,120.00	£3,795.00	£11,385.00
6	HOSIERY			145.00	£1,148.67	£3,446.00
7	MISC			68.00	£1,569.33	£4,708.00
8	TOILETRIES			54.00	£2,898.33	£8,695.00
9						
10	Total					
11	Monthly Sales	£15,017.00	£15,146.00	£15,367.00	£15,176.67	£45,530.00
12						
13	Managers					
14	Commission	£375.43	£378.65	£384.18		
15		2.5				

Named cells and ranges

So far you have used cell addresses, e.g. A15, C15, etc. to refer to cells, and of course it works. There is however an often more convenient method of referring to cell addresses and ranges of cells. This method is known as naming.

Excel allows the use of named cells or ranges of cells and these can be moved, copied or entered in formulas, just like cells with ordinary addresses.

Picture this: you could give the absolute reference a name, such as *Commission* and use that reference in other worksheets. When an adjustment in the commission rate is called for, it only has to be made at the one located, in this case in the workbook ECDL1, worksheet 1, cell B15. The adjustment will automatically update all referenced worksheets.

Clearly one can see minor problems in this instance. Previous months' commission, which will have already been paid at the previous rate will be amended by the change and show an incorrect figure. There are ways and means of dealing with this situation, but this area is outside the realms of this book.

We have talked a great deal about naming cells or ranges of cells, so how do we do it? We will use the absolute reference recently created in the ECDL1 workbook.

Basic steps

1   Ensure that the workbook ECDL1 is open and that you are at worksheet 1.

2   Select cell A15, the one used in the absolute reference, then point to the Name box, to the left of the Formula bar. It will already have the cell reference A15.

3   Click into the Name box. The cell reference will be highlighted ready for you to overtype the existing name, in this instance A15.

4   Type in a name (up to 255 characters) – call it *Commission* – and press [Enter].

4 Enter the name

3 Click into the Name box

2 Select the cell

Using names in formulas

You will recall that we used the absolute cell reference \$A\$15 in the formula for cells B14, C14 and D14 to calculate the commission due. The fact that we gave the Absolute Reference will have no bearing on this factor, the formula will still function.

We will now create a new calculation based on the absolute reference name and the Total Monthly Sales figure in cell F11.

Basic steps

1 In A17, enter *'Managers'*.

2 In A18, enter *'Quarterly'*.

3 In A19, enter *'Commission'*.

4 In B19, enter the formula:

=F11/100*Commission

Press [Enter] and you should have the result: £1,138.25.

Excel recognised that the name *Commission* was an absolute reference, and used it in the formula to perform the calculation.

Save the changes.

Take note

When creating named cells or ranges, Excel automatically changes the cell or ranges to an Absolute Reference.

You may have noticed that when you created the charts, earlier in the course, that the Chart Wizard step 2 dialog box, shown opposite, displayed the selected range as an Absolute Reference.

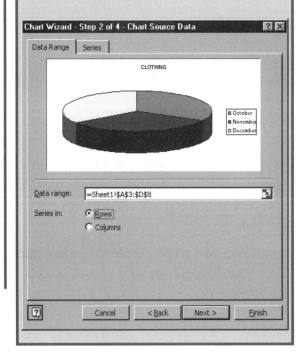

Take note

Valid names can include letters, numbers, periods, and underlines, but no spaces. A Name cannot begin with a number.

Integration with other applications

Information stored in an Excel workbook can easily be copied or linked to any of the other applications in the Microsoft Office 97 suite. A chart or data can be inserted into a Word document, an Access database or a PowerPoint presentation. It is also possible to import data from these applications into Excel.

Exchange data with Access

To analyse the data from an Access table in Excel, you can use features in Access to export the data automatically to a new Excel workbook. You can also import worksheet data into Access. If you want only a few records from an Access table, you can open the table and copy and paste selected records into Excel.

If you're working in Excel and have installed and loaded the AccessLinks add-in, you can convert a list to an Access database file. For more information about add-ins use the on-line Help system.

You can create a PivotTable to analyse data from Access just as you would from any external data source.

Practice

It will only be possible to practise the following if you have already completed the module on Access.

Basic steps

1 Open the Access database ECDL2 and then select, but do not open, the table ECDL Table2.

2 Open the Edit menu and select Copy.

3 Open Excel with a new workbook.

4 Ensure cell A1 is selected.

5 Open the Edit menu and select Paste.

6 The table selected in Access will be pasted into the workbook and you may then format the worksheet to suit your requirements.

It is almost certain that the pasted version of the table will require some reformatting once within the worksheet – in particular cell widths will require some adjustment to display long entries or field names.

Using the online Help system

The online help system in all Microsoft applications is similar in its style, appearance and operation. We are going to discuss the online help by accessing it using Excel. You should remember that the procedures discussed here are the same for Word, PowerPoint and Access though this latter has some special features.

We will look at only one avenue of the Help system, based on the Index tab.

Basic steps

1 Open the Help menu and select Contents and Index.

2 Select the Index tab if not already selected.

3 Type in one or more words relating to the subject that you want help on, e.g. type in 'Help' to find out more about the system.

4 Click the Display button.

5 The Topics Found dialog box will open, listing any relevant pages. Select a topic and click the Display button.

6 A dialog box will open, displaying the topic. Use the scroll bars to reveal more of the text, if appropriate.

7 To continue the search, or to locate another subject, click the Help Topics button, and you will be returned to the Index.

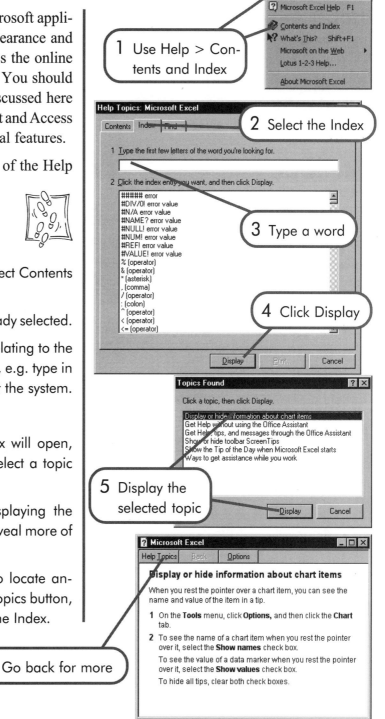

1 Use Help > Contents and Index

2 Select the Index

3 Type a word

4 Click Display

5 Display the selected topic

7 Go back for more

Printing the Help Topic

If you wish to print out the current Help topic click the **Options** button and select Print from the menu.

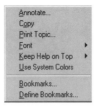

Annotate...
Copy
Print Topic...
Font ▶
Keep Help on Top ▶
Use System Colors

Bookmarks...
Define Bookmarks...

Annotating Help pages

You can add your own annotations to the current Help topic.

Basic steps

1   Click Options and select Annotate.

2   Type in your comments, then click Save to save your annotations.

3   When you return you to the Help topic, you will note that a little green paperclip has been added, next to the topic title. To view an annotation, click the paperclip symbol.

4   To delete an annotation, open the Annotate dialog box and click Delete.

The F1 Help key

Help can also be obtained through the use of the **[F1]** key.

Place the cursor in any cell and press **[F1]** and the Office Assistant will appear.

Type in your question and Excel will attempt to match your question to its data bank. If successful, it will usually offer you a number of options.

This Help feature can be a little on the hit and miss. Keep your questions simple.

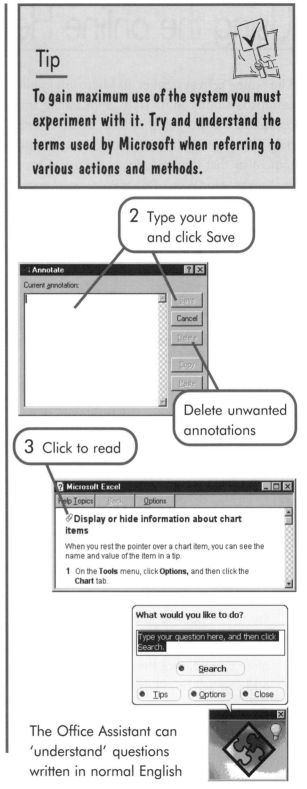

Tip

To gain maximum use of the system you must experiment with it. Try and understand the terms used by Microsoft when referring to various actions and methods.

2 Type your note and click Save

Delete unwanted annotations

3 Click to read

The Office Assistant can 'understand' questions written in normal English

Sample paper 4: Spreadsheets

1	How many worksheets are available when Excel opens a new workbook?	1. 1 2. 3 3. 16
2	How is an active cell indicated in a worksheet?	1. It has a label saying 'active'. 2. It has a thick black line around it. 3. It is a different colour to all the other cells.
3	In simple terms explain the formula: =sum(D2:D6)	
4	Access tables can be copied or imported into an Excel Worksheet, True or False?	1. True 2. False
5	List the two methods which will permit you access to the Format Cells dialog box.	1. The Edit menu 2. The Tools menu 3. Right -lick on cell 4. Format menu
6	To obtain Help when working in Excel, you can select Help on the Menu bar. What is the other way Help can be obtained?	
7	After opening a new workbook in Excel, what is the first thing you should do:	1. Type in the column headings. 2. Save the workbook. 3. Type in the row descriptions.
8	What information is shown in the Formula bar?	
9	Describe the quick method of adjusting the column widths.	

10	List the two sort options available in Excel.	1. 2.
11	Write the formula for calculating the average of cells B4 B5 B6 B7 B8.	
12	In the calculation 3*4+6/2, what is the answer? Show how it was reached.	

5 Databases

Introduction to Access

What is a database?

A database is a collection of information organised in such a manner as to make the information easily accessible. The structure of the database should be simple in order to make storage and retrieval equally easy.

Some examples of databases in everyday use, which people may not think of in terms of a database are:

- A telephone directory
- A dictionary
- A catalogue

In the business world, databases are used for such things as:

- Stock control records
- Customer accounts
- Personnel records

Within a database, related information is stored in tables, organised in *columns* and *rows*.

The columns have headings, known as *field names*, which relate to their content.

Each row contains items of data, known as *fields*, under the different column headings and makes up what is known as a *record*.

In the example there are five records of six fields. They are shown here with their field names.

Planning your database

Before you start creating the components of your database, it is worth spending some time thinking about the information that you are dealing with and how you will want that information handled and displayed.

Following on from this, you should spend some time designing the database on paper, planning the table and designing the layout of the forms and reports, before finally building the database within Access. This way you will identify your requirements and take away the hit and miss aspect, which would occur if you did not spend some time beforehand thinking out the design and layout.

Field name   Field data

Name	Surname	Tel	Fax	Town	Post Code
Michelle	O'Leary	01934 418261	01934 418261	Glasgow	G2 6YH
Keith	Champion	0171 548 7285		Hackney	NW12 7RQ
James	Bates	01705 293176	01705 293176	Portsmouth	PO3 2PL
Joe	Smith	01705 275193	01705 275213	Portsmouth	PO5 2DG
Peter	Bloggs	0181 329 1122	0181 329 1123	Richmond	TW9 1QP

Record

Primary and Secondary keys

During the course of creating the database covered in this book, you will encounter the terms *Primary* and *Secondary keys*. When you have created a table and attempted to save it, for example, Access will warn you that 'no Primary Key has been assigned'. This fact will have no bearing on the database that you will shortly build. It is worthwhile however explaining what the functions of these keys are and why they are used.

If you later progress to creating more complex databases, you will be building in ways to link different tables together, hence the term *relational database*. The linking of tables typically involves setting up each table with a field common to tables. Although this means deliberately duplicating some data in the database, it is better to duplicate a limited amount than have a long set of fields within the database.

The fields that are used to create the links, from one table to another, are usually described as Primary and Secondary keys.

Primary keys uniquely identify a record. A good example might occur in personnel database. Each person has a unique National Insurance number. This number would be in a field which would be assigned as the Primary key. This field would be used to link data to other records in other tables within the database.

If you want to link data from one table to another table you will need to include a field in the second table that corresponds to the Primary key in the first table. This field is then known as the *Secondary key*.

This screenshot of the Relationships display was taken from the *Northwind* example database which is supplied with Access.

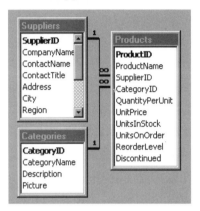

There are three tables: *Suppliers*, *Categories* and *Products*. Two tables have Primary key fields: *Suppliers* is **Supplier ID** and *Categories* is **Category ID**. You will see that there is a link from each of these to the table *Products*.

The *Products* table has two fields with matching names, **Supplier ID** and **Category ID**, and these are the Secondary key fields.

Primary and Secondary keys provide the links within relational databases and one cannot exist without the other.

These keys are discussed solely as background information. While working on exercises in this book, if you are prompted by Access that no Primary key has been assigned, ignore it.

We do suggest that, at a later stage, it would be worthwhile investigating the Northwind database. It can be found in the Folder: Microsoft Office\Office\Samples.

Viewing and editing data

There are three ways in which you will work with data:

1 You need to enter records into the database and these records are stored within tables.

2 You need a means of editing or updating the data within the tables.

3 You require a means of searching and viewing the records found.

These tasks are performed using the following components of the database.

Tables are used to enter new data, edit existing data and to find data within the table. Tables enable you to view numerous records at once.

Forms are the usual method of entering or editing data contained within tables. You can create forms that combine data from one or more tables and each table may have more than one forms associated with it. Forms are normally used to view one record at a time. They are based and dependent upon tables.

Queries are used to sort or select data using a set of criteria. Once the data has been selected, it can then be edited using a Datasheet View of a table or Form View, or used to find data or to create other tables and forms.

Reports are outputs from the database – typically printed – with the information sorted, selected and organised into a useful form.

The report can be produced with the information displayed in a table format or as single columns, or the user can design the report layout completely.

A report can be set up to perform calculations and print out the results. It may have multiple tables associated with it.

Access is a powerful relational database which allows multiple tables and forms to be created and linked together according to a given set of criteria. See the example on the previous page relating to Primary and Secondary fields.

Starting Access

As with most Windows applications, you can start Access a number of different ways. Here is one method.

Click on **Start** the **Start** button. Point to **Programs** to open its menu. Click on **Microsoft Access**. You will be presented with this dialog box.

Make your choice – in this instance select **Blank Database** – then click the **OK** button.

Creating a database

The File New Database dialog box will open. Access automatically creates a name for you in the File Name slot. Note that the name is already highlighted, which means that when you type in your choice of name for the database, the name that Access prepared for you will be overwritten.

Basic steps

1 Click the down arrow by the Save In slot and select 3½ Floppy (A:).

2 Click into the File name slot and type the name *ECDL1*.

3 Click the Create button.

4 At the Database window, ensure that the Tables tab is selected, then click the New button to create a new table.

5 The New Table dialog box will open. Select Design View and click the OK button.

We left the database with the **Design View**

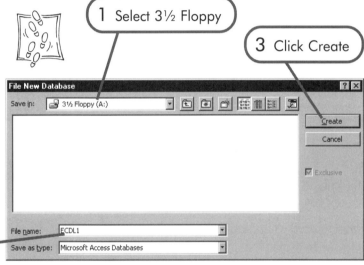

1 Select 3½ Floppy

3 Click Create

2 Type the File name

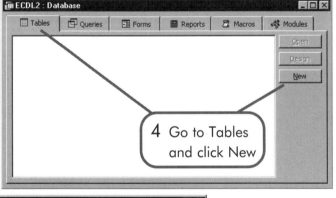

4 Go to Tables and click New

5 Select Design View

Views

Access databases can be viewed in several ways.

Datasheet View displays data from a table, form or query in a table format. In Datasheet View, you can edit fields, add and delete data, and search for data.

Form View displays one or more whole records. Form View is the primary means of adding and modifying data in tables.

Design View is used to design tables, forms or queries.

dialog box open, as shown below, and it is from here that you will create the relevant fields for this database.

An explanation of the three columns:

- **Field Name** is the column header that will appear in the table.

- **Data Type** defines and formats the type of column content. When the cursor is moved into this field a drop-down arrow will appear. Click on it to open up a list of options.

- **Description** is optional. It is there for you to include your comments to remind you, or others, at a later date, of the purpose and function of that particular field.

The Field Name and Data Type each have default and optional settings. For instance if the Data Type is Text, the default setting for the Field Name is 50 characters long. This can be increased to 255 characters or decreased as appropriate.

To learn more of these properties and their usage, consult the on-line Help, which is covered on page 137.

Entering the Field Names

Type in the following Field Names, with the Data Type options as indicated:

Field Name	Data Type
ID	AutoNumber
First Name	Text
Last Name	Text
Date of Birth	Date/Time
Salary	Currency
No of Children	Number

Field Properties

You may have noticed that as you selected the Data Type something happened in the lower area of the box, marked **Field Properties**. For the *Salary* and *No of Children* fields, click into the **Default Value** slot and delete the 0.

Once you have entered all the fields, click the **Close** button. You will now be presented with another dialog box, which will prompt you to save the table.

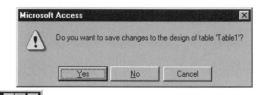

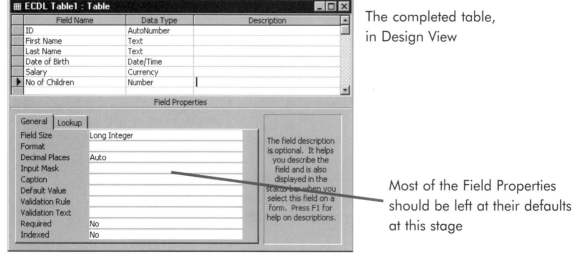

The completed table, in Design View

Most of the Field Properties should be left at their defaults at this stage

Click on the **Yes** button, which will open up the **Save As** dialog box. Enter the new name: '*ECDL Table1*' and click the **OK** button.

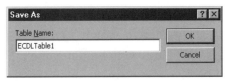

You will be warned that '*There is no primary key defined*'. We do not require a primary key, so click the **No** button. You will be returned to the database window.

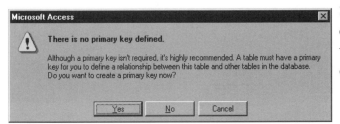

The Database Window

Imagine that the database window as a flat-face filing card system with six items stored within it. These items are identified by the tabs located along the top of the window. All items that make up the database are stored in this window. For example, to locate a form, assuming that one exists, click on the **Forms** tab and that tab will open revealing any content.

This is where you must go to create a new table, form, report or other component. Open the appropriate tab and click the **New** button.

Select *ECDL Table1* in the Database window and click the **Open** button. The table will open in Datasheet View, so that you can now start to enter data into the table.

Click the tabs to see the other sets of components

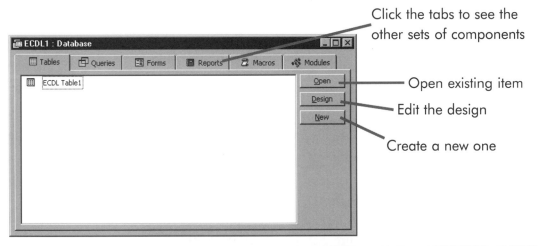

Open existing item

Edit the design

Create a new one

Our new empty table

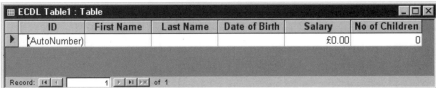

Entering data in a table

In the ID column you will see that Access is displaying word 'AutoNumber'. You will recall that this was the Data Type selected for this field at the design stage. As soon as any detail is entered into the File Name column, Access will automatically enter the ID number.

Access provides the AutoNumber data type to create fields that automatically enter a number when a record is added. Once a number is generated for a record, it can't be deleted or changed. AutoNumbers that increment by one are the most common kind and are a good choice for use as a table's primary key.

To enter the data press **[Tab]** and the cursor will move to the *First Name* field. Enter the name 'Simon'. Note that as soon as you typed the first letter, a new record appeared below the one that you are currently entering data in.

Moving between fields

To move to the next field, press **[Tab]** again and the cursor will move to the next field, *Last Name*. Continue entering the data relating to Simon Smith until you reach the last field, *No of Children*. After entering the number 3, press **[Tab]** again and the cursor will move to the ID field and start a new record. Continue entering the following data in the table, and ensure that you type the dates exactly as shown below:

Simon	Smith	12 Jan 71	£950	3
James	Bond	31 Oct 67	£1250	0
David	Jones	16 Aug 77	£1130	2
Angela	Mathews	18 May 70	£1180	0
Cherry	King	11 July 72	£1270	1

When you have finished typing in all the data, check the manner in which Access actually displays the date, which, for Simon Smith should be 12/01/71. You actually typed in 12 Jan 71, which is the way we want the date to be displayed in the table.

Changing the Data Type format

We will now ensure that Access displays the date the way we want it. To make any changes to the table we must revert to the Design View of the table.

Basic steps

1 Click the Design View icon 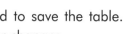 .

2 At the Design View window, click in the *Date of Birth* field.

3 In the Field Properties area, select the General tab and click in the Format slot.

4 A drop-down arrow will appear on the right. Click on it and a list will appear.

5 Select the date style and format required.

6 Click the Datasheet View icon to return to the table.

7 You will be prompted to save the table. Click Yes to save your changes.

8 The table will re-open Datasheet View. Check the format of the date displayed and it should be as follows: 12-Jan-71.

Note the arrow beside the currently selected field

2 Select the field

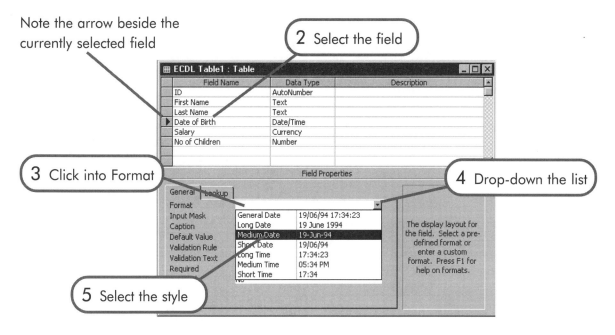

3 Click into Format

4 Drop-down the list

5 Select the style

7 Save the changes

Adding records

We will now add a further three records to the table. Click once in the empty field as indicated, and type in the data shown below.

George Brown   13 Jan 55   £940   0
Joe Hopeless   01 Apr 81   £890   2
Peter Brown   31 Jul 79   £930   3

Tip

As you enter the data into fields, the table is automatically saved. Access does **not** automatically save changes in Design View, so when working in **all** Design views, periodically save any changes made to the item you are working on.

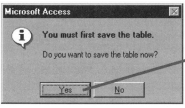

Click here and add the new entry

Print Preview

Before printing a table, it is advisable to preview it.

To do this, open the **File** menu and select **Print Preview**. The preview window will open.

Check that the layout is similar to the example shown below. Should the document open up rather small, click on the Zoom tool (the magnifying glass icon). The cursor will now change to a magnifying glass. Point at the document and click.

- If the glass had a "+" sign within it then the image of the document will enlarge. If it had a "-" sign, the image will reduce in size.

- Select **Close** on the Print Preview toolbar and when the window closes, open the **File** menu and select **Print**. The Print dialog box will now open.

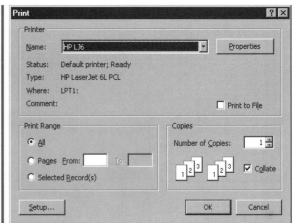

- Ensure the correct printer is selected, set the **Print range** and **Number of Copies** as required then click the **OK** button. The table will then be printed.

Print Properties

Various changes can be implemented from within the Print dialog box. We will not investigate these options at this stage, however you should, at a later stage, read the handbook relating to your printer and practise making changes to the way the document can be printed.

The Print Preview window

Click to zoom in or out

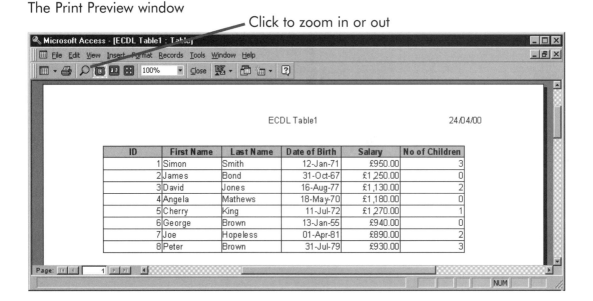

Saving a second copy of a table

You can export the table to another database or save a copy under a different name in the same database. To save the table in the same database, choose **Close** from the **File** menu, then **Save As/Export**, again from the **File** menu.

The **Save As** dialog box will open. Select the option **Within the Current Database as New Name** and the suggested new name will become highlighted.

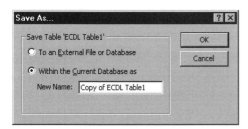

Access will offer you a name based on the current name of the table, preceded by 'Copy of'. In this instance the suggested new name is: *Copy of ECDL Table1*.

You may accept the suggested name, and it is recommend that you do because it is easier to identify the table. However, should you wish to change the name, you will have seen that it is already highlighted – simply type in the new name, and the suggestion will be over-written.

When you have entered the name, click the **OK** button. You will be returned to the Database window, which will now display, in the Tables pane, both copies of the table.

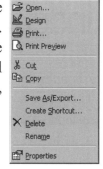

Renaming a table

You may wish to rename a table, or for that matter a Form, Query or Report, at some stage of your work. To do this Close the item and then select it in the database window.

● Right-click on the table and a menu will appear. Select **Rename**.

Or select the file then use the menu command **File > Rename**.

● The highlighted item will now have a flashing cursor within the name area. Replace or edit the name as required.

In this instance, select the table *Copy of ECDL Table1* and then **Rename**.

● Enter the new name '*ECDL Table2*'. Press **[Enter]** for the change to take place.

5: Databases

Right-click and select Rename

Tip

Access remembers the last four databases that were used and stores their names in the File menu. Just click on the name and the database will open.

Indexing records

An *index* is a pointer (an indicator) to a record. The index is placed on a field of a record. For instance if you had a database that was made up of addresses and you regularly run searches on the postal code, then you would place an index on the postal code field.

Indexing makes searches much quicker. The computer only has to read the pointers rather than each record in the database until it finds the required field.

Basic steps

1 Ensure that *ECDL Table1* is open.

2 Click on the Design icon 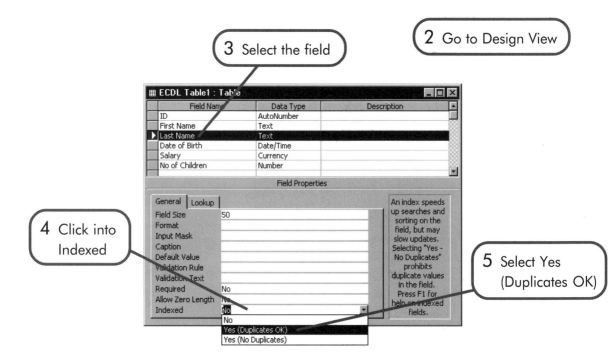 and the table will revert to Design View.

3 Select the field, in this case *Last Name*.

4 In the the Field Properties area, click in the Indexed slot and a drop-down arrow will appear on its right.

5 Select the option: Yes (Duplicates OK). The reason for selecting this, is that there may well be a number of people with the same surnames and had the other option been selected, you would not have been permitted to enter the same name twice. The Yes (No Duplicates) option should only be used where there will always be unique data in the indexed field.

6 Close the table, and save the changes when prompted. You will be returned to the database window.

3 Select the field

2 Go to Design View

4 Click into Indexed

5 Select Yes (Duplicates OK)

Deleting records

Though deleting records is quite a major action to undertake, and should be approached with caution, it is sometimes necessary.

Basic steps

1 If not already open, open *ECDL Table1*.

2 To select a record, click on the grey square at the left-hand side. In this case, select one relating to 'George Brown'.

3 Open the Edit menu and select Delete Record.

Or

4 Right-click on the record and from the pop-up menu select Delete Record. The record will be removed and the lower records rolled up to fill the gap.

5 A prompt will warn you that you are about to delete a record. Click Yes to confirm.

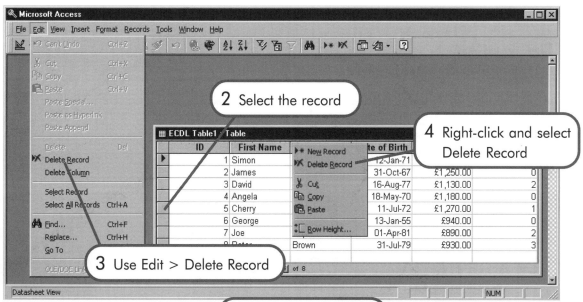

2 Select the record

4 Right-click and select Delete Record

3 Use Edit > Delete Record

ID field numbers are not adjusted when a record is deleted

5 Confirm the deletion

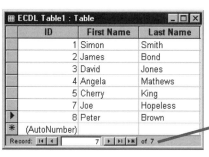

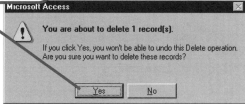

After a deletion, the record indicator shows the correct number of records in the database

Sorting records

An excellent feature of databases is that you can present the same information in a variety of ways. You may wish to display the information in the ECDL Table1 with the *Last Name* fields in alphabetical (or in Access terminology, ascending) order. Here's how to do this:

Basic steps

1 Select the field that you wish to sort by clicking on the field name. The column will be highlighted.

2 Click on the Ascending Order icon to sort the names into alphabetical order.

Insert additional records

To build the database up somewhat, we will now add a further two records. Enter this data into the table:

Gary Watson	20 Feb 76	£976	2
Linda Robson	19 Oct 78	£1100	1

Re-sort the table in Ascending order on the *Last Name* field.

> 1 Select the field to sort by

ECDL Table1 : Table

	ID	First Name	Last Name	Date of Birth	Salary	No of Children
	1	Simon	Smith	12-Jan-71	£950.00	3
	2	James	Bond	31-Oct-67	£1,250.00	0
	3	David	Jones	16-Aug-77	£1,130.00	2
	4	Angela	Mathews	18-May-70	£1,180.00	0
	5	Cherry	King	11-Jul-72	£1,270.00	1
	7	Joe	Hopeless	01-Apr-81	£890.00	2
▶	8	Peter	Brown	31-Jul-79	£930.00	3
*	(AutoNumber)					

Record: |◀ ◀| 7 |▶ ▶| ▶*| of 7

> 2 Click Ascending order

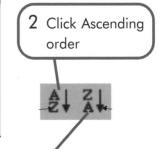

Descending order icon

The table with its additional records, sorted into ascending alphabetical order of the Last Name field.

ECDL Table1 : Table

	ID	First Name	Last Name	Date of Birth	Salary	No of Children
▶	2	James	Bond	31-Oct-67	£1,250.00	0
	8	Peter	Brown	31-Jul-79	£930.00	3
	7	Joe	Hopeless	01-Apr-81	£890.00	2
	3	David	Jones	16-Aug-77	£1,130.00	2
	5	Cherry	King	11-Jul-72	£1,270.00	1
	4	Angela	Mathews	18-May-70	£1,180.00	0
	10	Linda	Robson	19-Oct-78	£1,100.00	1
	1	Simon	Smith	12-Jan-71	£950.00	3
	9	Gary	Watson	20-Feb-76	£976.00	2
*	(AutoNumber)					

Record: |◀ ◀| 1 |▶ ▶| ▶*| of 9

Moving fields

After constructing a table you may realise that you would prefer to have two particular columns adjacent to each other. In this case we require *Salary* to be next to the *Last Name* column. Here's how to move it.

Basic steps

1 Click on the *Salary* header to select the column.

2 Keep the mouse button pressed. You will see a line appear to the left of the column and a small rectangle appear on the lower end of the cursor.

3 Drag to the left, towards the *Last Name* field.

4 As you drag, a black line will appear between the *Last Name* and *Date of Birth* fields. Release the button and the column will move next to the *Last Name* field.

At present, any time that we wish to view details of any of the personnel in our database we have to view this information in a table. The table has only six fields and is reasonably easy to view and use. Imagine if it included their addresses and the names of their wives and children. Not all of the detail would fit into the display window and we would be constantly using the scroll bars to see the detail.

There is an easier way to view the data and it uses *Forms*. We will be looking at those very shortly.

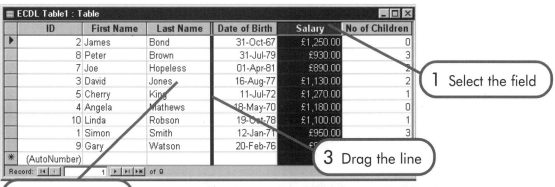

Salary is now next to the *Last Name* field

Modifying the database structure

Deleting fields

It is possible to modify the database structures long after the database was constructed. However such modifications should be carefully considered before being undertaken. This is particularly important when working with relational databases, where knock-on effects, from one table to another, may not have been considered or realised. Modification of smaller sized databases is somewhat easier but still require careful consideration and thought.

If the modification requirement is to remove a field, that is no longer required, select the relevant database table and go into Design View. Select the field and from the menu bar, click on **Edit > Delete Column**.

Access will warn you that deleting the field will result in a loss of data and allow you to either carry on and delete the field or to cancel the operation.

If you decide to carry on with the operation of deleting the field, the selected column will then be deleted. Close the Design View and when prompted save the changes.

If a form was based on the now modified table, if may be necessary to now modify the form and remove items relating to the deleted field.

Inserting fields

It is also possible to insert additional fields in an existing database. It is from the Design View of a table that additional fields are inserted, in a similar manner as when you were constructing the original table. Refer to page 146 if assistance is required. (Inserting additional fields will of course have knock-on effects on such items as Forms, Queries and Reports.)

Creating a form

Forms only display one record at a time, unlike tables, which display multiple records. They are all based on tables, and are not standalone items; therefore to create a Form a table has to be constructed first.

Forms can be constructed using a wizard or from the Design View mode.

Close *ECDL Table1* and save any changes. This will return us to the Database window. To create a form, follow these steps:

Basic steps

1   Click the Forms tab to open the Forms panel. It will be empty at present.

2   Click the New button.

3   In upper pane of the New Form dialog box, select Form Wizard.

4   Click the down arrow in the Choose the table slot and select *ECDL Table1*.

5   Click the OK button.

The Form Wizard

The next window to open will be one of the Form Wizard group.

A wizard is a semi-automated method of creating numerous items within Access and is an ideal way of creating a form for our database.

At various stages, the wizard will prompt you for information to assist with the design and construction of the form. You can often backtrack on a chosen option by clicking the Back button, which will take you back to the previous window.

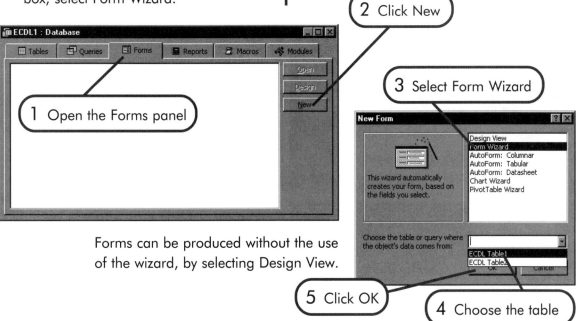

Forms can be produced without the use of the wizard, by selecting Design View.

5: Databases

Selecting the form fields

At the first panel of the wizard, you select the fields required for the form from the list of those in the table, *ECDL Table1*. You may not want all the fields, though in this case we do.

Fields are selected and moved from the **Available Fields** to the **Selected Fields** pane. They can be handled individually or *en masse*. Fields in the **Selected Fields** pane will be included in the form.

The table that the form is based on – you can change it if required.

Fields available in the table

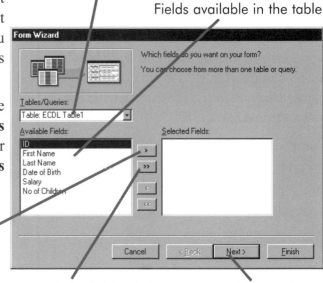

To move a field, select it and click on this arrow.

To move all the fields, click the double-headed arrow.

Click Next when you have done

Layout and style

The next two panels determine the layout and background style of the form. Select each option in turn and it check its appearance in the preview area.

● Select *Columnar* in this instance, then click the **Next** button.

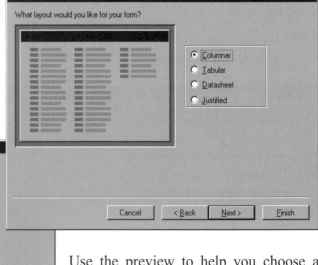

Use the preview to help you choose a background style – the example shows 'International'.

● Select Standard this time, and click the **Next** button.

158

The final stage of the Wizard prompts you for a name for the form.

- Call this form *ECDL Form1*.
- Do not change the options offered.
- Click once on the **Finish** button.

The wizard will now produce the completed form.

Navigating in Form View

The status line along the bottom of the form is for navigation through the database. It tells you where you are and contains arrow buttons that let you move between the records.

Using the guide outlined here, practise moving through the database and viewing different records. Remember what the various control buttons do, as they will save you considerable time with a large database.

Close the form window. The database window will remain open irrespective of whether you are using a table, form or query. At this stage you should only have the Database window open.

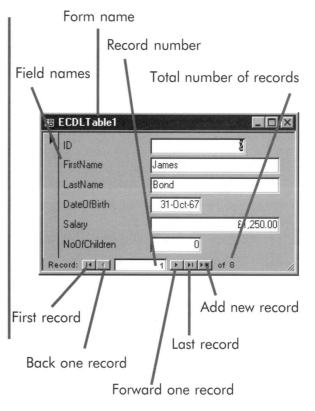

5: Databases

Using Queries

Queries are used to extract information from the database. They can also be used to create new tables based upon the extracted information, and can perform a number of other tasks, which we will not cover in this book.

Queries are powerful tools and, during this book, we are only going to skim the surface of queries. You should, in time, use the on-line Help for further information on their use.

We will now create a query, which will extract from the database information that matches set criteria. The first stage is to specify the fields that define the criteria and/or are wanted in the results display.

Basic steps

1 Ensure all tables are closed and that the database window is displayed.

2 Open the Queries tab and click New.

3 At the New Query dialog box , select the Design View option and click OK.

4 The Query Design window will open, with the Show Table dialog box in front. Select *ECDL Table1* and click Add.

5 Click the Close button.

6 Details of the table will appear in the Query Design window. In the Field name list, click on the *FirstName* field, drag it over to the first column and drop it in the Field row. The field's table will appear in the Table cell below.

7 Carry out the same action with the fields *Last Name* and *Salary*, placing them in the next two columns.

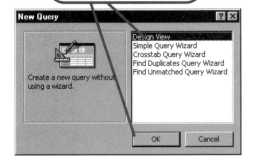

3 Select Design View and click OK

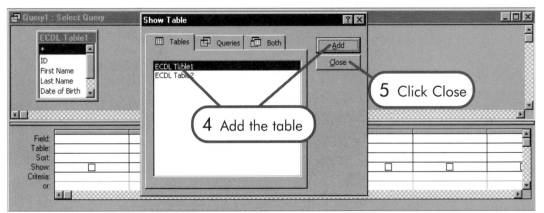

4 Add the table

5 Click Close

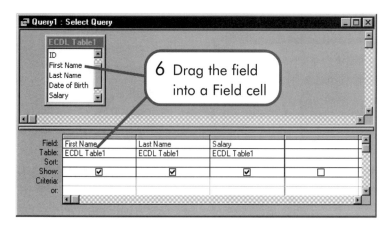

6 Drag the field into a Field cell

Take note

The table name is needed as you can use more than one table in a query.

As you progress and master Access queries, you may find that you have included a field in a query, which is an important element of the criteria, but you do not want the information, from that field, displayed in the query result.

In the example you will see that there is a check box in the *Show* row. By default Access always displays a tick in the box, but if you decide that the field should not be displayed in the query result, remove the tick. The field will still be used in the query but will not be displayed when the query is run.

● To remove the tick, click on the box. Click again on the same box to restore the tick.

We are going to define the criteria, using operators, to extract all the personnel who have a salary over £1000.

Basic steps

1 Click in the Criteria field under *Salary*.

2 Type a greater than symbol (>), then 1000 and press [Enter].

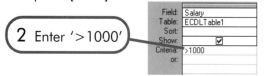

2 Enter '>1000'

4 Click the Run Query icon, [!], to run the query to produce the results.

Access will now search the database for all personnel with salaries over £1000 and present the information in a table format.

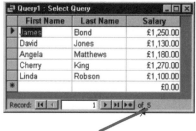

5 records met the criteria

The search was conducted extremely quickly due to the fact that there are only nine records. Access will still produce results very quickly even if it has to search several hundred records.

As we may want to run the query in the future, we will save it. Click the Close button on the top right of the window. You will be asked if you wish to save the query. Click **Yes**.

In the Save As dialog box, type a name for the Query, e.g. *Salary>1000*, then click **OK**.

You will now be returned to the Database window and you will see the query saved in the Queries tab. You may create any number of queries, each one saved under a different name.

Carry out the two short exercises below:

Exercise 1

- Create a query, in Design View, which will extract all the personnel listed in *ECDL Table1* who have 2 children.

  This time you should use the equals (=) sign, not the greater than (>) sign.

- Include the *First Name*, *Last Name* and *No. of Children* fields in the query as well.

- Save the query and call it *Children*.

The result table should look like this:

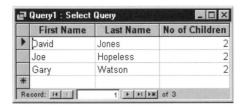

Exercise 2

- Create another Query, this time to extract all those personnel who were born after Jan 70 and have 3 children.

- Save the Query as Jan70.

The result table should look like this:

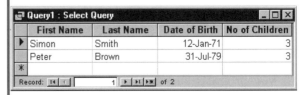

Reports

At some stage during the use of the database you will require some, or all, of the content to be printed for distribution. You could simply print a copy of the table but a table may be quite large and it does not lend itself to easy reading.

The best way to print data is to produce a report. You can created one using a wizard or do it yourself using the Design mode. In this instance we are going to create a report based on *ECDL Table1* using a wizard.

Basic steps

1   Close and open tables, forms or queries.

2   In the Database window, open the Reports tab and click the New button.

3   In the New Report dialog box, select *Report Wizard*.

4   Select *ECDL Table1* from the drop-down list of tables and queries, then click OK.

❑   The Report Wizard will start. The first stage is to select the fields which will constitute the report.

5   Ensure that the correct table name is displayed in the Tables/Queries slot.

6   Select *First Name* then click on the arrow to move it into the Selected Fields pane.

7   Repeat with *Last Name* and *Salary*.

8   Click the Next button.

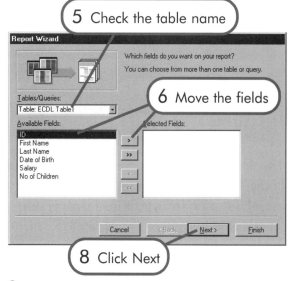

5 Check the table name

6 Move the fields

8 Click Next

9   The Wizard will ask you if you want to add any grouping levels. Experiment with this later. For now, ignore it and click Next.

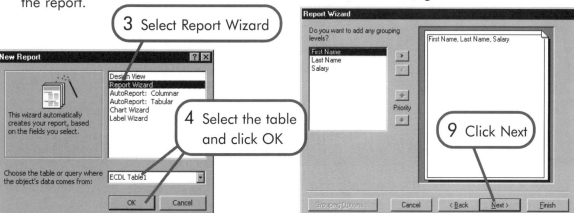

3 Select Report Wizard

4 Select the table and click OK

9 Click Next

The wizard will present you with a dialog box from which you may sort the records. We will only concern ourselves with the *Salary* field.

10 Select *Salary* from the drop-down list. The report will be sorted on the Salary field in ascending order.

11 Click Next.

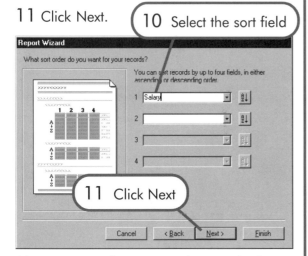

The next step gives you options on the layout of the Report. Do you want the fields laid out in Columnar or Tabular form, the paper orientation set to Portrait or Landscape?

12 Leave the settings as Tabular and Portrait and click Next.

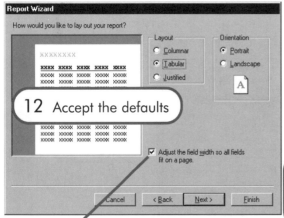

Leave the tick in the box. It will not affect us this time, but you should know of this facility.

13 The next step offers style options. Select *Soft Gray* and click Next.

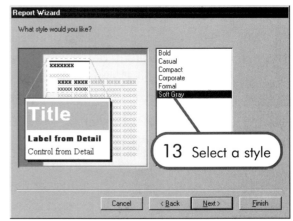

At the last step there are a number of options:

- A report title. Access has already allocated it a name based upon the table name. Type in a new name, *Salary*.

- You can Preview the report. This is the default setting – select it.

- You can have the on-line Help displayed while working with the report. Do not select this option.

14 Having set the title, do not make any other changes. We want to see how the report looks before going any further. Click Finish and the Preview window will open.

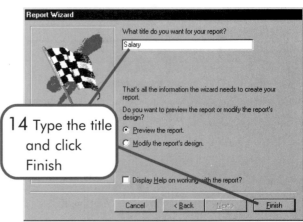

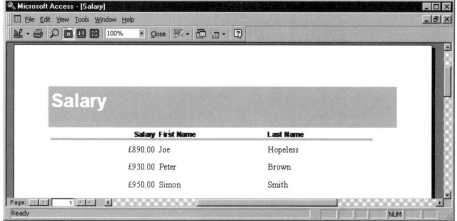

There is a problem with the layout. The *Salary* and *First Name* columns are too close and we need to make an adjustment.

Click 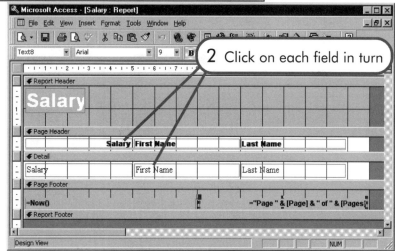 the Design View icon to change to the Design View where we may make the changes. We need extra spacing between the *Salary* and the *First Name* fields.

2 Click on each field in turn

Basic steps

1 Hold down [Shift] – this will allow you to make multiply selections.

2 Click on the *First Name* field in the Page Header section, then click on the *First Name* field in the Detail area.

3 Release [Shift]. Both fields will be selected.

4 Point to the centre handle in either field. When the cursor changes to a double-headed arrow, drag it to the right for half a square then release the mouse button.

Both fields are selected

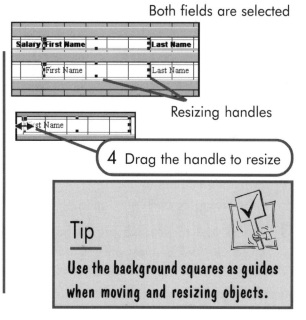

Resizing handles

4 Drag the handle to resize

Tip

Use the background squares as guides when moving and resizing objects.

165

5   On the Toolbar, click the down arrow to the right of the View icon.

6   From the drop-down list, select Print Preview.

(6 Choose Print Preview)

❑   The image will revert to Print Preview and you will see that there is a reasonable amount of space between the two fields.

Before spacing adjusted

Salary	First Name
£890.00	Joe
£930.00	Peter

Salary	First Name
£890.00	Joe
£930.00	Peter

After spacing adjusted

7   Close the Print Preview window and save the changes, then close the Salary report.

Printing the report

After previewing your report, you will probably want to print it.

Basic steps

1   Select the Reports tab on the database window and then select the *Salary* report. You can print the report without actually opening it.

2   Open the File menu and select Print. The print dialog box will now open.

3   Ensure that the correct printer has been selected. Your display will most likely be different to that shown here.

4   You can, if required, only print one page or all the pages within the report. As our report only has one page you need not make any changes in the Print Range area.

5   If you require more than one copy, you adjust the figure in the Copies area to that which you require. In this case leave it at 1 copy.

6   Click the OK button. After a short period of time your printer should start up and begin printing the report.

(3 Select the printer)

(5 Set the number of copies)

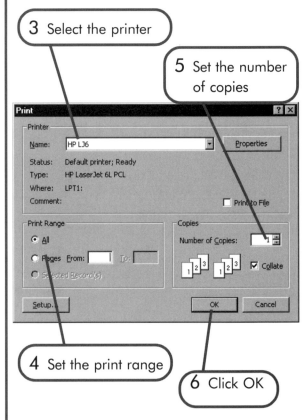

(4 Set the print range)

(6 Click OK)

Exporting a database

Earlier in the book we saved a copy of the *ECDL Table1* and renamed it *ECDL Table2*.

During the course of saving the table ECDL Table1 we were offered the opportunity to export it to another database. This is what we are about to do. We are going to use the existing database *ECDL1* and create a new database, which we will call *ECDL2*.

A table can be exported with data or as 'Definition Only'. 'Definition Only' means that just the table structure, without any data, is exported. A table structure may well be suitable for a series of tables, usually with just minor amendments. It is more logical to copy a table and make small changes to it rather than spend considerable time creating a new table from the beginning.

Basic steps

1 Close all tables, etc. then close the Database window.

2 From the File menu select New Database.

3 In the General tab of the New dialog box, select the Blank Database icon.

4 Click OK. The File New Database dialog box will open. Remember a database must be saved before you can start work on it.

5 If not already selected, in the Save In slot, select the *Floppy disk A:* drive.

❑ If you are using the same floppy disk that you saved the previous database on, you should now see *ECDL1.MDB* listed.

6 Type *ECDL2* in the File name slot.

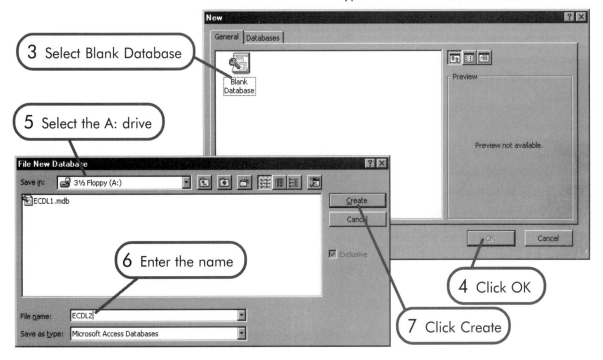

3 Select Blank Database

5 Select the A: drive

6 Enter the name

4 Click OK

7 Click Create

7   Click the Create button.

8   The dialog box will close and the database window for the *ECDL2* database will open. We do not want this at the moment so close it, then select File >Open Database.

9   At the Open dialog box, ensure that the Floppy disk drive is selected, then open the database *ECDL1.mdb*.

10 At the *ECDL1* Database window, click the file *ECDL Table2,* then click the Tables tab.

11 Open the File menu and select Save As/ Export.

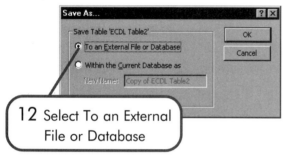

12 Select To an External File or Database

12 At the Save As dialog box, ensure that the option: *To an External File or Database* is selected and click OK.

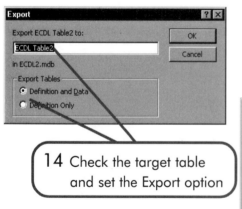

14 Check the target table and set the Export option

13 A further dialog box will open, offering you the option of which database to export the table to. As we only have two databases and the table is already part of *ECDL1.mdb*, the choice must be to export it to *ECDL2.mdb*. Select this by clicking Export.

14 At the Export dialog box , confirm that the target database is *ECDL2*, and select the option *Definition and data*. Access will now copy the table to *ECDL2.mdb*.

15 Close the *ECDL1* Database window, then select File > Open Database and choose *ECDL2.mdb*.

16 Go to the Tables tab and you should find a copy of the *ECDL2* table present.

17 Open the table *ECDL Table2* and add the following records :

Raymond Jennings	21 Mar 65	1350	3
Marie Rosenbloom	30 May 56	1175	2
Frank Robinson	25 Sep 57	1225	5
Richard Carson	15 Dec 60	1452	4
Clare Steine	21 Dec 61	1245	2
Rosemary Kline	15 Jul 59	1236	0

16 Go to Tables

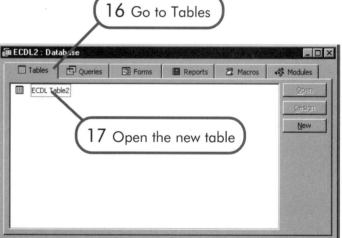

17 Open the new table

Changing the table structure

You can add new fields to a database if necessary. In this case we want to be able to list personnel by gender. A simple way to do this would be to add another field to the table which we will call *Gender*.

Basic steps

1 With *ECDL Table2* open, select the Design View icon on the Toolbar.

2 Place the cursor in the blank line under the field *No of Children*. Type in '*Gender*' and in the Data Type column accept the default setting of Text.

3 Switch to the Field Properties pane , either by pressing [F6] or by clicking into the required item slot.

4 We are only going to enter a single letter in this field. Delete the default setting of 50 and type in '1', then close the window. Save the changes when prompted.

5 Back at the database window, open *ECDL Table2*. The new field, *Gender*, will appear after *No of Children*. You may have noticed that even though we set the field size to one, there clearly is more space in the field displayed.

6 Place the cursor in the *Gender* field for 'Simon Smith' and type in 'Male'. You should find that you will only be permitted to enter the first letter as the field size is controlled to one character only.

7 It would make more sense to have the *Gender* field after the *Last Name* field. Move it now – see page 153, if you have forgotten how to do this.

8 Fill in the *Gender* column appropriate to the names in the *First Name* field.

ID	First Name	Last Name	Gender	Date of Birth	Salary	No of Children
1	Simon	Smith	M	12-Jan-71	£950.00	3
2	James	Bond	M	31-Oct-67	£1,250.00	0
3	David	Jones	M	16-Aug-77	£1,130.00	2
4	Angela	Mathews	F	18-May-70	£1,180.00	0
5	Cherry	King	F	11-Jul-72	£1,270.00	1
6	George	Brown	M	13-Jan-55	£940.00	0
7	Joe	Hopeless	M	01-Apr-81	£890.00	2
8	Peter	Brown	M	31-Jul-79	£930.00	3
9	Raymond	Jennings	M	21-Mar-65	£1,350.00	3
10	Marie	Rosenbloom	F	30-May-56	£1,750.00	2
11	Frank	Ronbinson	M	25-Sep-57	£1,250.00	5
12	Richard	Carson	M	15-Dec-60	£1,452.00	4
13	Clare	Steine	F	21-Dec-61	£1,245.00	2
14	Rosemary	Kline	F	15-Jul-59	£1,326.00	0

ECDL Table2 : Table

Record: 2 of 14

ECDL Table2 after the Gender field has been added and data entered

Exercises

1: Create a query to list all females

Create a query that will output a list of females in the table. Include these fields in the query:

- First Name
- Last Name
- Gender

The criteria should be on the *Gender* field.

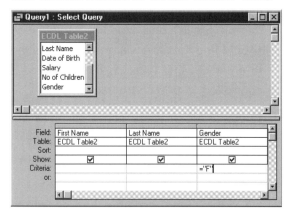

Run the query and you should find that it will return a table like this, with five females listed.

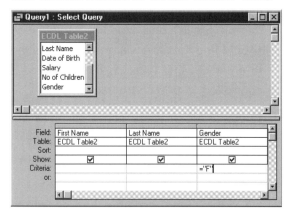

Return to Design View and modify the same query to include the *No of Children* field. Run the query, and you should see this result.

Save the query as *Females*.

2: Create a query to list all males

Create another query showing all males with children, this time including the fields:

- First Name
- Last Name
- Gender
- No of Children

Click on the **Show** check box to remove the tick. Access will use the criteria set in the *Gender* field but will not display the Gender column in the query results table.

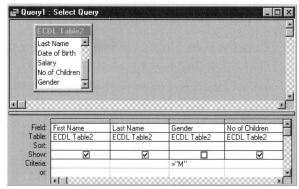

When run, the query result table should look like this:

Save this query as *Males*.

3: Create a report based on a query

Close all the windows that may be open except for the database window. Select the **Reports** tab then click on the **New** button.

The new report is to be based on the query that you recently created and saved as *Males*.

Use the Report Wizard to create this new report. It should include all fields, with no grouping, but sorted on Last Name, and with the default layout and style settings. Accept the suggested name for the report – *Males*.

Preview the report, and make any adjustments if necessary, then print out a copy of it.

4: Delete some records

Open the table *ECDL Table2* and delete the records for the following personnel:

David Jones and *Frank Robinson*.

Close the table, re-run the *Males* report and then click on Preview.

Compare the print copy from the first time that the report was run – before any records were deleted – with the Preview copy now on screen. The screen copy reflects the changes as a result of the action of deleting the two records.

What this indicates is that the report will always run the query on which it is based, so that the information displayed is always current or as reflected in the database.

Integration with other applications

Information stored in an Access database can very easily be copied or linked to any of the other applications to be found within the Microsoft Office 97 suite.

A table can be inserted into a Word document, an Excel spreadsheet or a PowerPoint presentation.

It is also possible to import data from the above mentioned applications into Access.

Exchange data between Excel and Access

To analyse the data from a Access table in Excel, you can use features in Access to export the data automatically to a new Excel workbook. You can also import worksheet data into Access. If you want only a few records from a Access table, you can open the table and copy and paste selected records into Excel.

If you're working in Excel and have installed and loaded the AccessLinks add-in, you can convert a list to a Access database file. For more information about add-ins use the on-line Help.

You can create a PivotTable to analyse data from Access just as you would from any external data source.

Using the online Help system

You can use the normal procedures for Help, as described on page 135, with one major exception. Access has a much more interactive **[F1]** Help function.

This **[F1]** key will assist you in a number of circumstances when designing a database. Follow these steps to discover the differences between the Access **[F1]** key and that for the other Office applications.

Basic steps

1 Open the table *ECDL Table 2* in Design View.

2 Place the cursor in the *First Name* field and press [F1]. The Microsoft Access Reference dialog box will open and display details relevant to the selected field, in this instance the FieldName property.

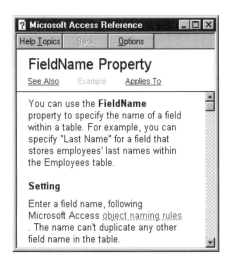

3 Close this box and you are returned to the Design View of the table.

4 Select the *Date of Birth* field.

5 Place the cursor in the Format slot in the Field Properties pane, and press [F1]. The Microsoft Access Reference dialog box will open again, this time displaying the Field Properties relevant to the *Date of Birth* Data Type, i.e. Date/Time.

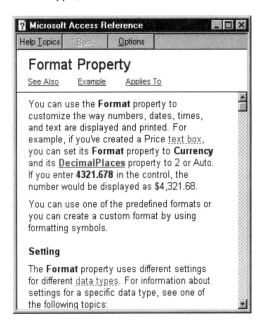

6 Close all dialog boxes.

Clearly the Access F1 online Help is much more interactive and does not require any input from you other than to select the appropriate field when in Design View.

Sample paper 5: Databases

1	Name three data types used in a database.	1. 2. 3.
2	What is meant by the term 'pointer' and what is the correct name for it?	
3	When running a query a certain field may be required for the query to function, but is not required to be displayed in the query result. What simple action will ensure that the field is not shown in the query result?	
4	What is the name of the view used to create the structure of a new table?	1. Datasheet View 2. Import Table 3. Design View
5	A field of the Text Data Type has a default length setting of 50 characters. What is the maximum length allowable in Access?	1. 100 2. 150 3. 200 4. 255
6	Describe the main difference between a table and a form.	Table: Form:
7	List the four main database components that the user can create and use.	1. 2. 3. 4.
8	If you decide that a certain field in a table has an incorrect default setting, what view would you use to change the setting?	1. Import Table 2. Datasheet View 3. Design View

9	When working in any of the Design views, Access automatically saves any changes made. True or False?	1. True 2. False
10	List the two sort options available in Access.	1. 2.
11	In simple terms, describe what a Wizard is?	
12	List two examples of a database in everyday use.	1. 2.
13	When viewing data, in Form view, what navigation controls does the user use to select different records within that database?	
14	You have completed a report and are ready to print the document. What feature is available to you to view the report before printing it?	
15	You see the following criterion in a query: =>250 In simple terms describe the condition the criterion has set.	

6 Presentations

What is PowerPoint?

PowerPoint is an application, in the Microsoft Office 97 suite, which is used to create presentations, also known as slide shows, to impart information to a wide variety of audiences.

- It can be used to produce a slide show on screen that will run unattended.
- PowerPoint has a number of preformatted templates to simplify the construction and design of presentations.
- PowerPoint has a range of coloured backgrounds and text formats that will suit most situations and presentations, but which can be easily adjusted to suit particular needs.
- You can also prepare a presentation that will be given using 35mm colour slides.
- PowerPoint can produce banners and overhead projector transparencies, both in colour and black and white.
- Sound and video clips can be incorporated into a slide show.

In this chapter we will create an on-screen presentation, and introduce some of the drawing and other tools to be found in PowerPoint.

Starting PowerPoint

There are a number of ways to start PowerPoint. In this book we will use the Start button method. You, in time, will develop your own preferred method of starting programs.

Basic steps

1 Click on the Start button on the Taskbar.

2 Click on Programs on the pop-up menu.

3 A sub-menu will open to the right. Click on Microsoft PowerPoint. The application will open and run. You will then be presented with the PowerPoint screen.

Take note

PowerPoint, like most Windows applications, can be customised in many and varied ways, so our examples may not match your own display. This should not distract you. The images used here were taken from PowerPoint using its default settings. Simply follow the instructions and you will achieve the required result.

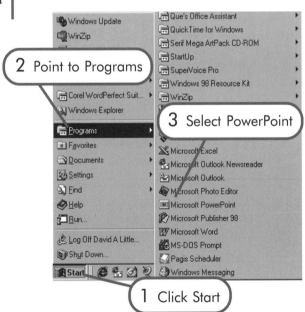

2 Point to Programs

3 Select PowerPoint

1 Click Start

A guided tour of the screen

When PowerPoint is first started, the opening display should be as shown below. The name of the presentation is normally displayed in the Title bar. As none is currently open, no name is displayed.

The PowerPoint dialog box opens on the initial start-up, and offers a number of options:

- **AutoContent wizard** brings up a number of templates from which you may select a topic suitable to your requirements.

- **Template** offers you a series of coloured background Presentation Designs.

- **Blank presentation** will open up another dialog box from which you may select from a number of slides with an outline structure, but no backgrounds or text. It is this selection which we will make shortly.

- **Open an existing presentation** will open a previously saved presentation.

The **OK** button will carry out your selection, whereas the **Cancel** button will close the dialog box without carrying out any action based on the selection.

Leave the dialog box open for a moment.

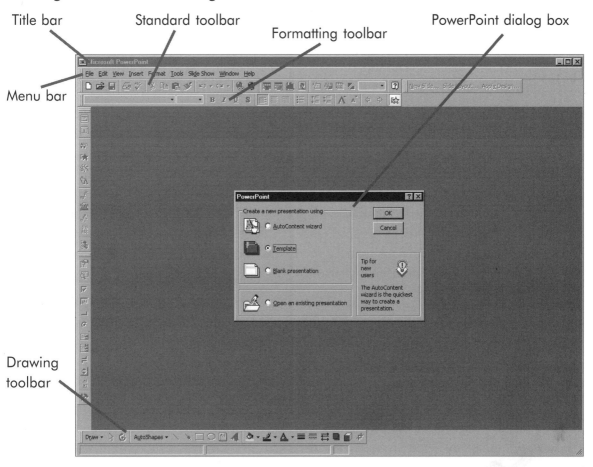

Title bar Standard toolbar Formatting toolbar PowerPoint dialog box

Menu bar

Drawing toolbar

6: Presentations

179

Slide show scenario

Our objective is to create a number of slides to introduce a new member of staff to a department within the company. This new member is in fact the new departmental head, hence the presentation to a particular department.

This company, *Tec-com*, specialises in computer training for companies and the general public, and recently underwent quite a major expansion investment. Previously *Tec-com* only ran courses on common applications, but have now started computer networking courses.

The original staff were not qualified in networking, and a whole new department was formed to teach these courses. This has resulted in an increase in trainers who specialise in networking, with back-up and support staff. The company has also invested a considerable sum in a number of different network systems, which will allow the students to install and run various types of networks during the courses.

Jonathan Morgan Richards is the new employee. He prefers to be known as 'Jon'. He is 38 years of age and is married to Katherine, known as Kathy, who works as a consultant website designer. They have been married for ten years and have two children, an 8-year-old son and a 6-year-old daughter.

Jon has a degree in Computer Sciences and went on to qualify as a Certified Novell Engineer, a Microsoft Systems Certified Engineer, and a Microsoft Certified Professional in a number of MS Office applications.

Jon completed a number of years' working in the field, designing and supervising the installation of various types of network systems, during which time he found himself instructing support staff on how the network was assembled and functioned.

Jon realised that he had a particular skill in teaching network subjects and then spent some time attending college to learn more of the art of instruction, and was later to gain the Microsoft Certified Trainer qualification.

Jon was initially employed in the UK with a large multinational company; Samson's United Systems as a systems engineer. During this time he was assigned to the company's US office, where a year later he was headhunted by an American organisation; Anglo-American International, who specialised in developing remote computerised control systems.

After two years Jon found he much preferred the hands-on experience of networking and people contact and returned to the UK where he joined the staff of one of the newly converted banks, Collins plc, as deputy systems engineer. It was during this time that his interest in teaching was re-awoken and he gained the Microsoft Certified Trainer qualification.

Jon was approached by a specialised recruitment agency and asked if he would be interested in a career divergence, retaining the network aspect but with an emphasis on training. Jon agreed to the offer and that brings us back to the current situation, the briefing.

Keep this information close to hand, as we will be referring to it within the presentation.

Creating the presentation

We are going to create the presentation using a number of the preformatted slides available in PowerPoint. Before we went into Jon's background we left PowerPoint open and displaying the dialog box.

Basic steps

1   Select the Blank presentation option and then click the OK button.

2   At the New Slide dialog box select the *Bulleted List* slide, then click the OK button.

3   PowerPoint will now open the slide, and we can edit the slide to our requirements.

❑   Before we proceed any further we will save the presentation.

4   Use the menu command File > Save. The Save As dialog box will open when saving the file for the first time.

5   We are going to save the presentation to a floppy disk. Click on the down arrow, and select the 3½ Floppy (A:).

6   Enter '*Jon's Intro*' into the File name slot.

7   Click the Save button.

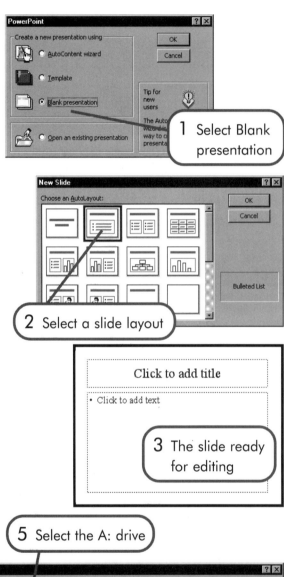

1 Select Blank presentation

2 Select a slide layout

3 The slide ready for editing

5 Select the A: drive

6 Enter the name

7 Click Save

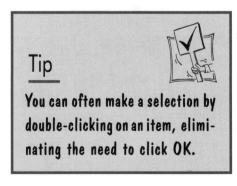

Tip

You can often make a selection by double-clicking on an item, eliminating the need to click OK.

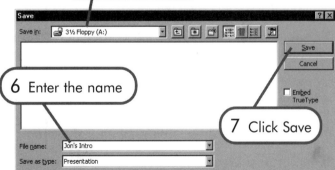

Editing the Slide Master

There are a number of sub-headings that we want on all the slides, and the way to do this is to edit the Slide Master. This is where you should put any graphics or text that you want on every slide. It also sets the default text formats and styles, colours and backgrounds.

We require the following on each slide:

- The company name: Tec-com.
- The date the presentation was created.
- The slide number.

Basic steps

1 Use the menu command View > Master > Slide Master to go into Slide Master View.

2 Double-click over the <date/time> text to highlight it, then from the menu bar select Insert > Date and Time.

3 At the Date and Time dialog box, select a date/time format and click OK.

❑ You will be returned to the Slide Master view. The last item that we wish to add to the slide is the company name.

4 Double-click on the <footer> text to high-light it. Type in 'Tec-com plc'.

5 Click on <#> in the Number area, then use View > Header and Footer.

6 At the Header and Footer dialog box, select the Slide tab.

7 Tick Slide number then click Apply to All.

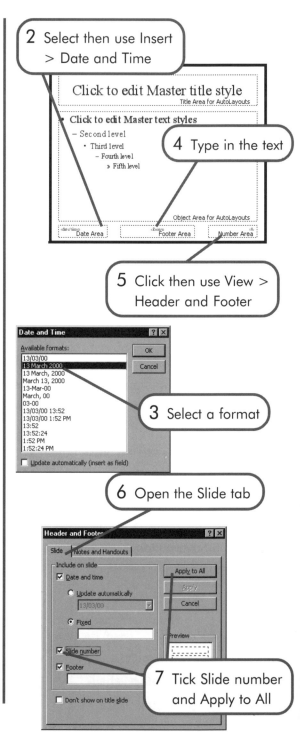

2 Select then use Insert > Date and Time

Click to edit Master title style
Title Area for AutoLayouts

Click to edit Master text styles
– Second level
• Third level
– Fourth level
» Fifth level

4 Type in the text

Object Area for AutoLayouts

Date Area   Footer Area   Number Area

5 Click then use View > Header and Footer

Date and Time
Available formats:
13/03/00
13 March 2000
13 March, 2000
March 13, 2000
13-Mar-00
March, 00
03-00
13/03/00 13:52
13/03/00 1:52 PM
13:52
13:52:24
1:52 PM
1:52:24 PM
☐ Update automatically (insert as field)
OK
Cancel

3 Select a format

6 Open the Slide tab

Header and Footer
Slide | Notes and Handouts
Include on slide
☑ Date and time
 ○ Update automatically
  13/03/00
 ● Fixed
☑ Slide number
☑ Footer
☐ Don't show on title slide
Apply to All
Apply
Cancel
Preview

7 Tick Slide number and Apply to All

❏ You will not be able to see the numbering until you return to Slide View. PowerPoint will insert a slide number in a similar way as Word does for page numbering.

8 Save the changes.

9 Select View > Slide to return to Slide View.

The detail that we have just entered on the Slide Master will now appear on each slide in the presentation.

Titles and bullet lists

We are now ready to enter the title for the first slide. At the top of the slide is the Title area.

> Click to add title

Click into here and the prompt will be replaced by a flashing cursor in the middle of the area.

Type 'Staff Briefing'.

Note that the font is Times New Roman, size 44 pt, and that the text is centred in the area. You can change any of these format settings if so desired. We will retain them at this stage.

Click anywhere on the slide, outside the title area and the display should change to that as shown below. Notice that title area no longer has an outlined box around it.

> Staff Briefing

We will now move on to the lower area of the slide where that we are going to type in the aims and objectives of the briefing. This section is preformatted as a bullet point list.

You can change the style of the bullet point from the deafult ● to that of an arrowhead, a hand and many other symbols.

> • Click to add text

The bullet points are formatted in font type and size – in this case Times New Roman at 32 pt.

Click at the prompt and type in 'Aims and Objectives'. Press [Enter] and a new bulleted line will automatically be inserted.

'Aims and Objectives' is the title line for this area. Press [Tab] once and the cursor will be indented to the right and the text size reduced, in this instance to 28 pt. Type in 'Introduction of departmental head'.

Press [Enter] to insert a new line. PowerPoint always inserts new lines at the same indent level as the previous one. Press [Tab] to further indent the text. Note that the bullet point has changed.

Type in: 'Jon M Richards' and press [Enter]. PowerPoint has inserted a new line based on the previous line, but this time we want to return to that of the line starting 'Introduction'.

On the Formatting toolbar are two icons which can increase ▶ (promote) or decrease ◀ (demote) the indent. Click ◀ and the indent will decrease, moving one tab setting to the left.

Type in: 'Introduce Departmental Organisation', and press [Enter] once.

Retaining the same settings type in: 'Instructional Programme'. Do not press [Enter], or you will end up with an empty bullet line.

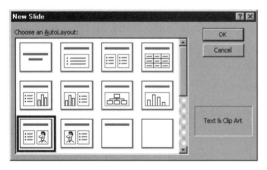

Staff Briefing

- Aims and Objectives.
  - Introduction to departmental head.
    - Jon M Richards.
  - Introduce Departmental Organisation.
  - Instructional Programme.

23 March 2000   Tec-comple   1

That is all we are going to place on the first slide. Save the changes

Insert a second slide

We are now going to insert a second slide.

- Use the command **Insert > New Slide** and the New Slide dialog box will open.

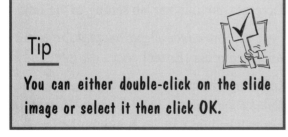

- Select the *Text & Clip Art* slide. This slide is preformatted with a title area, a bullet area and a graphic placement box.

Tip

You can either double-click on the slide image or select it then click OK.

Click in the title area and enter '*Staff Briefing*'.

Click in the bullet area and type '*Jonathan Morgan Richards*'. This is too wide for the box and '*Richards*' will be automatically moved to the next line. We need to make the box wider.

- Select the Bullet list area and point to a resize handle.

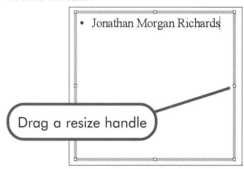

- When the cursor changes to a double-headed arrow, drag to the right until all the words fit on the one line. Release the button.

The frame for the bullet list may have overlapped the Clip Art frame. If so, adjust the left frame size for the Clip Art box in a similar way.

Carry on typing in the text, as shown in the example below. Ensure that you indent the relevant sections, as shown.

Staff Briefing

- Jonathon Morgan Richards
  - Prefers to be called Jon
  - 38, married with 2 children
- Qualifications:
  - Computer Sciences degree
  - Microsoft MSCE and MCP
  - Microsoft Certified Trainer
  - Novell CNE

23 March 2000   Tec-comple   2

Inserting a graphic

We should now to insert photograph of Jon, but as you won't have a copy of his picture, we'll cheat a little and use Clip Art.

Basic steps

1 Double-click on the Clip Art box on the slide.

2 At the Clip Gallery dialog box go to the Clip Art tab and find an image with more than one person in it. The one used here comes from the *People at Work* category.

3 Select the image and click on the Insert button.

> 2 Look in the Clip Gallery

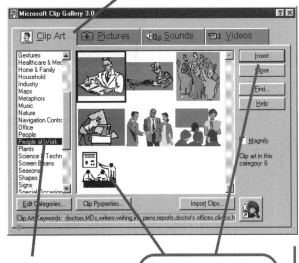

Click on the name to switch category

> 3 Insert the image

4 If the image is too big or too small, right-click on it and from the pop-up menu select Format Picture.

> 5 Go to the Size tab

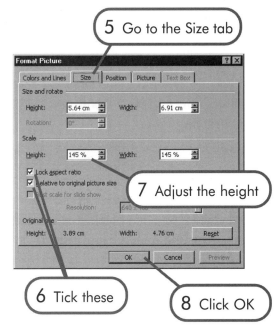

> 7 Adjust the height

> 6 Tick these

> 8 Click OK

5 At the Format Picture dialog box, click on the Size tab.

6 Tick the Lock aspect ratio and Relative to original size boxes.

7 Adjust the Height as necessary. The width will automatically adjust in relation to it.

8 Click the OK button to close the box.

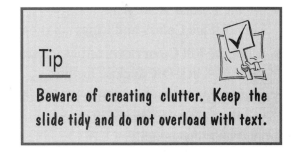

Tip

Beware of creating clutter. Keep the slide tidy and do not overload with text.

The Drawing toolbar

We are going to add a circle around the image to indicate which of the figures is Jon. The Drawing toolbar has the tools we need.

- If you do not have the Drawing toolbar visible, select **View** > **Toolbars** and click on **Drawing**.

Line   Circle/oval

- Click on the **Circle/oval** icon and the cursor will change to a thin black cross. Place the cross over the image. Hold **[Shift]** down, and drag the cursor down to the right to draw a small circle.

Holding **[Shift]** while drawing ensures that you to draw perfect circles every time. **[Shift]** also functions with other drawing tools. Experiment with these later.

You may now find that your image has been partially obscured by the circle. This is due to the fact that the circle has a *Fill* applied to it. This may be white or a colour, possibly green. If this is the case, we will now correct it so that we can see the image below it.

- The circle should still be selected – if not re-select it. Right-click and from the pop-up menu select **Format AutoShape**.
- At the Format AutoShape dialog box, ensure that the **Colors and Lines** tab is open.
- Click the **Fill Color** down arrow and select *No Fill*. Click **OK** to close the box.

You should now be able to see the image below the circle. Adjust the position of the circle to sit around your image tidily.

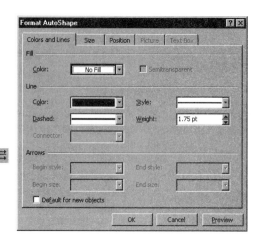

We need to draw a line from the end of the name 'Richards' to the new circle.

- Click on the Line icon. Place the cross cursor just behind the name 'Richards', click and drag the cursor to the edge of the circle. Release the mouse button.

Save the changes. The final appearance of the slide should resemble the example below.

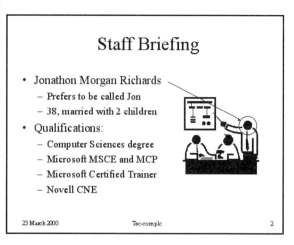

Staff Briefing

- Jonathon Morgan Richards
  - Prefers to be called Jon
  - 38, married with 2 children
- Qualifications:
  - Computer Sciences degree
  - Microsoft MSCE and MCP
  - Microsoft Certified Trainer
  - Novell CNE

23 March 2000   Tec-comple   2

Insert a third slide

We still have to include Jon's employment history, so we will use a new slide. Select **Insert > New Slide** and select a *Bullet list* slide layout.

This slide has a title area and a larger bullet list area.

Complete the slide with all of the detail as shown in the example below.

Save the changes.

Staff Briefing

- Jonathon Morgan Richards
  - Employment History
    - 1987 - On leaving university, recruited by multi-national company: Samson's United Systems
    - 1993 - Joined Anglo-American International, worked stateside for two years
    - 1995 - Returned to UK and joined the newly converted bank: Collins plc
    - 1999 - Tec-com

23 March 2000   Tec-comple   3

Adjusting and editing objects

Graphics, list boxes, organization charts and other objects that can be inserted onto slides can all be handled in similar ways.

First click onto the object, selecting it. It will be given a grey outline with sizing handles at the corners and mid-sides.

- Move the mouse cursor over the object and the cursor will change to a four-headed arrow, which indicates that it can be moved around to a different position on the slide.

- Move the mouse cursor over any of the sizing arrows and it will change to a double-headed arrow, which indicates that it can be resized as appropriate to your requirements.

If you wish to change any of the detail on the object, simply double-click on it. You will be returned to the Clip Gallery, Organization Chart (see next page) or whichever other application was used to create the object. It can then be replaced or edited as required.

Organization Chart

We have now reached the stage of the presentation when the organisational structure is about to be discussed. PowerPoint has a slide layout designed to create organisation charts with the minimum of effort and fuss.

- Use **Insert > New Slide** and from the **New Slide** dialog box select the *Organization Chart* layout slide. You should be get a slide like this:

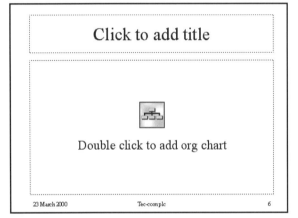

- In the slide title area type: '*Staff Briefing*'.
- Double-click on the icon and the Organization Chart window will open. Adjust it to a good working suitable size.

The Chart window

Add notes or headings

Change the Zoom level

Use these icons to add boxes to the chart

We are not going to make any changes to the existing chart at this stage, but will simply replace the '*Type name here*' prompts with other text.

To enter text into a box, click in it. The box will open out like this. We will only use the first two lines. Ignore the remaining lines – they will disappear when the box closes.

To move from one line to another, e.g. from the *Name* to the *Title* line, use **[Tab]**.

Start by clicking on the uppermost box and type in the detail as shown in below. Continue until all the detail has been entered.

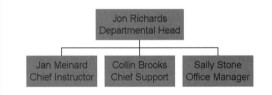

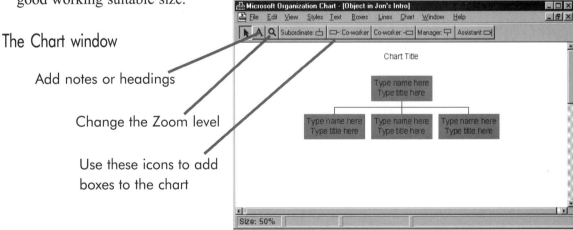

Inserting additional boxes

In retrospect, it would be advantageous to inform the staff of the changes and additions to the company, so we will add another two boxes. These are both at subordinate levels.

- Select the **Subordinate** icon on the Chart Toolbar. The cursor will change to ⬜.
- Point to the box that you want to attach it to, in this case, the *Jan Meinard* box and click. The new box will attach itself as shown here.

- Click into the new box and when it opens out add the detail as shown below.

Repeat to add a box beneath *Colin Brooks*.

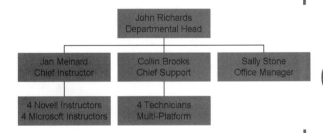

Deleting boxes

If you place a box on the chart and later decide that you do not want it, you can delete it easily by selecting it and pressing **[Delete]**.

Saving the chart

The chart will be saved as part of the presentation, but it is also possible to save it as a separate file, which can be used in other applications, for example Word or Excel.

Basic steps

1 On the Organization Chart menu bar select File >Save Copy As.

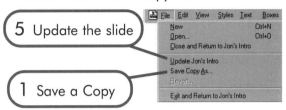

2 At the Save Chart dialog box, click on the down arrow and select the 3½ Floppy (A:)

3 Type in the name: *Tec-com Chart*.

4 Click the Save button.

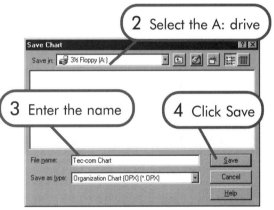

5 Reselect File and click on Update Jon's Intro, then close the chart window. You will be returned to the normal PowerPoint window, with the chart on display.

Save the changes to the presentation. This is particularly important at this stage. **Do not** save any changes from this point onwards unless specially instructed to do so.

Experiment with resizing, moving and re-opening the Chart window. **Do not** save any changes that you may make. Close the presentation and click **No** when prompted to save changes.

Slide Sorter View

We are now going to re-open the presentation. You may recall that Office applications remember which files were used recently. Open the **File** menu and you will find the presentation listed. Click on the name to open it.

The presentation will open up at Slide 1. We want to move to Slide 4 and this is the ideal opportunity to introduce the Slide Sorter View.

In the lower left-hand area of the presentation window is a set of icons.

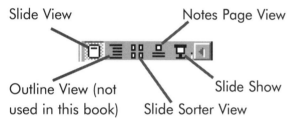

Slide View

Notes Page View

Outline View (not used in this book)

Slide Sorter View

Slide Show

Click on the Slide Sorter View icon.

Slide Sorter View displays all of the slides in a miniature format. It is here that you can change the position of slides or insert a new slide in the appropriate position within the presentation.

First save the presentation, then practise the following.

- Select Slide 4, that is the one that contains the chart. When selected, the image will have a thick border surrounding it.

- Place the mouse cursor over the image, left-click and hold. The cursor will change to an arrow with a small rectangle attached to it.

- Keeping the left button depressed, drag the cursor to the left until it is between the first and second slides, then release the button.

Slide 4 will now be Slide 2.

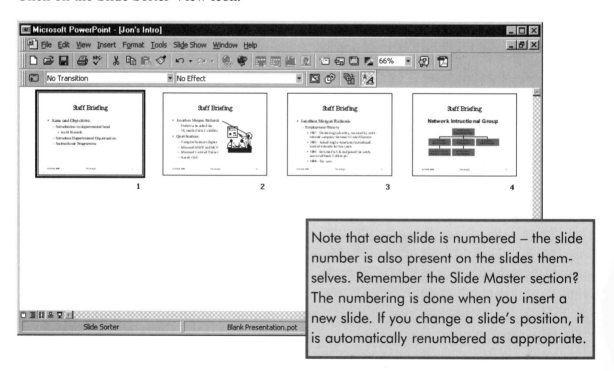

Note that each slide is numbered – the slide number is also present on the slides themselves. Remember the Slide Master section? The numbering is done when you insert a new slide. If you change a slide's position, it is automatically renumbered as appropriate.

You may have noticed that as the cursor was dragged to the left and when it arrived between the various slides, a vertical line appeared between the slides. This indicates that you may, if so desired, release the button and the slide will be moved to that location.

Practise the above actions, but **do not** save any changes at this stage.

When you feel confident moving slides as described above, Close the presentation but **do not** save the changes when prompted.

The reason for not saving the changes at this stage is that we wish to retain a common presentation throughout the book, and there is still more to be done.

- Re-open the presentation and move to the fourth slide, then double-click. So that we may modify the chart, double-click on it to open the Organization Chart.

- With the chart window open, highlight the chart title and type in 'Network Instructional Group'.

- Reselect the chart title then use **Text > Font** to open the Font dialog box.

- The Font Size is only 14, rather small for our requirements, so change the Size to 36 and Font style to Bold.

- When the selections have been made, click on the **OK** button. Select **File > Update Jon's Intro**, then select **File > Exit and return to Jon's Intro** for the changes to be implemented. You are now returned to the Slide View of the chart slide. Save the changes.

Tip

You can return from Slide Sorter View to Slide View simply by double-clicking on the appropriate slide image.

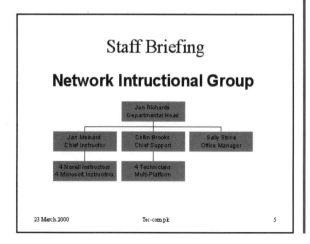

191

Running a slide show

At this stage it would be well worth checking the overall appearance of the presentation when run as a slide show. A slide show is the combination of all the slides assembled in the presentation, shown in full screen size, without any of the menu bars, toolbars, etc. being visible.

Slides can be either manually changed or set to run automatically. We will use the manual method during this presentation.

Click the Slide Show icon. The show will start at Slide 1. It is now up to the presenter to decide when to move onto the next slide.

To move onto the next slide, either:

· click the left mouse button, or

· click the icon in the lower left of the screen. A pop-up menu will appear and it is from here that you may control the slide show.

Practise both methods.

If you want to stop the show before reaching the end, you can select End Show from the pop-up menu or simply press **[Escape]**.

Now that we have previewed the show we realise that we have forgotten to include any details of Jon's family. Also the slide background was rather plain – just white. We can improve this easily because PowerPoint has a number of preformatted background designs.

Before we proceed, use **File > Save** to ensure the file is completely up to date. Another reason for saving at this stage is that we are going to experiment with a background design, but we will not retain it, as this book is published in black and white and some of the designs are rather dark and would not print particularly well.

Click to open the control menu

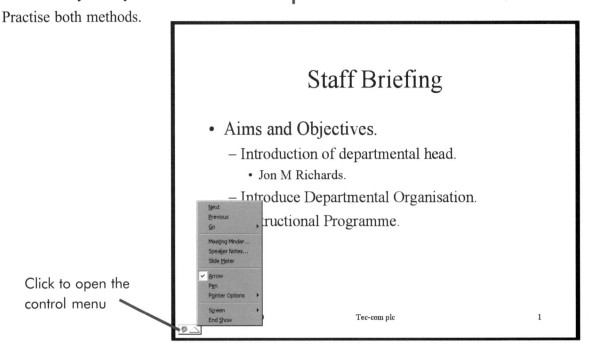

Applying a design

Go to Slide 1 of the presentation.

To apply a design use **Format > Apply Design**. The **Apply Design** dialog box will open. It is here that the design selections are made.

We will only to discuss the basics in respect of selecting a design. Experiment later to learn the other features and options available.

In this instance select *Dads Tie.pot*, and click the **Apply** button. This design will give you a good idea of the colour aspects. Remember **do not** save any changes.

If your slide show is to be run from an overhead projector, practise the show on the projector.

Projectors usually have a background colour, and this colour, often blue, may cause colour clashes with your display. Practice may not always make perfect, but it will help eliminate embarrassing moments for the presenter.

Formatting individual slides

It is possible to format individual slides with different colour displays and though we are not going to cover this option here, you should be aware of it. To format an individual slide, select it then use **Format > Slide Color Scheme...** Experiment with this at a later date.

We are now going to close the presentation and when prompted **do not** save the changes, because we want to return to the stage before any designs were applied.

Re-open the presentation and move on to the next page where we will insert the slide relating to Jon's family and make some changes to the font, font size and apply some colour.

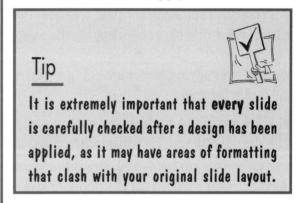

Tip

It is extremely important that **every slide** is carefully checked after a design has been applied, as it may have areas of formatting that clash with your original slide layout.

The folder in which PowerPoint stores all the default designs.

Design names – the currently selected design is *Dads Tie.pot*. The *.pot* extension identifies a file as a presentation design.

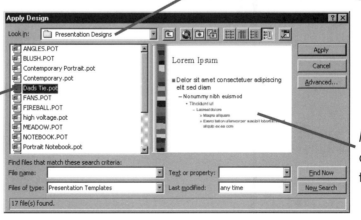

Miniature display of the design

Inserting a Text Box

Change to the Slide Sorter View – it is from here that we will insert the additional slide.

The new slide is to be inserted between Slides 3 and 4. Click between them and a thin vertical line will appear.

Use **Insert > New Slide** and at the **New Slide** dialog box select the *Bulleted list* slide.

Double-click on the new slide to return to Slide View, where we will start entering the family details (see page 180).

In the slide title area type '*Staff Briefing*'.

We want an additional, separate text box, but where will it fit without overlapping the existing two areas? At the moment it cannot fit without overlapping, so we are going to resize the bullet list area first.

● Click anywhere on the bullet list to select it – the resizing handles will appear around it.

The easiest way to change the size is to use the handles. As we only want a little more space between the two existing areas, point to the top, middle handle. When the cursor changes to a double-headed arrow, drag it down to just below the words '*Click to add text*' and release the button.

> • Click to add text

This is the level to which the box should be re-sized.

We will now insert a new text box between the two existing areas.

● Select [icon] the Text box icon from the Drawing toolbar. The cursor will change its shape to a thin inverted cross, ⊥.

● Place the cursor roughly mid-way between the two existing boxes and then press and hold the left mouse button. Drag the cursor down and to the right to create the additional text box, as shown in the example below, and then release the mouse button.

Be careful at this stage not to click outside the text area just inserted, because if you do, the text area will simply disappear. This is due to the fact that there is no text inside it, and PowerPoint thinks that it is no longer required and deletes it.

Staff Briefing

> • Click to add text

Tip

Use the spellchecker regularly.

194

Fonts and borders

When you insert a new text box, PowerPoint will automatically format it as left justified, i.e. with the text in the extreme left of the box. You can confirm this by the location of the flashing cursor.

The font type and size is the same as that used throughout the presentation, i.e. Times New Roman, at 24 pt. We will return to this shortly.

Type in '*Jon's Family*'.

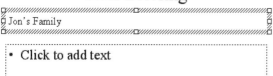

If you investigate the three text boxes, you will find that each has the same font type, i.e. New Times Roman, but each is a different font size.

The slide title is set to 44 pt, the new text box is set to 24 pt while the bullet list is set to 32 pt. It is convention that the slide title is the largest of the three. However, the new text box font size is too small. We want it to be the same size as shown in the bullet list.

Changing font size and type

● Click and drag over the text '*Jon's Family*' to highlight it.

● Right-click on the text and from the pop-up menu, select **Font**.

● At the **Font** dialog box change the size to 32

● To change the font type click on the **Font** down arrow and select a new type.

● Click the **OK** button when you have done.

Changing the alignment

With the text still highlighted, click on the **Centre** icon, on the Formatting toolbar. The text will now change its location and become centred in the text box.

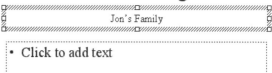

There is still more to do to this text box. Highlight the text again and this time click on the **Bold** icon on the Formatting toolbar.

Borders

You can, if you wish, include Borders around the various types of boxes used in PowerPoint. We will include a Border around the text box that we recently created. Follow the sequences outlined below:

Select the text box by clicking in it. Remember that when a text box is selected, a hatched outline appears around it.

With the text box selected, right-click over it and a pop-up menu will appear.

Select **Format Text Box**.

The Format Text Box dialog box will open. Ensure that the **Colors and Lines** tab is open.

195

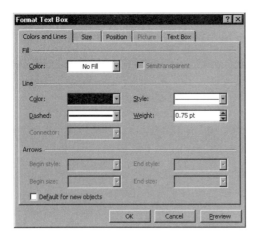

Adjust the settings in your dialog box to match those shown above. Click the down arrow besides **Color** and select *Automatic*.

When you have done, click the **OK** button.

You will be returned to Slide View. The text box should still be selected – click anywhere on the slide to deselect it. You can now clearly see the border surrounding the box.

The box is too wide for the amount of text it contains. We will now re-size it.

Staff Briefing

Jon's Family

• Click to add text

Click once within the box area. The outline will change and the resizing handles appear.

Point to the middle handle on the left border of the box. When the cursor changes to a double-headed arrow, drag the cursor to the right. The box will shrink as you drag. Continue to adjust the size until you are satisfied with the way the text appears within the box – leave a little space at each end of the text.

The box appears to have moved to the right side of the slide. It has not actually moved – it was simply resized.

The box should at this stage still be selected. Move the cursor up and over the lower border line of the box. When it changes to a four-headed arrow, drag it to the left until the box appears central below the slide title.

Staff Briefing

Jon's Family

• Click to add text

Save the changes. Select the bullet list and enter the text, complete with all formatting, as shown in the example below.

Once you have completed typing in all the text, Save the changes.

Staff Briefing

Jon's Family

• Katherine, prefers to be called Kathy
  – Consultant Web Designer
  – Married to Jon for then years
    • Two children
    • Richard 8 years of age
    • Hazel 6 years of age

23 March 2000   Tec-compk   4

Practice slide show

We are now at the stage to do a re-run of the slide show to check the layout and presentation of the slides. This time use the menu command **Slide Show > View Show** to run the show.

On viewing the slide show, we see that the chart, on Slide 5, appears rather small, so we are now going to increase its size somewhat.

- Ensure that the chart slide is on display.

- Select the chart by clicking over it and the resizing handles will appear around it.

- Point to the top left handle, and drag up to the left. Release the button when the border is about 3cm from the slide's left edge.

- The chart is still not quite large enough. Repeat the same actions, only this time drag the lower right handle to the lower right of the slide.

- Release the button when the handles are about 1.5 cm from the right slide edge.

- Re-run the Slide Show to ensure that you are happy with the final size and positioning on the slide.

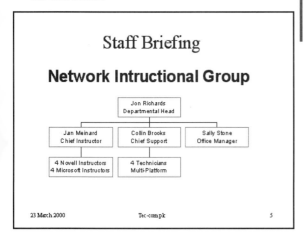

The fourth slide, with Jon's family details, has an oddity on it. The first bullet item has the text '*Katherine, prefers to be called Kathy*'.

The name 'Katherine' is okay size-wise, but the rest of the text should be in a smaller font.

- Highlight the text '*prefers to be called Kathy*' and change the font size to 24 pt.

Save the changes to the presentation.

That completes the overall presentation. However, to practise one or two other procedures, we are going to insert a sixth slide.

Insert a new slide after Slide 5. Select the *Title only* slide.

In the slide title type '*Practice Slide Only*'.

Switch to Slide 2, which has the image that we used to identify Jon to the audience.

Select the image and Copy it, either by clicking the **Copy** icon on the Standard toolbar, or by right-clicking on the image and selecting **Copy**.

Switch to Slide 6 and click the **Paste** icon on the Standard toolbar. The image will be placed on Slide 6. Practise moving and sizing it.

Save the changes to the document.

Tip

If you wish to run the complete presentation, as a Slide Show, always ensure that you are looking at the first slide in the presentation, otherwise PowerPoint will start the Slide Show from whichever slide is being displayed at that time.

Integration with other applications

Information in a PowerPoint presentation can easily be copied or linked to any of the other applications in the Microsoft Office 97 suite.

Data can be inserted in a Word document, an Excel worksheet or an Access database.

It is also possible to import data from the above mentioned applications into PowerPoint.

Exchange data between Word and Powerpoint

This is provided as an 'interest only' section. You do not have to carry out the exercise if you don't want to. You should, however, be aware that it is quite easy to use existing data, from other applications, in a PowerPoint slide show.

You can use text created in other programs to make a new presentation or add slides to an existing one. The text you import is in Outline format. This format is beyond the scope of this book – use the on-line Help to learn about it.

When you import text, PowerPoint uses the outline structure from the styles in the document. Heading 1 becomes a slide title, and heading 2 becomes the first level of text, and so on. If the document contains no styles, PowerPoint uses the paragraph indentations to create an outline. In plain text documents, tabs at the beginning of paragraphs define the outline structure.

Practice

It will only be possible to practise the following if you have already completed the module on Word.

To insert a Word table:

- In Slide View, display the slide you want to add a table to.
- Click the Word Table icon, on the Standard Toolbar, then drag to select the number of rows and columns you want.
- Enter the data in the table cells.
- Use the Word tools and menus to format the table. For example, to add borders to the table, use **Table > AutoFormat**.
- Click outside the table to return to PowerPoint.

Take note

You can easily create a presentation from an existing Word outline. In Word, open the document, point to **Send To** on the **File** menu, and select **Microsoft PowerPoint**.

Tip

PowerPoint comes with a slide layout that includes a placeholder for a table. To use this layout, look for the Table slide in the New Slide dialog box.

Sample paper 6: Presentations

1	Explain how to add the date to the Footer of a slide so that it appears on each slide.	
2	List three examples of preformatted slides	1. 2. 3.
3	List two of the PowerPoint Views	1. 2.
4	You have created a chart in PowerPoint, the chart can be used in Microsoft Word and Excel. True or False?	1. True 2. False
5	You are about to insert a new slide. What is the quickest method of selecting a slide from the New Slide dialog box?	
6	List the two methods that can be used to resize an object on a slide.	1. 2.
7	List the two methods, discussed in the book, to move from one slide to another while running a slide show.	1. 2.
8	Briefly describe what a Design is when applied to a presentation.	
9	Once a Design has been applied to a series of slides, it is impossible to change the design for an individual slide. True or False?	1. False. 2. True.
10	When a chart has been created and placed on a slide, it cannot be modified. True or False?	1. True. 2. False.
11	List three examples of any AutoShapes.	1. 2. 3.
12	The drawing tools found within PowerPoint are common to other Microsoft applications, such as Word or Excel. True or False?	1. True. 2. False

7 The Internet

The Internet

This module will introduce you to the Internet and the World Wide Web and demonstrate a number of key features and uses of both.

The module has been split into two sections: *The Internet*, which will show you how to navigate the World Wide Web to find information and Web sites of interest; and *Electronic Mail*, which will demonstrate how to send and receive mail using your computer.

The Internet section has been designed using Internet Explorer versions 4.0 and 5.0. If you are using a different browser, you may find some differences between the screenshots in the exercises and what you see on your computer. However, the concept of the exercise and results should be the same.

Similarly, the Electronic Mail module has been designed using Outlook Express version 4. If you are using a different version of Outlook Express or different e-mail software you may find some differences.

If you are unsure what software version you are using, please seek advice.

The background

Although the Internet has only become popular in recent years, it was designed back in 1969 by the US Department of Defense. For many years it remained an academic and military network, but in the 1990s people started to realise its commercial potential. As we enter the new millennium it has approximately 100 million users worldwide, and this is increasing exponentially.

The Internet actually consists of many networks round the world passing data to each other using a protocol called 'TCP/IP'.

- **TCP/IP (Transmission Control Protocol/Internet Protocol)** – developed in 1974 by Kahn and Cerf and allows computers to communicate over the Internet.

No single organisation manages or polices the Internet, and any individual can access, and post information to the Internet as long as they have the necessary equipment.

The Internet is changing the way we live – the way we communicate with each other, the way we find information, the way we shop and the way we do business.

Information delivered via the Internet can be current and dynamic. For example, a Web site dedicated to news, sport or weather can be updated every few minutes providing information as it happens, unlike traditional media.

But taking your first steps on to the Internet can be a puzzling experience. You will have heard all about Web sites on TV and in magazines telling you how simple the Internet is to use. There are now many journals and magazines dedicated to the Web, along with many guidebooks. But for the first-time user it can be difficult to cut through the technical jargon.

This module will show you how to take your first steps on the Internet, and prepare you for making the most out of its services. However, the best way to find out what is available over the Internet will be for you to explore it.

Getting Started

Before we discuss what the Internet can do for you, let us establish *how* you get on the Internet. Internet access these days is much simpler than it used to be, but you will still need these:

 A computer – this would seem obvious, but we are now seeing the introduction of Internet-compliant televisions, allowing you to connect your television to your telephone line, and 'surf' the Internet via this medium.

A modem - this will enable your computer to 'talk' over the Internet via your telephone line. Modems are available at different speeds and prices, so when deciding which to buy you need to balance the cost of the modem, against the cost of telephone calls that may be longer when using a slower modem.

- **Modem (MOdulate/DEModulate)** – converts digital data into analogue signals to pass down the telephone line, and then back into data at your PC.

A telephone line – note that most lines will not allow you to make voice calls while you are logged on to the Internet, so you may wish to consider having a separate telephone line, for use with the Internet. An alternative is to install an ISDN line, which can handle both voice and data and can communicate at a far quicker rate.

- **ISDN** (Integrated Systems Digital Network) – a digital telephone line.

An account with an ISP (Internet Service Provider) – this allows you to connect to the Internet via the ISP's communication equipment. Some ISPs charge a monthly fee for the service, but many offer a free dial-up service where all you pay for are the costs of the telephone call – usually at Local Rate charges. A new breed of ISPs is emerging offering a totally free service using a 'Freephone' telephone number. When deciding which provider you wish to use you need to balance level of service against the cost.

Once you have all the items above, and have decided upon which ISP to use, access is simple. Your ISP will either provide you with all the information you require to set-up your Internet connection, or more likely will supply you with a disk that will automate the whole process.

Take note

You will find that on occasions the Internet may be a little temperamental, or appear to run slowly. This may be due to the site you are visiting, or the volume of traffic, so patience is also required during your early days of exploration.

Surfing the Internet

The most popular part of the Internet is the World Wide Web (WWW) – which allows people to publish pages, or Web sites, from anywhere in the world. A Web site can be read at any time by anybody, anywhere.

The phrase 'surfing the Internet' is generally used to describe an undirected type of Web browsing in which the users jumps from page to page on the WWW whimsically, as opposed to searching for specific information.

The best-known Web sites are large-scale professional services packed full of information, entertainment and with the capability to purchase items on-line – anything from buying flowers, to booking a holiday, to ordering concert tickets. However, anyone can be a publisher on the Internet. Many Web sites are the work of small groups or individuals talking about their hobbies or interests.

So how do you get to these sites? The Web is viewed through a *'browser'*. These are free, and if your PC was not supplied with one you can easily obtain one on a disk from your ISP.

- **Browser** – the software you use to view the World Wide Web. We are using Internet Explorer in this book, but other browsers are available, such as Netscape Navigator.

Logging on to the Internet

You connect, or *log on*, to the Internet via your ISP. To log on you need to open your browser by clicking on Internet Explorer's icon or by selecting it through your Programs menu.

If your browser is configured to automatically connect to the Internet upon opening, you may be asked for a *Username* and *Password*. These will have been supplied by your ISP when you first registered with them.

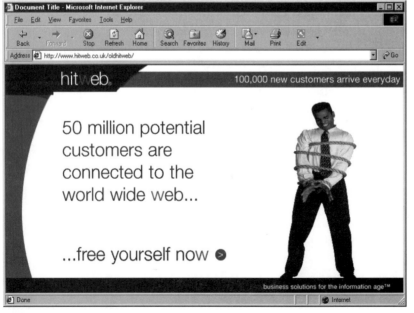

HitWeb – a new company with new solutions for business

You can configure your computer to save your Username and Password, so that every time that you log on you do not have to type them in. There are security implications though and anyone who has access to your computer, can use the Internet without your permission.

During logon, a dialog box displays the progress while your Username and Password are being verified. Once your computer has successfully completed this, you will be on-line and able to access the Internet and the World Wide Web

Interflora – a established organisation, but one that is making excellent use of the Internet

The Tate Galleries – old masters, new masters in a slick, modern setting

205

Finding a site

Uniform Resource Locator

Web site addresses (or URLs) are everywhere these days – in newspapers, on television adverts and even on your breakfast cereal packets. Although addresses may look daunting, you will soon get the hang of reading and remembering them.

- **URL** (Uniform Resource Locator) – the address of a Web site.

Addresses usually begin with '**http://www**' followed by more letters, dots and slashes. Most browsers do not need you to type in the '**http://**' part; you can just start with the '**www**'.

- **HTTP** (HyperText Transfer Protocol) – the method used by browsers to view and download Web pages. That's why Web site addresses begin with 'http://'

Following the 'www.' you will then usually find the name of the organisation or company which publishes the site. For example, you would expect IBM computers to start '**http://www.ibm.**', or the Wembley site to start '**http://www.wembley.**'.

The end of the URL indicates the type of organisation that publishes the site. For example:

- International businesses end with '**.com**' (commercial)
- Non-commercial organisations end '**.org**'
- Network and Internet specialists use '**.net**'

These are referred to as *global domains*.

Where sites are country-specific the extension is followed by an international country code. For the United Kingdom this is '.uk'. Other examples include '.de' for Germany, '.us' for USA, and '.fr' for France. Every country has their own international country code.

Therefore within the United Kingdom

- Commercial sites end '**.co.uk**'
- Government sites end '**.gov.uk**'
- Academic sites '**.ac.uk**'
- Non-profit sites use '**.org.uk**'

Sometimes the URL will have a further part that works in the same way as a sub-folder in Windows Explorer. For example, at the Hitweb site '**www.hitweb.co.uk**' there are a series of pages with information about a company called Perkins Slade. These pages can be found by going to the Hitweb site and using the site navigation to find the appropriate pages, or alternatively and much simpler, the address '**www.hitweb.co.uk/perkins-slade**' will take you directly to the required pages.

Take note

Web sites are constantly being updated and changed. If at any time, you are directed to a site, and when that site opens you find that the first page is different, don't worry. Some organisations change the appearance of their sites every couple of months.

Practice session

The best way to understand the Internet is to explore it. Let's get on-line.

Basic steps

1 On your desktop, double-click on the icon that connects you to the Internet. This is probably 'Internet Explorer', but may be 'Netscape' or some other, depending on which browser you are using.

2 Your computer will now connect to the ISP, and open the default home page.

3 In the address line at the top of the browser type 'www.bmw.com', and hit [Enter].

4 There will be a slight delay while the computer searches for this site. When the page opens, select English and you will be taken to BMW's English section.

5 The page will load a bit at a time with text being downloaded first followed by the images. If the images are big it may take many seconds, or even a few minutes to complete. You will know when the page has finished downloading, as the message 'Done' will appear in the Status line of your browser.

Exercises

● Find the Web site of Hitweb, a UK based business. *co.uk*

● Find the Web site of the ECDL foundation, an international business. *com*

● Find the Web site of the RNIB, a UK based charity. *org.uk*.

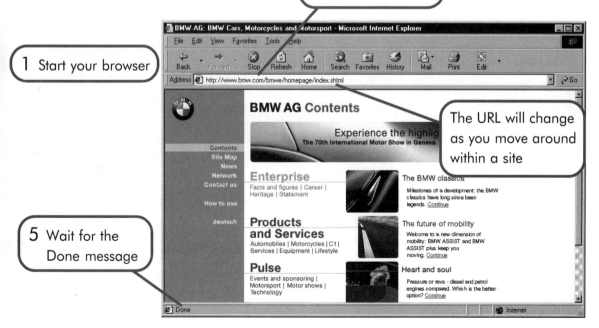

3 Type the address

1 Start your browser

The URL will change as you move around within a site

5 Wait for the Done message

7: Communications

207

Home Page

Every time you start your browser, it will head for your 'home' page. This is the Web site you have chosen as your regular starting point. When using Internet Explorer, the default home page is '**www.msn.com**', but you can change this to a page of your choice.

If you get lost on the Internet, click the **Home** button in your browser to go to your home page.

Basic steps

1 Go to 'www.bcdtraining.co.uk'.

2 When the page opens, open the View menu (I.E. 4.0) or the Tools menu (I.E. 5.0) and select Internet Options.

3 At the Internet Options dialog box select the General tab.

4 In the Home Page area, click Use Current. BCD's URL will appear in the Address slot.

5 Click OK.

❏ The BCD site is now your home page and will appear every time you start your browser or click its 'Home' button.

Exercises

● Set 'www.hitweb.co.uk' as your home page.

● Visit another site, and then return to your home page using the 'Home' button.

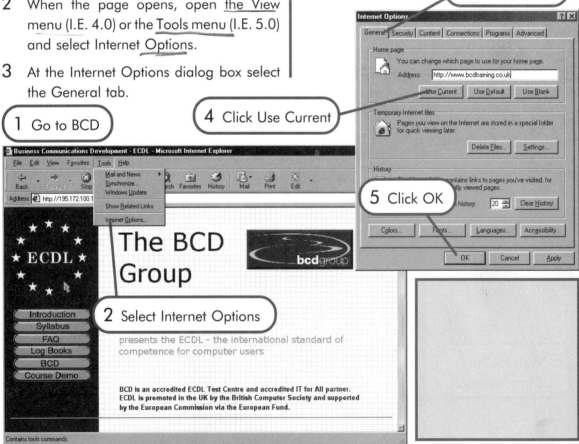

1 Go to BCD

2 Select Internet Options

3 Select General

4 Click Use Current

5 Click OK

Favourite sites

As you start to use the Internet on a regular basis, you will want a quick way of getting to your favourite sites without having to remember their addresses. One of the most useful browser tools is 'Favorites' (or 'Bookmarks' in Netscape), which stores site addresses.

When you arrive at a site you want to bookmark, add it to your Favorites. When you want to return to it, you can then simply click it in the Favorites list. If your list starts to get out of hand, you can organise it into folders – one for news, one for your hobby, and so on.

Note: The screenshots are from Internet Explorer (IE) 5. If you are using IE 4, you will find that the dialog boxes are slightly different, but still allow you to carry out the instructions and complete the exercise.

Basic steps

❑ Adding Favorites

1 Find the Web site of 'madesimple.co.uk'.

2 Open the Favorites menu and click Add to Favorites'.

3 At the Add Favorite dialog box, enter 'Made Simple books' in the Name slot and click OK.

❑ Organising Favorites

4 Open the Favorites menu again and select Organize Favorites. The Organize Favorites dialog box will open, listing your folders and favourite sites.

5 Click on 'Made Simple books', then click the Move to Folder button.

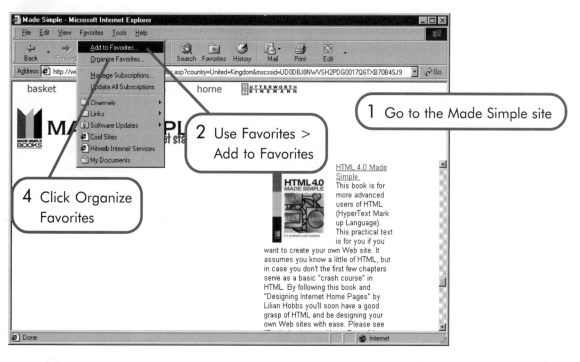

6 At the Browse for Folder dialog box, select the '*Cool Sites*' folder, then click OK.

7 Back at the Organize Favourites dialog box., click on the '*Cool Sites*' folder. When the folder opens, you will see '*Made Simple books*' is now in it.

❏ Using Favorites

8 The next time you wish to visit this site, click on Favourites, select the '*Cool Sites*' folder, then double-click on '*Made Simple books*'.

Exercises

● Go to the Website 'www.itforall.org.uk' and add it to your list of favourites, named 'IT for All'

● Organise your list of favourites so that 'IT for All' is kept in the 'News and Weather' folder.

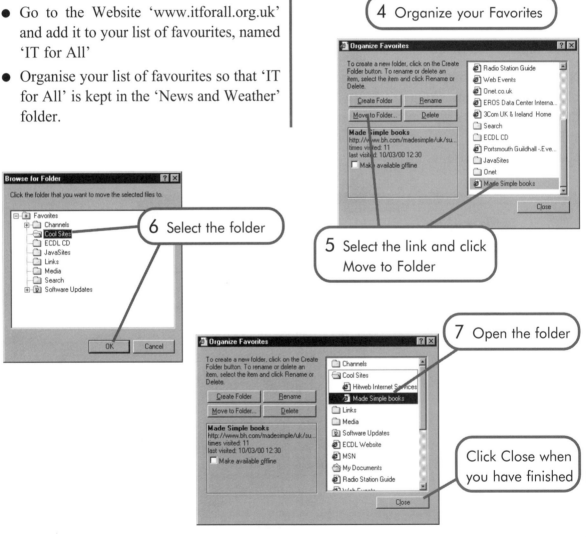

3 Enter the name

4 Organize your Favorites

6 Select the folder

5 Select the link and click Move to Folder

7 Open the folder

Click Close when you have finished

Surfing

You need to get to know your browser buttons to become more proficient in your surfing.

- **Back** takes you to the Web page you were looking at last. You will be surprised how often you want to retrace your footsteps.

- **Forward** use this if you do go back, then want to return to where you just came from.

- **Stop** click this if you wish to stop downloading a page that you selected either by accident, or are having trouble loading.

- **Refresh** will download the current page, all over again. This is useful if some images have failed to load properly, or if the page is likely to be updated frequently.

- **Home** as we discussed in the last section, takes you to your home page.

- **Favorites** open your Favorites list in the same way as the Favorites menu command.

- **Search** opens the default search engine within your browser window. We shall discuss search engines later in this document.

- **History** provides a listing of all the sites you have visited over a set period of time, allowing you to click on the URL and be taken directly there.

In addition you can return to a site you visited the last time you were on the Web by clicking on the arrow at the end of the box containing the current Web site address. This will drop-down a list of the Web sites you have looked at most recently. You can click on the one you want, to go directly there.

Most browsers have many other tricks you can use to help you navigate the Net – experiment with the controls to find out extra features.

Your browser may have other icons to open related applications

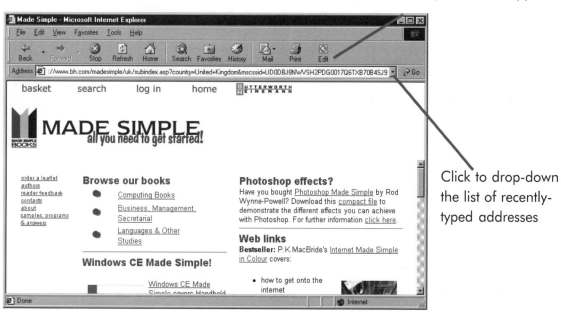

Click to drop-down the list of recently-typed addresses

Search engines

Many newcomers to the Internet worry about how they are going to find the addresses of Web sites that might be of interest to them. There is no equivalent of a phone book for the Internet – but you will find it remarkably easy to find what you are looking for.

The nearest you will get to a telephone book is one of the major search engines. These have indexed millions of Web pages to allow you to track down topics by typing in keywords.

Try it out on the Ask Jeeves search engine that features on the Hitweb site.

- Go to **www.hitweb.co.uk** and when the page is loaded, click on '*Links*' then on '*Help Me*' to reach the page shown below.

- Type into the search box some relevant words to describe what you are looking for.

- Ask Jeeves will return a long list of Web sites that match your criteria, with the closest matches at the top of the page.

Now you can surf to your heart's content.

You may find that you get too many results, or that you are not getting the information you require. It is important that your search is specific as possible, for example:

- If you require information about your nearest branch of Boots the Chemist, don't simply type 'Boots' as this will return boot and shoemakers from around the world! Instead you should use keywords such as 'Boots', 'Chemist'', Pharmacy', 'UK', etc.

- Most search engines have an 'Advanced' feature, which will allow you to include and exclude certain criteria, or search with strings of words, e.g. 'Boots the Chemist'.

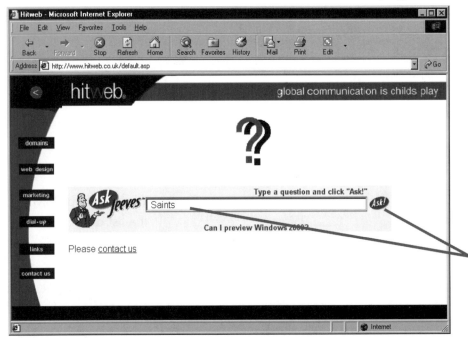

Type one or more relevant words and click Ask

Retrieving information from the Internet

On occasions you may find information on a Web site that you wish to save to your computers hard disk for future reference. This can be achieved in a number of ways.

Download

There are thousands of sites on the Internet offering all sorts of files you can download. Popular examples would be the MP3 music files, movie trailers and the latest games demos. You can download files from any Web site simply be finding the file and following the instructions contained on the Web page. When you start to download, you will usually encounter this dialog box.

After you have made your selection and clicked the OK button, this dialog box will appear.

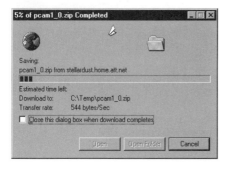

You can stop a download at any time, simply by clicking the **Cancel** button.

● Create a folder and call it '*Download*' and always save your downloads in it.

Downloading files can take some time and transfer rates can vary widely. Try to download during off-peak hours, that is early in the morning or late at night.

If you are interested in attempting a download, try the following Web sites:

> http://www.download.com
> http://www.shareware.com

Take note

Files downloaded from the Internet may contain computer viruses. See Chapter 1 for further information on viruses.

Save an image

To save an image that is on a Web page, simply right-click on it and select **Save Picture As** from the pop-up menu.

You will need to specify which folder on your hard disk you wish to save the image to.

It's easy to copy just about anything from the Internet, but sometimes it may not be legal.

Before you copy any text or images, which you intend to use on your own Web page, make sure that you have permission from the original author. If you fail to do this, you could find yourself with a costly legal problem.

Save a Web page

To save the Web page you are currently viewing, first click the left mouse button on the page – this is known as 'anchoring' – then open the **File** menu and select **Save As**.

The page will be saved in HTML format and can be viewed at a later stage using your browser. It should be noted that this would not save any graphics on the page.

Print a Web page

To print the Web page you are viewing you again need to 'anchor' the page, then open the **File** menu and select **Print**.

Note that many sites are constructed using 'frames', so that what appears to be a single Web page is actually constructed from several components. After selecting 'Print' you may be asked whether you want to print all the frames, or just the one that you 'anchored' to.

Exercises
● Go to the www.hitweb.net site, anchor on the home page, and then print the page.
● Go to the www.bcs.org.uk site, anchor on the home page, and then save in your download folder or on your 'A:' drive. Using Windows Explorer, find the saved page, and then by double-clicking on the file name, view the page.

Hyperlinks

As you move from Web site to Web site, you will get used to clicking on text, pictures and graphics to link through to more information or other Web sites. These links are known as 'Hyperlinks'.

- **Hyperlinks** are connections between Web pages, or different parts of the same page, and provide a shortcut method of navigating around the Internet.

Links are usually designed to stand out from the rest of the page. A text link will be highlighted in some way – often in blue underlined text when the rest of the text is black. Links might also take the form of graphics, or even pictures. With practice, you will soon work out how to spot a link.

When you have discovered a link on a page, the 'Cursor' on the screen will change, as it moves over the link, from an arrow into a little hand, with the finger pointing upwards. Click the mouse button, and the browser will whisk you off to another site or page.

Exercises

- Go to the Ask Jeeves search engine at www.hitweb.co.uk, as described previously, or the Yahoo search engine at www.yahoo.com
- Enter a keyword of your choice relevant to a subject you are interested in
- Select the result most appropriate to the topic you are interested in from the list returned.

7: Communications

215

Five sites of interest

Going online is an adventure to start with. Surfing the Web is great fun and can be very informative. But you will soon discover that the practical uses of the Internet will make it increasingly central to all aspects of your life.

Communicating with family, friends and business associates by e-mail is quicker, cheaper and easier than writing letters.

Online shopping is taking off as companies prepare to do more and more of their business over the Internet. If you want you can do all your Christmas shopping from the comfort of your home. Sometimes, with such as CDs, books or even a new computer, you will be offered extra discounts for buying online.

Your children will use computers at school and can use the Internet to help with homework and make e-mail pen-friends in other countries.

Detailed below are our top five sites to visit, showing you what the Internet can do for you. Take the opportunity to visit the sites, and also search for a few of specific interest to yourself.

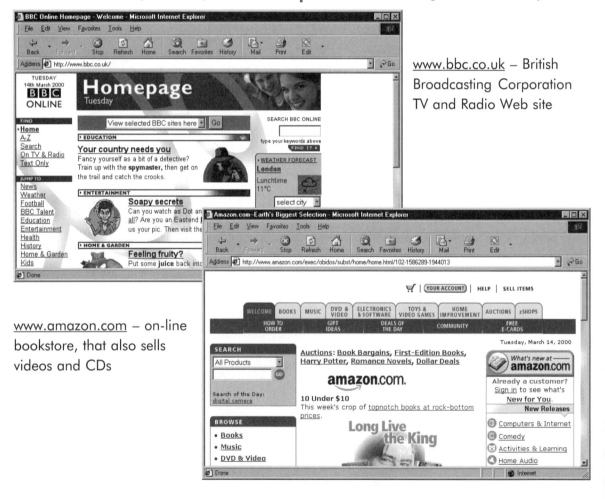

www.bbc.co.uk – British Broadcasting Corporation TV and Radio Web site

www.amazon.com – on-line bookstore, that also sells videos and CDs

www.itforall.org.uk – DTI 'IT for All' initiative with information for the beginner

www.hants.gov.uk – a local government Website, as recommended by Bill Gates!

www.virgin.com – a commercial site, the Virgin company's Website

Web site development

Once you have spent a few hours looking at other people's Web sites, you might decide you want one too. The following pages will show you how to build a very basic Web page. *Note that you will not be required to know this as part of your test.*

Large, commercial Web sites that have good design and complex functionality are usually designed by professional Web development companies. It is recommended that if you require a Web site for a professional organisation, that you approach one of the many Web development companies that specialise in all aspects of site design.

However, most ISPs these days provide you with free Web space so that you can create your own personal Web site.

Web pages are created using a system called HyperText Mark-up Language, or HTML.

To make best use of your free Web space, you will need to learn the basics of HTML. It is simple to learn and with practice you can create Web sites quite easily.

HTML works by inserting tags into text. So an HTML file can be written entirely in a normal word processor or text-editing program, like Word, Notepad or Wordpad.

Each tag is surrounded by angle brackets like this < >.

Browsers display Web pages by reading through the text of an HTML file, and obeying the formatting commands given in the tags.

We are going to create a Web page in Notepad. Click onto the **Start** button and then select **Programs**, **Accessories** and **Notepad**.

You will be presented with a blank page ready to beginning typing in your HTML code.

Before we start, we will save the file. Open the **File** menu and select **Save As**. When the Save As dialog box opens, switch to the download folder and type the filename '*My web page.htm*'. It is important to include the extension '*.htm*' as this specifies the file is HTML and tells your computer that it should be viewed via a browser.

Using Notepad, enter the following text:

```
<HTML>
<HEAD>
<P><TITLE>My first web page</TITLE></P>
</HEAD>
<BODY>
<P><H1>Welcome to my home page</H1>
</P>
<HR>
<P>There's not much here at the moment, but
I am busy learning more HTML so that I can
create the web site <I>of my dreams.</I></P>
<P>You can e-mail me by <A HREF=
"mailto:me@myaddress.com"> clicking here
</A></P>
</BODY>
</HTML>
```

You can now view the Web page you have just created in two ways.

Using Windows Explorer, locate the file 'My web Page.htm' in the folder you have just saved it to, and double-click on the file name.

Alternatively, open your Internet Explorer window, and in the Address bar type the full path of where your file is, e.g. *C:\My Documents\Exercises\My web page.htm,* and hit **[Enter]** on your keyboard. You should now be viewing the Web page.

HTML tags

You will see that most tags have to be opened and closed. The closing tag has a forward-slash inserted before the word, so it looks like this: </HTML>.

A Web browser will format everything between two matching tags in a particular way.

Each tag in the exercise on the previous page has a function.

<HTML> shows this is an HTML document.

<HEAD> identifies the document header – it will not appear in the display, but gives each page an identity.

<TITLE> gives the page a name. The title will appear at the top of the browser, and will identify a page in Favorites lists.

<BODY> is the main part of the document – the part that will appear in the browser.

<H1> is a heading, size 1 – the biggest text the browser will display. Everything between the <H1> and </H1> will be displayed as a large title on the page.

<HR> draws a horizontal line across the page. It does not need a closing tag.

<P> is to show the start of each paragraph.

<I> </I> makes text between them *italic*.

<A...> creates a hyperlink to another page or e-mail address. Note that after the 'A' is more code that tells the browser to make a link to a specified e-mail address.

Exercises

- Build a new Web page with a file name of 'ECDL.HTM', saved to the temp folder.

- It should have:

  the heading, 'My exercise page';

  a title of 'ECDL exercise site';

  and the text 'This is my completed ECDL exercise Web page. To congratulate me, mail me at', followed by a hyperlink to your mail address of 'yourname@acme.co.uk'.

There are many guides on the Internet to help you learn HTML and assist with Web site design. Remember to keep things simple and add to your knowledge slowly over time.

Web design software

There are many Web authoring tools which allow you to build Web sites in a simpler manner than coding in HTML. Users of Windows 95 and 98 have an application called FrontPage Express, which is ideal for building simple Web pages.

● FrontPage can normally be found at **Start > Programs > Internet Explorer > FrontPage Express**.

Shown below is FrontPage Express, displaying the first page of the BCD Group ECDL CD course.

FrontPage Express is a cut-down version of the full product and you will not have full access to all of the software facilities. Practise and learn how to use FrontPage Express and don't forget to use the online Help, provided as part of the application.

Uploading to the World Wide Web

Uploading is the opposite of downloading – transferring files from your computer to a site on the Internet, e.g. your ISP Web computer.

Having successfully built your Web page(s) you may wish to consider putting your site on to the World Wide Web so that your friends, colleagues and the whole world can see your work! Your ISP has probably allocated free Web space to you, if not, Business Communications Development Limited have teamed up with Hitweb Internet Solutions to enable you to do this free of charge, as follows:

● Complete the form at www.onet.co.uk/hitweb and you will be instructed on how you can upload your site onto the World Wide Web making it visible to 100 million plus Internet users around the world.

Special tools for creating forms

Formatting tools – almost identical to those in Word

Browsing tools

Estimated download time for the page – keep an eye on this, as visitors prefer fast-loading pages.

Electronic mail

Electronic Mail or e-mail is a method of sending and receiving messages, from or to a computer or specialist telephone, via the Internet.

Sending and receiving e-mail is very cheap and is very fast.

The most commonly used program for sending and receiving e-mail is Outlook Express which is distributed with the Windows operating system. Double-click on the Outlook Express icon on the desktop to start it. Depending on which version of Outlook Express you have, your screens may appear a little different from those shown.

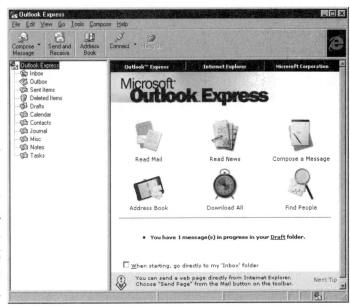

Basic steps

❑ Composing a message

1 Click the Compose Message (or New Mail) button.

2 The New Message window will open. If it is too small, click on the Maximise button.

3 Enter the e-mail address of the the recipient in the To box., e.g. *info@bcdtraining.co.uk*

4 In the Subject line, type a subject, e.g. *'Next meeting of the Wine Drinkers Appreciation Society'*.

5 Type your message.

6 Click Send.

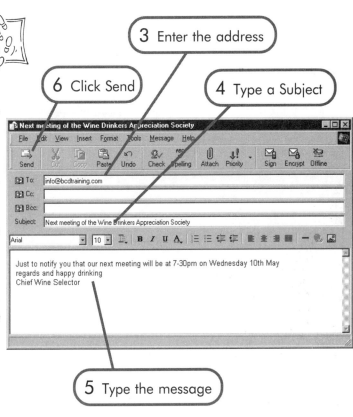

Attaching a file to a message

Files such as Word documents or Excel workbooks can be attached to e-mail.

Basic steps

1   Click the paperclip icon.

2   At the Insert Attachment dialog box, select
    the file(s).

3   Click the Attach button.

❑   A new slot will appear below the Subject
    line, showing the attached file .

4   Click the Send button.

Take note

**Messages are normally typed in lowercase,
with uppercase used for emphasis. Typing
in uppercase is considered the equivalent of
shouting and is best avoided.**

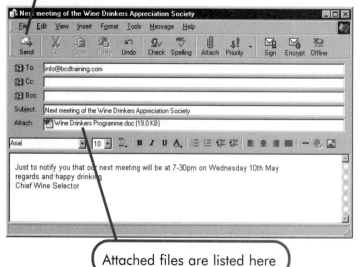

1 Click the paperclip

2 Select the file(s)

3 Click Attach

4 Click Send

Attached files are listed here

Cc and Bcc

Cc as shown in the example to the
left stands for Carbon Copy and is
sent as information to a third party.

Bcc stands for Blind Carbon Copy.
Only the sender will be aware that
the person shown in the Bcc address
line has received a copy.

Incoming mail

To receive e-mail

To receive e-mail click ![Send/Recv button] the **Send/Recv** button. If you are not connected to your ISP, you will be prompted to connect and when online, your e-mail will be sent to you.

Whenever you send an e-mail, Outlook Express checks your mail box at your ISP, to see if there is any mail waiting, and to collect it, if there is.

Received messages are stored in your **Inbox**. You can tell how many unread messages there are by looking at the Folders list. The number of unread messages is displayed next to the **Inbox** label.

Click a header to open the message in the lower panel

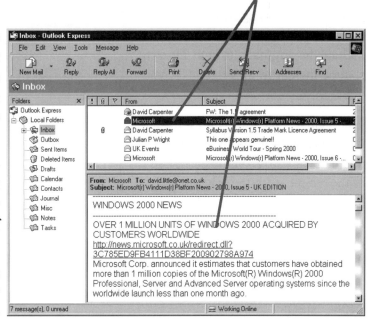

Copying a message

To copy a message to another application highlight it, then open the **Edit** menu and click on **Select All**.

The entire text will then be highlighted, as shown here.

From the **Edit** menu select Copy, and the message will be stored in the Clipboard ready for further use.

The copied text can then be imported into a second application, such as Word. With the application open and a new or existing document open, right-click in

the appropriate area of the document and select **Paste** from the pop-up menu. The message will appear in the document and you can, if so required, edit it.

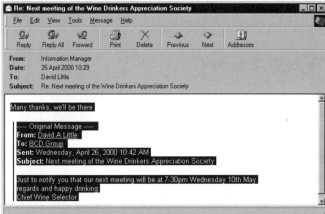

Replying to mail

The Reply feature has the option to copy the original message into your reply. The default setting is for this to be on, and it can be very useful. Imagine the scenario, you wish to respond to an e-mail, and include the original message. Do you re-type the entire message? No, you use Reply.

This copied message feature means that there is little room for error or misunderstanding, on the part of any of the recipients, if the original text is included in the response. The recipients can easily refer back through the messages at any time and re-read them.

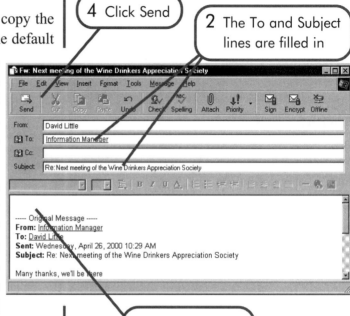

4 Click Send

2 The To and Subject lines are filled in

3 Type your reply

Basic steps

1   Select the message that you wish to respond to and click Reply.

2   At the Compose window, note that Outlook Express has completed the To: and Subject lines for you.

3   Type in your response.

4   When finished, click Send.

The Reply All feature

Another Reply feature is the Reply All. If you receive an e-mail, which was sent to a number of people, and you wish to respond to it and you want all of the recipients to see your responses, you can use the Reply All feature.

● Select the message and click the **Reply All** button.

● The Reply All dialog box will open and you will find that all the addresses from the original message have been copied into the 'To' slot for you.

In the message section, type in your responses and when finished, left-click on the Send. Outlook Express will send the message to all the addresses listed in the 'To' slot of the message. You do not have to send each of the message addressees an individual message. A real-time saver.

Forwarding a message

You can send a message that you have received on to another person. This feature is very useful and a time saver.

To forward a message, first select it then click on the **Forward** button.

The Compose window will open.

Enter the mail address of the recipient in the 'To' slot.

Add your own message, and amend the Subject and the original message if required.

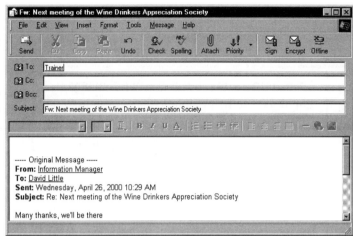

Filing e-mail

The more e-mail you get – and keep – the more important it is that you store it in an organised manner. Filing is simple, and should be done regularly.

Basic steps

1   Open the Inbox, and highlight the message to be filed.

2   From the Edit menu select Move to Folder. The Move dialog box will open

3   If you need to create a new folder, click the New Folder button.

4   At the New Folder dialog box , type a name for the folder and click OK.

5   When you return to the Move dialog box, select the new folder then click OK.

❑   The dialog box will close and the message will be moved to its new folder.

5   Select the folder and click OK

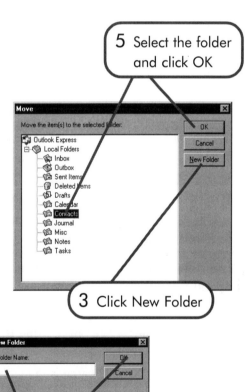

3   Click New Folder

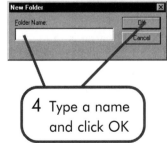

4   Type a name and click OK

7: Communications

225

Sample paper 7: Communications

1	Apart from a computer name two things you require before being able to access the Internet?	*modem* *ISDN Integr. Systems Digital Network* *ISP Internet Service Provider*
2	In what format does an ISDN line transmit data:	1. Analogue 2. Digital *telephone line*
3	What does 'HTTP' stand for?	*Hyper Text Transfer Protocol.*
4	What extension to a URL (Uniform Resource Locator) is a UK based company likely to have?	
5	What is the name given to the first page your browser opens when logging onto the Internet?	1. Index Page 2. Favourites Page 3. Home Page ✓
6	In Internet Explorer, the navigation toolbar allows you to perform a number of tasks. 'Search', and 'Stop' are two, name a third.	
7	What function do 'Hyperlinks' provide?	
8	Before saving or printing a Web page you first need to click onto the page. What term is used to describe this process?	
9	Name three practical uses of the Internet or World Wide Web?	1. 2. 3.
10	When developing a Web page using HTML, formatting commands are written in angle brackets – '< >'. What name is given to these commands?	1. Tags 2. Brackets 3. Prompts
11	When sending an e-mail, what does Cc mean in the address section?	

12	You wish to respond to an e-mail. To avoid any confusion as to which e-mail you are referring to, what facility of Outlook Express would you use?	1.	Copy
		2.	Edit
		3.	Reply to Author
13	You have received an e-mail and wish to use the content in a Word document. What facility would you use rather than retype the message?	1.	Move
		2.	Copy
		3.	Forward Message
14	You wish to send an e-mail to a number of people, but you do not want everyone to know that it was sent to a particular person. Which address line would you use for this person?	1.	Cc
		2.	To
		3.	Bcc
15	You have received an e-mail and you wish to send it to another colleague who was not on the original mail address listing. Which facility would you use?	1.	Reply to Author
		2.	Forward
		3.	Send and Receive

Index